Banking, Lending and Real Estate

This book deals directly with the risk/return multiple trade-offs coming out of the closely intertwined relationship between banking and real estate. The authors explore how banks could embrace a more proactive approach to make the most of their, mostly "long-only," exposure to real estate, and create positive spillover effects on their real estate counterparts and the sector as a whole. It provides a "state-of-the–art" representation and analysis of the strategies that best practices in banking are adopting to manage these issues and plan for a new set of interrelations, driving a "virtuous circle" as opposed to the current one.

Banking, Lending and Real Estate is built on the academic know-how and professional expertise of the authors, who have been researching, writing and working on this joint topic for over a decade. With its pragmatic approach, it allows the reader to capture which leading hedge active and holistic approaches are available today and proven to treat, e.g., the banks' overexposure to this asset class; to manage "unlikely to pay" and sub-performing positions; and to optimise the recovery value coming from the workout of real estate–related NPL (and underlying assets). Case studies and relevant examples are provided, leveraging on the authors' experience in consulting projects in the EMEA region and from working with global, regional and domestic banks and the real estate players acting across its value chain.

This book will appeal to both academics and business practitioners within the banking, financial services and real estate sectors, as well as professionals from financial and strategic/industrial advisory working in those fields.

Claudio Scardovi is a managing director and global co-head of the financial services practice for AlixPartners, a global consultancy focused on restructuring, value recovery, transformation and growth. Claudio has specialised in the financial services sector for the past 24 years, primarily (for 19 years) as managing director and country or regional head of financial services for a number of companies, including KPMG, Accenture, Intervaluenet.com, Oliver Wyman, Lehman Brothers, Nomura, Advent International and AlixPartners. He is also a professor at Bocconi University and at SDA Bocconi, specialising in capital markets, financial systems, restructuring and transformation, and for Imperial College's master's in management programme. Author of over 200 articles and papers and 17 books, Claudio is also one of the strategic advisors to the master's programme at Imperial College in London and is part of the strategic advisory board/Future of Banking for the World Economic Forum. He has also been a board member of Risanamento SpA and Consorzio AMI in Italy.

Alessia Bezzecchi is an Associate Professor of Practice di Corporate Finance and Real Estate and the Program Director of the Executive Master's in Finance (EMF), focused on asset/wealth management, corporate finance & control, banking transformation, and real estate transformation at SDA Bocconi School of Management. She is also teaching professor of "capital markets" at Bocconi University and director for the Executive Program in Real Estate Finance and Real Estate (EPFIRE).

Banking, Money and International Finance

9 **Price and Financial Stability**
Rethinking Financial Markets
David Harrison

10 **A Comparative History of Bank Failures**
From Medici to Barings
Sten Jönsson

11 **Expert Systems in Finance**
Smart Financial Applications in Big Data Environments
Edited by Noura Metawa, Mohamed Elhoseny, Aboul Ella Hassanien, M. Kabir Hassan

12 **Equity Home Bias in International Finance**
A Place-Attachment Perspective
Kavous Ardalan

13 **Frontier Capital Markets and Investment Banking**
Principles and Practice from Nigeria
Temitope W. Oshikoya and Kehinde Durosinmi-Etti

14 **French Banking and Entrepreneurialism in China and Hong Kong**
From the 1850s to 1980s
Hubert Bonin

15 **Banking, Lending and Real Estate**
Claudio Scardovi and Alessia Bezzecchi

For more information about this the series, please visit www.routledge.com/series/BMIF

Banking, Lending and Real Estate

Claudio Scardovi and Alessia Bezzecchi

Routledge
Taylor & Francis Group
LONDON AND NEW YORK

First published 2019
by Routledge
2 Park Square, Milton Park, Abingdon, Oxon OX14 4RN

and by Routledge
605 Third Avenue, New York, NY 10017

Routledge is an imprint of the Taylor & Francis Group, an informa business

British Library Cataloguing-in-Publication Data
A catalogue record for this book is available from the British Library

Library of Congress Cataloging-in-Publication Data
A catalog record has been requested for this book

ISBN: 978-0-367-23547-5 (hbk)

Typeset in Times New Roman
by codeMantra

Contents

Contents

List of figures

List of tables

1 Banking and real estate

A difficult relationship

Claudio Scardovi and Alessia Bezzecchi

1.1 Intertwined destinies

Banking and real estate have always enjoyed a very close relation, apparently cosy but actually, most often, turning out to be built on shaky foundations (Scardovi and Bezzecchi 2014). Banks have developed their business model out of many intangible things. Intangible as, in fact, the money they manage as basis of their own commerce, as intangibles are the information advantages that have allowed to banks to profit from an easy intermediation game ("buy the money – sell the money – make a hefty spread"). And intangibility is the ultimate production factor of banking and of the financial services industry – i.e. risk, be it of a financial or non-financial nature (e.g. pure risks like morbidity or mortality).

Risk is the ultimate production factor as banks originate, structure, underwrite, hedge, intermediate, insure, syndicate and sell a lot of it and of many different natures, most of them interconnected. The bank's intermediation game (the basic "buy the money – sell the money") has developed also by stretching and leveraging risks. The bank has to manage the leverage inherently built into its "money multiplier" business model (on the back of 1 Euro of capital, it raises so many in liabilities that then it uses to extend loans to multiple counterparts), and it faces therefore a "liquidity risk" – should a sudden withdrawal of its funds happen. It also faces a credit or market risk, as it starts to employ those funds to derive some yield, either by extending loans or by trading on the financial markets.

Also, as typical average maturities of liabilities and assets differ (with the first one much shorter than the second), banks also must face this equity duration mismatch and bear reinvestment and refinancing risks. The further velocity created on the usage of the bank's equity capital – obtained by securitising the assets in the banks' portfolio and in their sale via secondary markets, in order to restart anew the lending cycle – is also adding further intangibility and instability to the banks' business model – as almost anything that can wrong could potentially wipe out most of its capital.

Almost as an answer to face this "intangibility to the core," banks have developed through time a very much close and intertwined relationship with the real estate sector – an almost incestuous one, as the interconnections have become so extreme – both in width and depth – so as to make banks the largest real estate players of all, at least in continental Europe, and ultimately dependent on the fortunes of this sector (as, of course, the real estate sector has, in turn, become ultimately driven by the fortunes of the lending business, if not – directly or indirectly – owned by the banks themselves).

It may look like an exaggeration in principle, but let's just think of the balance sheet of a typical universal bank, in the continental European context, where banks' lending still pretty much dominates the funding of small- and medium-sized enterprises (SMEs), small businesses and individuals and even more so in the real estate sector – as they finance real estate developers, new development projects and, of course, mortgages.

This typical universal bank will own real estate assets for its own use: "trophy" assets for its headquarters, owned less for their functionalities as for their ability to impress perspective clients and the collective imagination of societies, so as to convey the (usually unfounded) message relating how rich, safe, credible and hence stable the bank is; and other real estate assets used for their own branch network, becoming more irrelevant by the day as digital banking expands making the cost structure of traditional distribution channels more uneconomic and less useful by the day.

The idea of owning and not renting real estate assets has also been so engrained that banks have thought of "capitalising" their financial strength by buying instrumental real estate assets, on the assumption their volatility was much lower than other financial assets, or actually almost non-existent and with upward trends expected in the long-term – you would just need to wait long enough, to see their value double or triple in time and with no mark-to-market in the meantime.

1.2 A "low, upward volatility" fallacy

Of course, the real estate volatility has indeed been pretty low, until measured properly or at all. And the prevailing, almost universal, accounting treatment of instrumental real estate (at historical costs, with revaluations so rare to almost ensure that they were all upward-looking – you just wait enough, and the inflation will do the rest) has certainly favoured this "low, upward volatility" paradigm. On this basis, banks have become even more eager to be long on real estate assets and on its cycle – almost a one-way bet on the value of bricks, no matter what the cash flow is.

They are the owner (albeit not end users) of the real estate assets they finance with their leasing portfolio, and as such, they bear all the operational risks associated with them as well. And they are almost co-owners of the real estate assets that are part of the reserves their insurance business has to put aside, to cover future claims of policyholders, be them of a life or P&C (property and casualty) nature. Banks are also the owner of real estate assets that are entering their books as component of principal trading or investment strategies, or as they come from the exchange of sub-performing debt into equity, or from the repossession of real estate assets that were put as collateral to loans that, as they have become non-performing, have left these properties as the only chance to recover.

The long position of banks on real estate assets does not, however, stop here as another, even greater and more influential exposure typically comes from performing loans and other sub- and non-performing ones (and including the so-called "grey area") where the real estate assets are representing the "lion share" of the collateral in use, driving in a significant way its "probability of default" (PD) and partially related "exposure at default" (EAD) and "loss given default" (LGD). The case is obvious for retail mortgages and for loans to SME backed by real estate assets, and it's even more direct and plain for the loans extended to real estate developers and usually tied to a special purpose vehicle (SPV) that is the owner of the building being developed (sometimes just a portion of land, or a half developed urbanisation plan), with no recourse allowed on the real estate company itself.

Ultimately, not many assets from the bank's balance sheet are left that could be deemed as neither directly nor indirectly related to the real estate sector. It is also true that the massive backlog of non-performing exposures/non-performing loans (NPE/NPL) left after the global financial crisis has left banks with a larger share of repossessed real estate assets, most of them with limited liquidity and dubious quality, vis-à-vis the initial appraisal that was confirming their contribution to the "loan-to-value" at the origination and inception of the loan.

Indeed, the perfect storm of the global financial crisis was mostly driven by the prick of the bubble in the real estate sector, initially in the USA and then elsewhere. Following this, banks found out that, indeed, not all is good in real estate, as the sector is not always going up and even when it does so, over very long-time horizons, it can barely match the loss in purchasing power determined by the inflation registered over the same period. Banks also found out that real estate assets are surely unmovable, but their prices are moving a lot – hence, they have a very high volatility – if you just can find a way to measure their mark-to-market on a more objective and frequent basis.

Real estate is also very "cyclical," as it is driven by the cycles of saving and investment of the people and companies in an economy, not to mention fiscal policies (on one side, housing is a sensitive topic, so a number of expansionary fiscal policies are often used to manage the election and political cycle; on the other side, houses are easy to tax and it's very difficult to avoid taxation when a tax hike needs to be performed in extremis). All in all, it is not unreasonable to state that real estate is then contributing very little to the diversification of the risks underwritten by banks in their lending portfolio – hitting harder when things are bad and capital cushions are thin.

It then looks like that this "designed to be virtuous" relationship has been turning "vicious," with the materiality of real estate contributing other headaches to banking and vice versa. This close and intertwined relationship is then turning out to be built on shaky foundations – and this is more relevant for our discussions on credit workout, and for the recovery attainable from the active management of the NPE/NPL real estate collaterals. Not to mention the future credit underwriting and the active and holistic management of the overall exposure of banks to the real estate sector.

1.3 Bricks after the storm

What else could go wrong for the "bricks after the (first) storm" of the global financial crisis that started in 2008 with the default of Lehman Brothers (also largely due to its real estate undertakings and fatal bets)? And what could go wrong for the banks that have been unwillingly turned – "obtorto collo" – into real estate owners and property developers-in-chief? Digital transformation and the so-called "Fourth Industrial Revolution" brought about by new technologies could not certainly impact such a "high-touch, unmovable and concrete" component of the global economy. Or, are these also going to change its dynamics in the absolute and relative performance of its valuations?

For example, with the diffusion of the "shared economy" (where everybody rents something, on the spot, so there is no more need to buy and hold a real estate asset… or where hotels and hospitality are just crowded out by extended value proposition of the likes of AirBnB)? And with the continuously changing scale and scope and value dynamics of large and small cities, urban areas and of the countryside (with the gentrification trend driving the polarisation between high and low end on one side, and augmented reality, super digital connectivity, faster and faster travelling and commuting changing the way we work – more and more from home – and live our mobility)?

It would be dangerously naïve to assume that the "second" storm of the digital and technological transformation (and of the many "social" and "behavioural" changes driven by this) is going to have limited impacts on the real estate sector and on the banks' exposure on this. It could (and should) certainly – and this is a safe bet – change the way banks approach, the way they value and monitor, repossess and manage real estate assets, using data and machine learning/artificial intelligence (ML/AI) applications as a force for good and as an opportunity to rethink their governance, organisation, management, risk underwriting and commercial strategies as well. The reference to the alternative asset management professional industry comes again as handy.

Banks are, de facto, for all the above-mentioned reasons, almost like hedge funds, with a long position on the real estate sector and cycle. It may appear (or they may hope) that they have bought a call on the real estate underlying to their loans. In fact, and most likely, they usually end up selling a put to the borrowers, potentially getting hold of the worst kind of repossessed assets at the worst possible moment and with limited opportunities to even touch the precious, valuable ones (that the debtor will retain, will long judicial processes require to reposes them). As real estate long-only hedge fund, the volatility driven by their large exposure (either direct or indirect) on real properties drives a lot their regulatory, economic and market value of equity (whether properly measured and monitored by regulators and investors alike, it is another matter) and their future success or failure.

Given this critical relationship and oversized exposure, it is striking to observe how banks still tend to measure, control and manage their exposure on real estate assets in a very traditional and unsophisticated way – they may have very complex modelling and databases and software for managing the few exotic derivatives they may have been left with, but then they end up relying on valuations on real estate assets that are driven by appraisals done by third parties that still use such rough proxies like "price per square meter" or "price per bedroom" etc.

These "independent" third parties, whatever the sophistication they may develop in the future in their valuation approaches, also run the "client's capture" risk, ending up ratifying whatever value is expected and hoped for by the banker that is hiring them in the first instance. The overall set of valuation methodologies, active management initiatives and, finally, organisational and governance approaches are, therefore, worth a full revisit – as the day of reckoning of this dangerous relationship is approaching and is already manifested in the banks' challenge to recover value from NPE/NPL.

1.4 Fifty shades of grey

For a start, a real estate asset valuation should be addressed with a clear understanding of the value derived by its final, best owner. Basically, the analysis should start with the question regarding "which kind of value are we trying to measure and for what stakeholder?" The answer will be different if we want to place a flat to a family that is going to use it as first or second house, or to a long-only, long-term investor trying to rent it as part of a strategy to build some decent, predictable yield over a very long-timed horizon. Or to a real estate developer that wants to buy many of them to change their end use and refurbish the entire building. Or to an asset manager trying to aggregate assets for a Real Estate Investment Trust (REIT) to be then IPO-ed and listed in the stock market.

Figure 1.1 shows how a correct approach to valuation should address both the "who is the potential best and available buyer?" and the "what is the final end use foreseen for the asset?" questions. Based on the answer to the first question, we could likely segment the potential bidders into retail or institutional, and into end users or investors, driven then by different holding periods and trading strategies – and related risk/return profiles.

End uses could then be multiple and include the individuals/ families' own use – to be addressed by market comparable and Discounted Cash Flow (DCF) analysis or the investors' asset sale – to be analysed with a DCF that

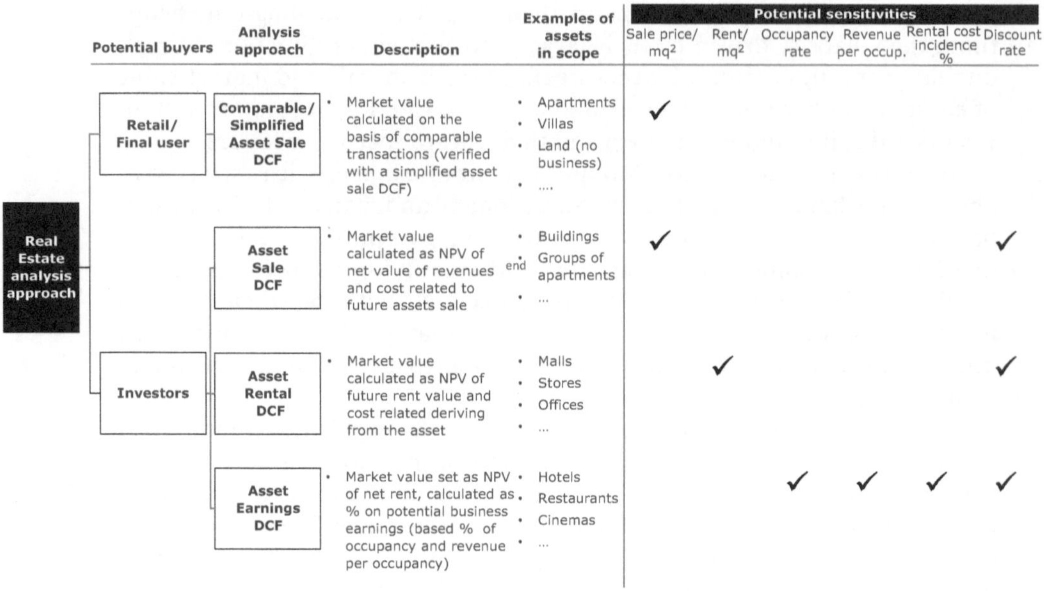

Figure 1.1 Valuation approach is driven by the potential buyer counterpart and final use of the asset.

takes into account the sale costs, the income perceived in between and the discount on full price to be considered, given the market liquidity and the deepness and abundance of potential bidders. Vice versa, an asset held by investors as income producing should be addressed as the net present value (NPV) of future income net of operating costs, with specific hypothesis on occupancy rates and idle times between different contractual renting agreements, etc.

Whilst confirming the superior approach derived from the use of DCF valuation models, the main point we want to raise here is that value is not, as many other things in life, absolute and fully objective, as it needs to consider the overall market conditions, the investors' behaviour and expectations and any other kind of social development that could change – even in a significant way – the subjective perception of a real estate "fashionableness" (see Figure 1.1).

Their substitution value (or cost of construction, net of amortisation) is usually uncorrelated to this subjective value, and to the market one, that is emerging as a result of the interplay of the many subjective considerations played by the market participants. Hence, the approach to segment and determine which potential end users are the best owners and likely available buyers, and which end uses they could consider for the asset, is a critical component of the approach – determining what is "trophy" and what is "worthless."

It's then not usually a question of black or white, as many real estate properties may be worth a lot, given the right market conditions, a supporting lending supply, a proper end use, a consistent refurbishing and a cunning marketing plan that is addressing the potential "best and highest available users." There have been "trophy asset" (such as castles) that are now irrelevant and in need of a change of end use to be able to find any kind of buyer, and crap, industrial warehouses now turned into highly sought-after "fashionable" properties gaining from and contributing to positive externalities.

"Fifty shades of grey" would stand as a better approach to characterise the revaluation opportunities of real estate assets. And that is partly explaining (aside from the typical accounting gimmick) why such a high degree of volatility exists in the valuation of a loan to the same counterpart and with the same underlying real estate collateral amongst different banks – specifically for the so-called "grey area" of loans that are in between the performing and the non-performing status.

It's not just the window dressing or the different view (half-full, half-empty) on the future of the world, but it also depends on the active and holistic asset management plan the bank may have identified for the real estate collateral – even more so if it is a greenfield or brownfield development plan. That is in the hands of banks, at least partially, and to be controlled in full after repossession.

1.5 Active management: not unmovable

The revaluation work done on the real estate assets, following the best end-investor/best end-user approach, should then form the basis to develop an active asset management strategy for the properties that the bank already owns, for its own use, or coming from past debt-to-equity conversion or, most likely and in a much more abundant way, from the repossession activities carried out by its Real Estate Owned COmpany (REOCO) as part of its credit workout activities.

For the properties in use, the active asset management strategy should be set by starting to answer few simple questions: is the bank the best user, let alone the best owner of each and every single asset it has classified as "instrumental" on its balance sheet? And are these assets really "core" and for how long? Given digitisation trends, a business plan on future branch closures should be considered, as well as similar considerations on headquarters, given reduction in the head counts expected and the robotisation, outsourcing, offshoring trends also implied in future competitive scenarios. As a general rule, we should see less and less bricks in use for the bank of the future.

Then, assuming these properties are truly instrumental and for a certain future timeline, are they the right ones for the bank (i.e. is the bank the best user) or should they be swapped with others which are cheaper, more convenient and bespoke to the real and relevant use justified by the bank's financials? For example, is a branch located in Via Monte Napoleone in Milan best used to run a bank's branch, or should D&G, Armani or Hermes be the best end users? With the bank's branch relocated to the much cheaper and more convenient – for access, parking slots etc. – Corso Venezia?

As a quick and dirty key performance indicator (KPI), we should consider, e.g., the revenues generated by the bank or any other end user per square meter, and weighting the square meters employed with their open market value, to get a better sense of the real invested capital and related opportunity cost – not only to get to the best user but also to think of ways to improve the KPI: either incrementing revenues (very tough) or keeping them put and relocating somewhere else (Figure 1.2).

And, finally, if the branch in Corso Venezia is truly required to run the commercial strategy of the bank and justified by its financial performance, should the bank own the asset, or just rent it, or consider other financial and contractual solutions, including lease back or rent to buy (or rent to sell – in case the bank wants to sell the asset guaranteeing a certain yield to the end buyer for the period it is planning to use it, anticipating the reduction in the number of its physical branches footprint)? The question seems obvious to answer as, even assuming the bank has a positive outlook on the value of real estate, the principal investment activity in real estate is hardly a core business for a financial institution and – anyway – it should be done in different ways, with a clearly defined trading portfolio, monitored and managed for what it really is and given its risk/return objectives.

Also, renting is making more visible the cost structure of this bank's distribution strategy that would otherwise see its profitability boosted by an artificial (and wrong) assumption that the real estate asset, as owned, comes for free. It would then allow more flexibility in changing the location (as customers' flows changes through time or the best format differs in time, based on the changing customers' behaviours at point of sale) or in shutting it down for the inevitable progressive reduction of "high-touch" distribution strategies, in banking and in financial services in general.

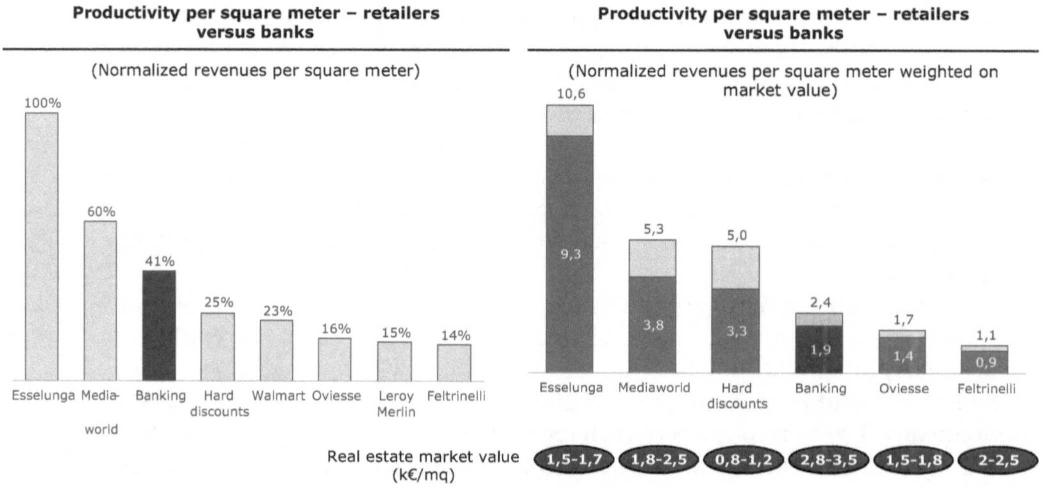

Figure 1.2 Valuation and productivity of real estate assets.

All of these questions, and other ones, and a more strategic one that is related on "how to make the use of a given real estate asset more productive?" (e.g. redesigning its layout, managing the empty space with sub-location, concentrating staff from exited, more expensive properties, promoting smart/shared-office practices, optimising the workflow and the customers' footfall at the point of sale and maximising the revenues generated per square meter, weighted by its market value) are part of an "active space management" strategy and approach that can help the bank in optimising the yield obtained on the real estate assets used (either as owned or as rented) for its own core business, and as part of its current operating model (and invested capital strategy).

1.6 Obtorto collo

The properties that are coming from previous "debt-to-equity" swaps and conversion may be more complex to manage, as the objective of the bank is not as much (or not only) to maximise the yield on those assets whilst reducing their cost contribution, as it is to defend their value (avoiding further depreciations down the road and accounting losses on day 1) on their equity and debt pieces, ideally recovering some of the upside still embedded in those assets – likely requiring some investments.

The typical situation relates to real estate development assets that are under construction, and at different stages as such: from "greenfield" lands and basic infrastructure supporting a real estate development business plan that needs to be "restructured" (considering, aside from a different financial structure, also different development plans – end use of assets, pricing and marketing strategies, target clients, property managers and service partners), to "brownfield" buildings at some stage of development, but still requiring significant capital expenditures to be completed and a relevant "execution risk" in the development itself, to properties already in place but with the need of a heavy uplift – some significant refurbishing and potential "change of destination."

In all these cases, an "ad hoc" approach should be considered, as any dossier is almost like a company in itself, and with a balance sheet and a profit and loss component. They may be "small ticket," but a large real estate development project could be very sizeable with respect to its overall financing needs, and given the impact it could have on new mortgages, cross-selling of property insurance policies and the like. In all this cases, the bank, with its "debt-to-equity" swap decision, has decided (most often "obtorto collo") that this property development is worth a try, with an exposure to its returns as well as risks, and that the "entrepreneurial" and managerial role should be left to itself for some time, as de facto the main financier of the project (as the initial equity has usually been gone for some time). It will have to manage this "hot potato" temporarily and try not to get its fingers burned – sometimes with the help of new partners with fresh ideas and resources.

A tactical approach for the bank is then to hire real estate professionals as "ad interim" managers to run the asset and turn it around, changing its development plan as required and then executing this. A more strategic approach, in governance and organisational terms, is then discussed later in the chapter – when we reference to the opportunity for the bank to create a dedicated Real Estate Integrated Service (REIS) company – as the dossiers are many and sizeable – either by itself or in joint venture (JV) with an industrial partner and the bank could make a business out of it.

Whatever the stage of the real estate or related development, it is worth to focus the most critical case, when the loan has clearly ended in an insolvency status and has been denounced, and the bank has a few options left – with main one taking possession of the real estate collateral, to try to recover as much value as possible out of it. This "repossession strategy" is hardly a panacea, as the number of real estate owned (REO) assets coming from the repossession activities of banks has become very high, specifically in Mediterranean Europe (Spain, Italy and Greece), in the aftermath of the global crisis and as a consequence of the credit workout activities it had to carry over to manage the resulting large volumes of NPL and the limited options to get to extrajudicial compensation. Having possession of an asset is just the start of the journey, with no easy way out and the risk of further losses in value and even of new, potential liabilities – hence worth further discussion.

1.7 Real estate enhancement strategies

An analysis of the best real estate strategies should start well before the properties are repossessed. Actually, based on the analysis's outcome, the best option may well be the avoidance of their repossession, as any asset will bring with them not only some value but also related costs (for the basic maintenance), risks (that will lose most of its value when in the hands of the bank) and potential liabilities (once owned, the bank will become liable of anything it may happen – to things and people that may use the property, whether legally or not: take the example of a fire and accidental death at an owned repossessed hotel property that was temporarily and abusively inhabited by nomads).

Hence, in order to properly define the best recovery a strategy, the issue tree should start at loan level. As a first step, it should be considered the likelihood, related costs and recovered value of a successful financial restructuring achieved in agreement with the borrower. An agreement could be reached at an early stage, or after denouncement, used as a "stick" to force some extra judicial agreement in extremis and that would allow to the bank to get to a better NPV vis-à-vis any alternative judicial paths leading to the judicial enforcement for the repossession of the asset and its future sale – usually through a competitive bidding process where the bank itself (as it has largely been the case in Greece lately) is the only "interested" buyer to bid for such a deal. A summary of main real estate enhancement strategies for considerations is presented in Figure 1.3.

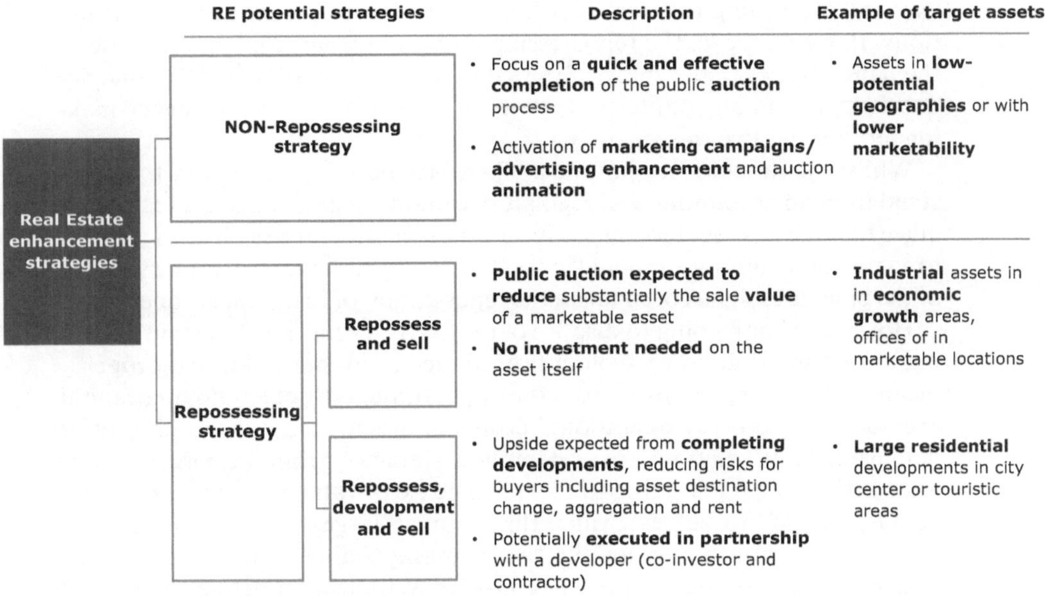

Figure 1.3 Valuation and productivity of real estate assets in the distribution value chain and at point of sales, across sectors.

In more detail (as per Figure 1.3), assuming the best way forward is represented by the judicial path and that most of the valuable collaterals are made of real estate assets (a very likely case), the bank will pursue the sale of these via a regulated, competitive auction process – running a simplified sale process for all related collaterals to a loan. In liquid and well-functioning lending and real estate markets, most of the auctions will be left for the free market forces to execute, with transactions finalised with end investors and with end users (in a competitive, liquid, transparent and well-functioning market, the best available investors/users will end up bidding the highest price, matching the NPV of the highest yield they could attain from its use of the asset or from its renting).

In reality, most of the auctions end up with sale prices very far from such values, as markets are typically dislocated – picks in NPE/NPL portfolios auctioned by banks are usually the result of distressed markets in the first instance – and, even if they are not, the auction process is not typically maximising the transparency and liquidity required to get the best price (it's driven by fire sale objectives, allowing minimal matchmaking amongst assets and end buyers and it's typically very opaque in the mechanisms and in the way market participants participate to this).

In this instance, the bank could then decide to play an alternative strategy, participating directly to the auction process with its own REOCO, to create a greater competitive tension in the first place, and to ensure it has a "floor" to the exit price of each and every asset, that is the one at which it is ready to place a bid and repossess the asset, to fully become its legal owner, with all the costs and risks and potential liabilities mentioned above. The way and the timing this repossession is done changes a lot across jurisdictions. In Greece, e.g., the repossession with full ownership from the side of the bank implies that a share of the sale price will get allocated to minority debtholders and all counterparts "others-than-banks" anyway, hence making more expensive this strategy.

Whilst the rationale for putting a "floor" to the exit price is easy to understand from an accounting and regulatory capital perspective, it does not guarantee that the best net recovery value is attained. Several less obvious answers to a set of other questions should in fact be driving the active real estate strategy of the bank after it has been taken the repossession of real estate properties.

How is the bank going to dispose of the assets, eventually? Certainly, buying more time is good to avoid a fire sale scenario, but holding a property means having further costs (from the opportunity cost of employing capital and funding, to other operational costs and associated risks) and a lot of management distractions are also implied – far away from the core business. How is then the bank going to create some extra value out of those asset – i.e. targeting a "to be" exit value that is much larger than the current "as is" fair value, not to mention, its "as is" market value? What would be the best asset management strategy to consider? With what timeline and related property management in the mean time? What would be the best exit to target, in terms of final buyers and destination?

1.8 Active: reactive, proactive – if bricks could talk

In the aftermath of the lending meltdown that happened in 2008–2012, and of their REO repossessing activities, most continental European banks (in Portugal, Spain, Greece, Italy specifically but also in Austria – not to mention other Central and Eastern European Countries and other non-continental ones such as Ireland, Cyprus or Iceland) have ended up owning portfolios of thousands of properties – fulfilling even more our initial proposition of "banks as the biggest real estate players of all." In some cases, the balance sheet of their "bad bank" has become as sizeable as the remaining good one, and the value of the repossessed, owned real estate assets bigger than the value of the remaining outstanding performing loans – a truly real estate long-only hedge fund, selling current accounts, payment services and asset management products as a side business!

Given this high number of REO assets, and their typical heterogeneity, a top-down, segmentation approach is required for the bank to start designing the right active asset management strategies and to put them in place. Some of them will be "reactive" in nature, mostly trying to address the operational issues that are preventing the properties to be sold at something near their current, implicit, fair value: e.g. some of the buildings need to be restored to a well-functioning state and refurbished to that end; others will need some basic urbanisation work to be done, or some infrastructural one, or some variation with respect to the current city planning requirements. Others will instead need to be put back as fully compliant given various legal requirements (such as safety standards, energy usage standards, ecological impact, and usability for handicapped people) that would prevent their "all-clear" sale. A capital budgeting on capital expenditures and on the operating expenses that the bank will need to run during its holding period as owner will then need to be considered in their overall business plan to ensure that a proper return is achieved on this.

Other strategies will instead need to be more "proactive" in nature, trying to address the potential value uplift coming from specific clusters or on specific, large value potential, assets. To this end, a typical approach is presented, for a potential, segmentation that covers the location of real estate assets (location is a key driver of value in real estate, and value uplifts are usually larger for properties proactively managed in high-end places), the current (or prospective) end use and also the final end buyer or investor (whether final end user or simply financial investor then interested to put those assets at use to get some recurring yield via rents – see Figure 1.4).

Several proactive strategies could then be logically identified. For example, industrial assets could be converted into social housing residences in depressed areas, or residences turned into shops or offices, if worth the change in destination. Or, a number of flats and other properties already rented could be pooled into a fund (an REIT, or something similar) that could be offered to long-term institutional investors like pension funds or insurance companies, that would be happy with a lower yield (and hence higher price on the acquisition of the fund shares) – the longer its duration, the lower

	RE Strategy	Description
	0 Liquidate	• Focus on effective completion of the auction process, though the public auction process • No/ low upside expected from active Real Estate management – Example: assets in low-potential geographies or with lower marketability
	1 Repossess and sell	• Public auction expected to reduce substantially the sale value of a marketable asset • No investment needed on the asset itself – Example: Industrial assets in economic growth areas, offices of in valuable locations
Repossess, Develop and Sale	2 Repossess, develop and sell	• Significant upside expected from completing developments, reducing risks for buyers • Potentially executed with developers, with role of co-investor and contractor – Example: Large residential developments in city center or touristic areas
Repossess, Develop and Sale	3 Repossess, rent and sell	• Value maximized by putting in place tenants and sell • Multiple assets can be bundled in a single portfolio to attract larger investors – Example: Large residential, retail and office spaces
Repossess, Develop and Sale	4 Repossess, aggregate and sell	• Creation of a package of businesses to enhance complementary asset values • After repossession, management of the businesses while identifying the best "package" – Example: Hotels and restaurants in city center/ touristic areas
Repossess, Develop and Sale	5 Repossess change and sell	• Assets that can benefit from higher marketability after conversion to a different destination – Example: Case-by-case basis

Figure 1.4 Real estate repossession strategies.

its yield volatility. Or, several hotels, of similar characteristics and family owned, could be grouped into a sizeable, consistent network and managed by a professional operator (like an international hotel chain) to maximise the value of the hotels as operating companies, as this would drive the value of the real estate assets in turn.

In the traditional approach, the bank's REOCO is just acting to sustain the auction price and ensure there is an accounting "floor" price for the properties. Most of the REOCO have then been used to buy time and as a new, more creative way to "kick (again) the can down the road," hoping that the real estate sector will eventually recover and some high inflation will do the rest (no matter what the loss in purchasing power parity – it will not be recorded in the bank's books). In the new, active approach, they need then to develop critical real estate internal capabilities, with new people mastering a different set of skills and experiences – from asset to property to facility management, to the management of most of the final sale process via direct or indirect channels, but not only.

The REOCO could then become a strong tactical, organisational solution to address the bank's wind-down urgency, and be paired by other initiatives, also of a tactical nature, like the set-up of a real estate web and branch-based real estate agency business at the bank, or the development of new, dedicated investment vehicles (like the REIT). The bank could then even consider managing internally, on a temporary basis, few of the real estate development companies where it has become (obtorto collo) a leading shareholder, and then seek a partnership with an industrial partner.

This focalisation on real estate strategy and management, born out of urgent needs and of a tactical nature, could then in turn become something more strategic and permanent in nature, to address not just the wind-down priority but also the unavoidable real estate exposure that the bank will have to manage anyway, through good and bad times, expansionary and recessionary cycles, optimising not only the risks but also the returns associated with this critical "real" asset class – as if it were a business opportunity for the bank to be addressed in the open market, as discussed in the following chapter.

Reference

Scardovi, C., and A. Bezzecchi, 2014, Banking & real estate. Active real estate management per le banche, gli investitori e gli operatori immobiliari, EGEA.

2 Real estate strategy for banks

Not an oxymoron

Claudio Scardovi and Alessia Bezzecchi

2.1 Real estate strategy: holistic, active and integrated

New, smarter approaches for banks to their real estate management are not just possible, but urgently and critically required to truly turn around their interlinked destinies and for the good of both sectors. Most of the global financial crisis issues were engrained in this apparently cosy, intertwined relationship between banking and real estate – old problems were then made just more evident by the perfect storm of the investment and commercial banking markets.

Since then, several tactical solutions have been designed and executed almost in waves – we have shared some of these experiences working with banks and other financial intermediaries and in multiple key markets, such as Spain, Italy, Greece, Austria and in other CEE Countries, and we have experienced not only some of their earlier successes but also unfinished turnaround and transformation.

A first wave has been focusing mostly on the "holistic" component, making evident how large and deep these interrelationships were, encompassing, as we have commented, most of the bank's asset side – as either loan or ownership. Some numerical analysis has then been done, usually to quantify, in nominal terms, the direct and indirect exposure of the bank to the sector – a far cry from anything related with its real downside risk and tail risk exposure (not to mention any consideration on the diversification effects on the key factors influencing the real estate risk/return trade-off). As a result, banks are still far from quantifying any value at risk (VaR) related to their real estate exposure and are not doing any capital allocation, portfolio planning, diversification and hedging and risk-based pricing on new loans on this basis. But some steps in this direction are at least now being discussed.

In the best cases, some international best practices have started developing "banking and real estate" dashboards that try to compare the overall yield attained on those assets and their associated costs (such as capital expenditure, operating expenses and risks, and opportunity costs) with the capital invested or regulatory capital absorbed by them, to get to some kind of "value creation" (most likely "value destruction") indicator – to compare again with the real estate VaR underwritten. By comparing yields and costs, and net returns versus their cost of equity, they are setting the basis to make more informed strategic decisions, linking them with their internal capital management and business planning and commercial processes to incentivise better their managers.

From this basis, a second wave has then been focusing on the "active" component of real estate management, to identify, design and progressively execute a number of (as we have seen) either reactive or proactive initiatives aimed at better managing the bank's real estate risk exposure. Notably, they are not addressing the "return" dimension, as most of the initiatives are so far just aimed at managing the post-mortem rundown – in most cases, they are not even focused on the potential value uplift the bank could obtain on the real estate assets it has ended up owning.

2.2 Alphabet soup

These initiatives have then quickly turned into an alphabet soup (to which we have certainly contributing, maybe to create more confusion), including the active real estate management (AREM), which is based on the three key pillars of developing a property database, a monitoring dashboard and a predetermined set of corrective actions (as shown in Figures 2.1 and 2.2). Following a proactive approach to the AREM, banks can develop dynamic business plans for the main real estate assets linked to real estate development – setting on top of them KPI and "early warning signals" (EWS) that are then included in a report used to monitor and proactively manage their risk, mostly driven by the value dynamics of the underlying asset being built and commercialised.

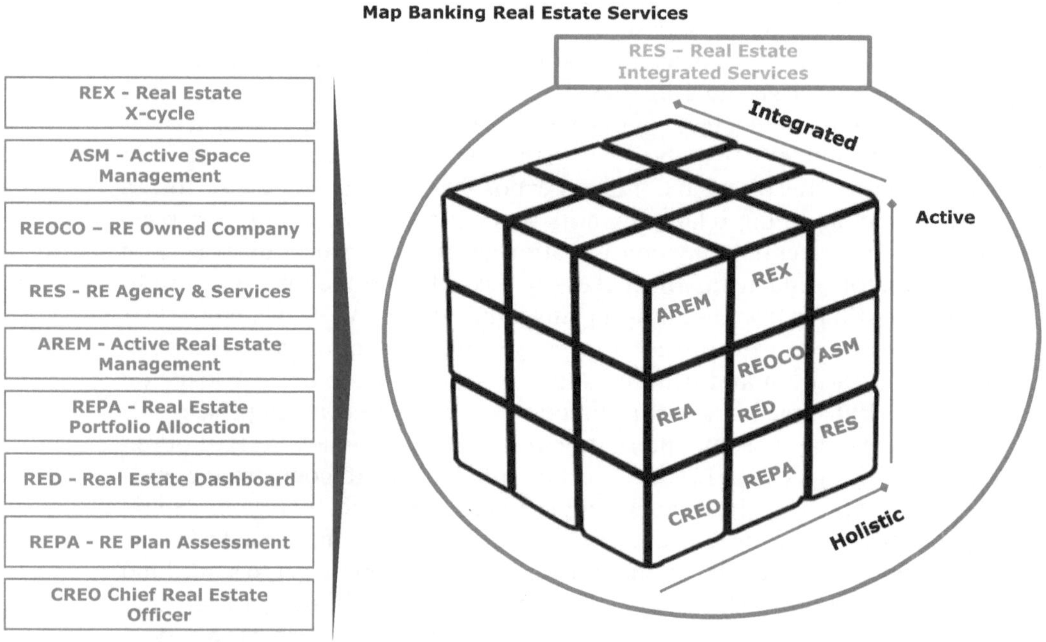

Figure 2.1 A Rubik's cube for banking and real estate.

Active Real Estate Management: Key Elements

Property Database

- Type of property (residential, office, retail, logistics)
- Status (new, to be refurbished, development)
- Property location (city and location)
- Liens in favor of the bank / other existing encumbrances
- Property appraisal and date (and, if available, valuation method and appraiser)
- Building's conformity to building and zoning regulations
- Legal status, liens and any other actions in effect on the property
- Leases, if any, in effect

Monitoring Dashboard

- Identification of a set of "Early Warning Signals" (EWS) in order to determine in advance any possible deterioration in credit quality
  - Limited in terms of their number (5/6)
  - Specifics by property type and status

Corrective Actions

- Focused on the loans
  - that evidence critical aspects;
  - that are large enough to cover the costs of the actions
- Financial and/or industrial actions (the latter customized in relation to the property type and status)
- Actions may also lead to a new valuation of the property, based on a specific plan ('to be' status) and/or on the principle of the "best available use"

Figure 2.2 Active real estate management based on the three key pillars.

Another example refers then to the real estate agency (REA) initiative, where banks set up their own real estate intermediation business – working both online and off-line – to increase the liquidity of their repossessed assets and deliver a potential B2C commercialisation strategy, getting also sell-side mandates from the real estate developers they end up financing anyway. They can then get a hefty upfront commission from their brokerage activity, leveraging largely the same cost structure (their branches as point of sale and some of their employees becoming redundant as a consequence of the digitalisation of the business) and taking advantage of their dominant position along the real estate value chain (banks lend to developers and to end buyers and they also gave property insurance).

A number of initiatives of real estate brokerage promoted by banks have already been taken across multiple countries (Figure 2.3), and sometimes with different strategic objectives: from the acceleration of the deleveraging and de-risking action plans related to the bank's real estate related exposure, to the use of REA to actually increase the bank's market share in mortgages and then promote other cross-selling of financial and non-financial products, to the promotion of new services that are able to attract clients at the branches point of sales and occupy the bank's many redundancies – generating a new source of revenues as brokerage fees captured in the trade.

Banks have also set up their own REOCO, which aims to optimise the repossession of real estate collaterals (REO assets) being auctioned as part

Nation	Brand and Bank	Agency	Appraisal	Active Management	Energy Certification	Tech Services	Comments
	Crédit Agricole	✓		✓		✓	• Focused on 'second home' and added value services
	Sparkasse	✓	✓		✓		• Traditional RE agency with additional basic services
	BBVA	✓					• Pure RE brokerage agency
	Danske Bank	✓					• RE agency with information management services (market analysis, check list for acquisition,..)
	HSBC	✓					• Focus on 'facilitated' offers linked to NPLs (e.g. discounts/better mortgages rates compared to the market)
	Santander	✓					• RE agency • Financial brokerage with convenient rates

Figure 2.3 Real estate agency and related services.

Acquisition

- Participations to court procedures regarding real estate assets sales
- Involvement in bankruptcy agreements comprehensive of real estate assets transferring
- Focus on "captive" and "non-captive" NPLs portfolios, for:
  - Creating the adequate competitive pressure on pricing, reducing time, managing balance sheet floor ["captive" NPL]
  - Offering added value services to propose to other banks (small FIGs), to institutional investors and to Private/Affluent and SME/Small Business Clients ["non-captive" NPL]

Management

- Coordination (direct) and execution (direct or in outsourcing) of the following services:
  - 'Facility management', aimed at optimizing costs/effect of maintenance
  - 'Facility services", as of catering, documents management, security, utilities, space redesign and optimization
  - 'Property/administrative management', aimed at managing the assets in order to increase/maintain their value (e.g. by renters research, rent contracts renegotiation, etc...)
  - 'Asset management', to finalize strategic and economic/financial management of the assets, for increasing their «to be» value in line with the Highest and Best Available Use (HBAU)

Valorization

- Optimal valorization (sale) based on:
  - Best 'exit strategy' definition in line with each asset typology
  - Best channels mix activation (web, agents, corporate/retail – national/regional, advisors, digital marketplace etc.) and third parts
- Potential exploitation of the Group branches network as key distribution channel

Figure 2.4 REOCO can help sustain real estate sales and exit values.

Value added	Activity	Focus	Objectives	Examples of actions
	Asset management	Administrative management of real estate	• Maximize asset value • Increase return on invested capital • Manage the properties proactively	• Analysis of profitability and redefinition of asset allocation • Development of a strategic business plan • Initiate and run property and facility management services • Finalize financing
	Property management	Maintenance and optimization of the properties	• Keep property value intact and increase it • Maximize the value of business transactions in relation to the property • Guarantee occupancy of the property through an appropriate network of relationships	• Definition of budget and forecast for buying/selling properties • Active search for tenants/buyers • Analysis of lease maturities and start-up of commercial campaign • Preparation of administrative and accounting reports • Collection of rents • Technical, legal and administrative document management • Payment of taxes
	Facility management		• Maintain properties so as to avoid any interruption of the resident businesses • Guarantee efficient service, in line with the objectives of the businesses • Offer high value-added services to the users of the properties	• Building maintenance (electrical systems, HVAC systems, ...) • Space optimization (planning, furnishings, security, ...) • Personal services (environmental hygiene, food/beverage services, document management, security, auto fleet management, travel services, utilities, ...)

Figure 2.5 Asset, property and facility management capabilities.

of the judicial recovery process, and sometimes offering asset, property and facility management basic services on top, to help in managing the recovery of remaining value and even adding value to the assets during the holding period and optimise the future exit (Figures 2.4 and 2.5).

Of course, once the real estate properties are repossessed, the bank can pursue more freely all kind of different strategies to defend and enhance their value, using the capabilities highlighted above and leveraging also on other initiatives such as the REA. Still, the chances of success will vary highly and will be heavily dependent on the nature of the assets and on the performance of the respective, functional sub-segments of the market and on their location (Figure 2.6).

Also, as part of this alphabet soup, other initiatives have become progressively more forward-looking and encompassing, including the active space management, where banks try to optimise the use of their own properties, to reduce renting and facility management costs, optimise capital expenditure and increase revenues derived from them.

For example, in order to maximise the revenues per square meter of branches, some banks have started cross-selling other non-banking products and services – from REA to travelling – and have even considered sub-renting part of their space to commercial partners that – apart from the rents – can also contribute in creating traffic and footfall (i.e. UBI, in Italia, has hosted

Asset type	Potential actions	Success likelihood	Upside recovery potential*
Residential	Agency RE, co marketing, ad hoc financing for primary market, ...		15%-25%
Offices	Agency RE, co marketing, ad hoc financing, space management initiatives, etc.		5%-10%
Commercial	Agency RE, co marketing, finanziamenti ad hoc, servizi di space management, etc.		5%-15%
Industrial	Industrial interventions on the company that occupies the asset		0%-5%
Hotel/resorts	Limited levers		5%-10%
Land and development projects	Asset management, project review, co marketing, new investors		5%-30%

Figure 2.6 Best corrective actions driven by assets' features.

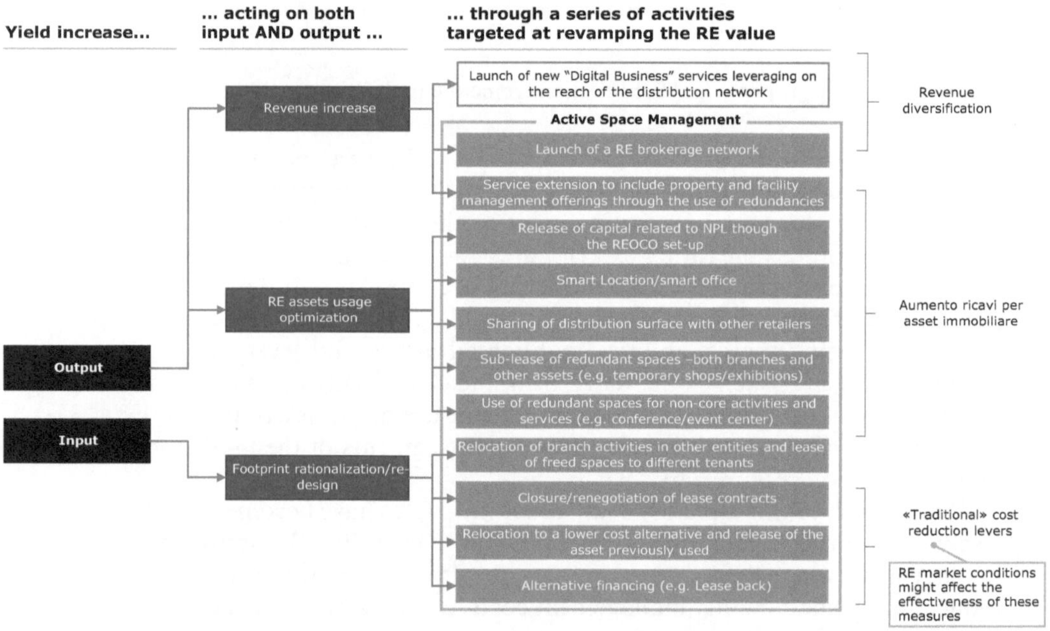

Figure 2.7 Active space management increases the yield per square meter.

Venchi, a producer and seller of high-end chocolates, and Intesa SanPaolo is hosting coffee shops at its "social" branches). Banks can also seek to enhance their productivity per square meter (weighted at market price) of headquarters and back offices using such techniques as "smart/shared office" (Figure 2.7).

A more innovative initiative to support the way banks approach their risk/return exposure coming from real estate is then related to the active

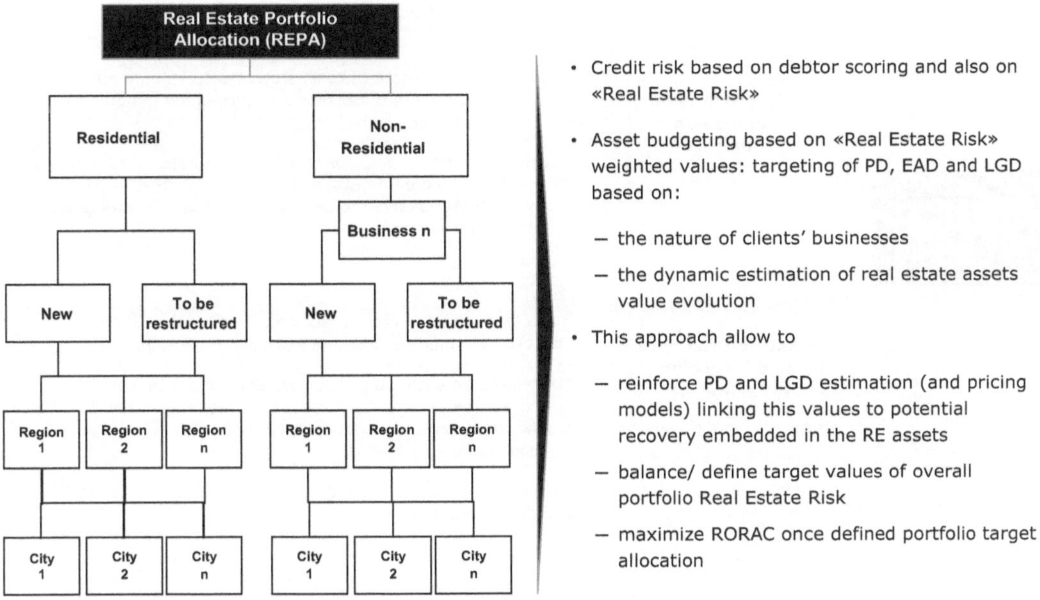

Figure 2.8 Real estate risk/return optimal portfolio allocation.

management of the "real estate portfolio allocation" (REPA) – mainly driven by the banks' overall lending portfolio via its property collaterals. Following approaches coming from the modern financial portfolio theory of diversification and optimisation, banks can aim to tailor their lending portfolios taking into consideration their exposure towards the real estate sector and related cycles, to design an ideal allocation of exposures towards real estate risk/return factors. This is then aimed at maximising their return on risk-adjusted capital. To this end, banks have also started to perform wider and deeper analysis of real estate cycles, to ideally define their "through-the-cycle" expected volatility and unexpected pick (or tail) one (Figure 2.8).

The analysis of the Real Estate sector performance across (X) the cycle (or REX) takes the aim at understanding and predicting trends for each stage of this at both county and regional levels, sub-segmenting also by asset typology and end use. Macroeconomic analysis can relate, e.g., how the lending supply, or the available income, unemployment rate, growth in GDP and in the consumption, and investment rates are ultimately influencing the prices of real estate (Figure 2.9).

Microeconomic analysis can then explain how customers' behaviour are influencing the way properties are used and valued (a fashionable part of the city can become less so, e.g., or a certain neighbourhood can become the best place for renting for high-flyers expatriates, or the spread of the "shared economy" could change the way second home are used and rented).

Whatever the macro- or microeconomic variable at play, the analysis on the aggregated data can be done either leveraging "traditional" statistical conjoint analysis or looking at historical trends and inferring a prediction

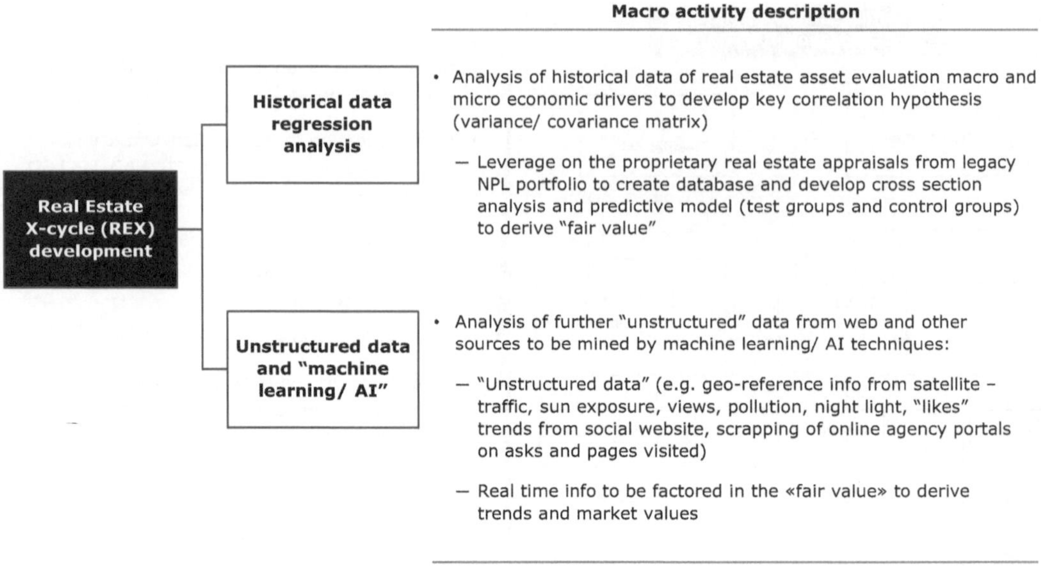

Figure 2.9 Real estate cycle analysis: backward and forward.

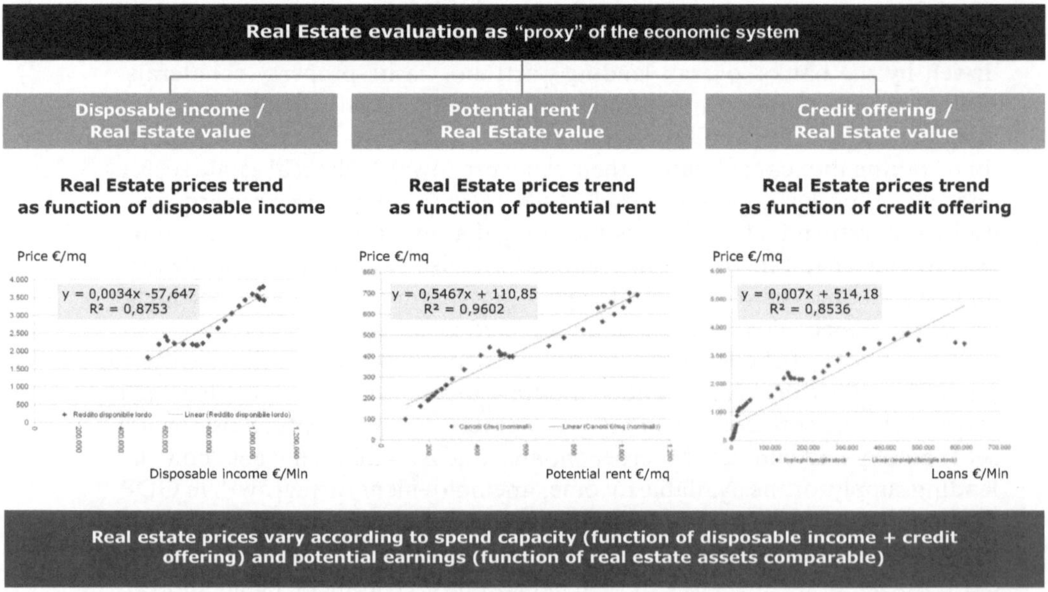

Figure 2.10 Backward-looking analysis based on structured data.

based on some hypothesis on the underlying distribution of frequency. This more traditional approach is mostly backward-looking, as it tries to see the future looking at the past, with regression analysis on disposable income, rent and lending supply (Figure 2.10).

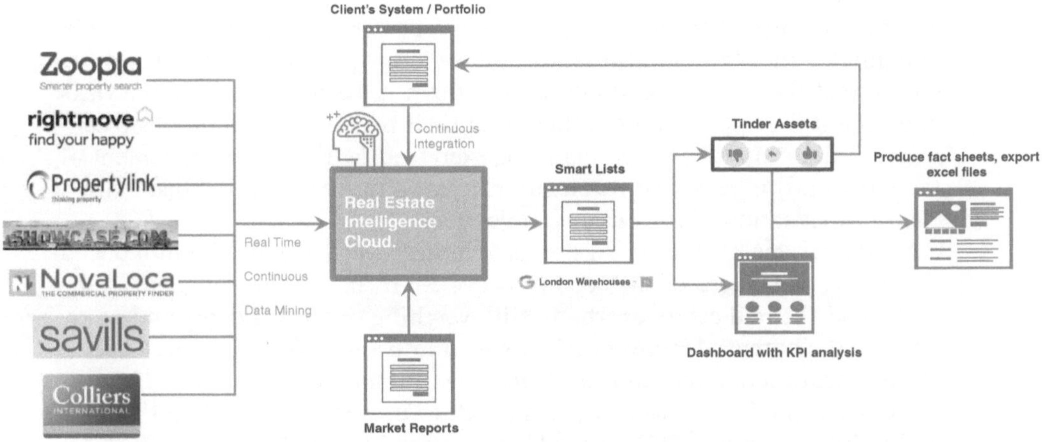

Figure 2.11 Forward-looking analysis based on unstructured data.

An alternative, more innovative and digital way now being tested trying to predict the evolution of the real estate economic cycle and the price of each property is also related to the use of big data, but of an "unstructured" nature. The unstructured data are mostly captured over the web and in real time and have often a "social" nature, as they express the views, beliefs and sentiments (the "like" or "thumbs up" of relevant cohorts of people) with regard to the properties themselves (e.g., by the way they look at them and ask for information on the ones listed for sale or renting on real estate online portals) or to factors (such as traffic, night life, quality of restaurants, and criminality) that can influence the value of the property's location or the way people would use it.

All these unstructured "big data" are then analysed by leveraging all kind of applied analytics techniques, including ML/AI applications. These applications can in fact read data and turn into more relevant information and then extract intelligence on trends and patterns and turn them into reliable predictions that would be hardly achievable by "traditional" regression analysis – even if usually though a "black box" process (Figure 2.11).

Many other examples could be found (and our alphabet soup extended) where banks are taking a holistic, reactive, or even proactive stance in understanding and managing their exposure to the real estate sector. Ultimately, their challenge becomes an integration one, to make sure that all these different initiatives are put at their most efficient and effective use by the way of an "integrated" strategy, tightly coordinated by a unique "real estate" centre of excellence – be it a "service centre" (a staff function, identified under a new tag name of chief real estate officer – CREO) or a "profit centre" (potentially developing its own business lines and value propositions for the open market, whilst serving their parent company as well, and as a dedicated division or – better – company: something we will refer to in the next chapter as REIS company).

2.3 Defining a real estate integrated strategy

Most of the initiatives described above can be very useful to help banks in managing better their almost unavoidable "long" position on the real estate sector. But they are not enough to help them in better managing the risks and exploit the opportunities inherent in their real estate dealings if no central coordination (if not command) is exercised by the top management of the bank on this issue and no clear strategy on real estate is defined, with a clear prioritisation of the targeted objectives.

Strategic objectives may, of course, change over time and be influenced by the relative stages of the economic cycle. Given the current stage of the cycle, and the real estate overhang still weighing on most European banks, but also the potential recovery of the sector into a new growth cycle, a useful exemplification of a relevant set of goals is summarised in Figure 2.12.

In this example, strategic targets include a further reduction in NPL/NPE and unlikely to pay (UTP)-related exposure (addressable with a mix of deleveraging and de-risking), a correlated limited or neutral impact on the P&L and regulatory capital of the bank, a potential progressive creation of goodwill (and hence capital gain) related to the development of a new centre of excellence and service/business platform dedicated to the real estate sector and, finally, an executable way to do all this "safely."

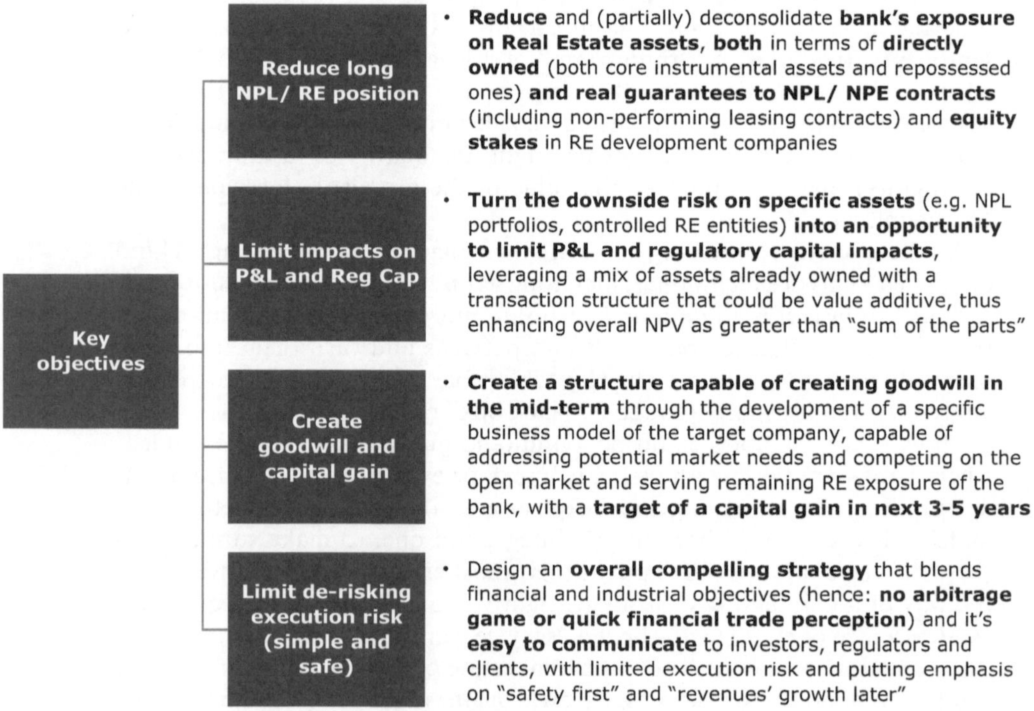

Figure 2.12 Key objective for the set-up of an REIS company.

Once a clear set of strategic objectives is set in stones and prioritised accordingly, it needs to be operationalised in the complex governance and organisational machine of the bank. The real estate strategy of the bank needs in fact to be closely embedded into its business and operating models and different initiatives, or "accelerators," need to work in line with the overall bank's strategy.

For example, a real estate strategy of a hailing bank, sandbagged by NPL and short of capital will likely be driven by a winding-down goal, where less real estate is better, and the issue is more "how to recover at best, in the quickest way, whilst pretending to keep doing new lending business as usual." And a real estate strategy of a clean, well-capitalised bank, positioned in a resurgent phase of the cycle will be more of an

> how to take advantage at best, positioning the balance sheet on the right properties sub asset classes, creating diversification but also leveraging a more aggressive exposure to sustain new fee-income producing sources and creating a new business out of it?

These questions need to be addressed starting from a clear understanding and quantification/qualification of the role played by the bank across the main value chains of real estate, including the ones related to its development or owning and renting. A target positioning can then help in clarifying

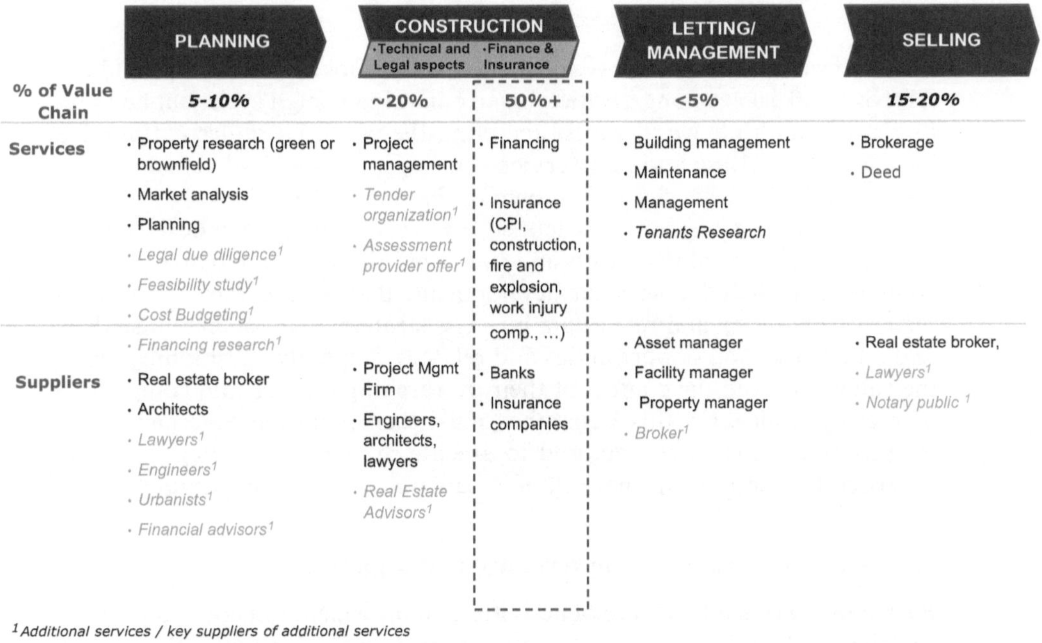

Figure 2.13 Real estate value chain: development.
Source: AlixPartners experience.

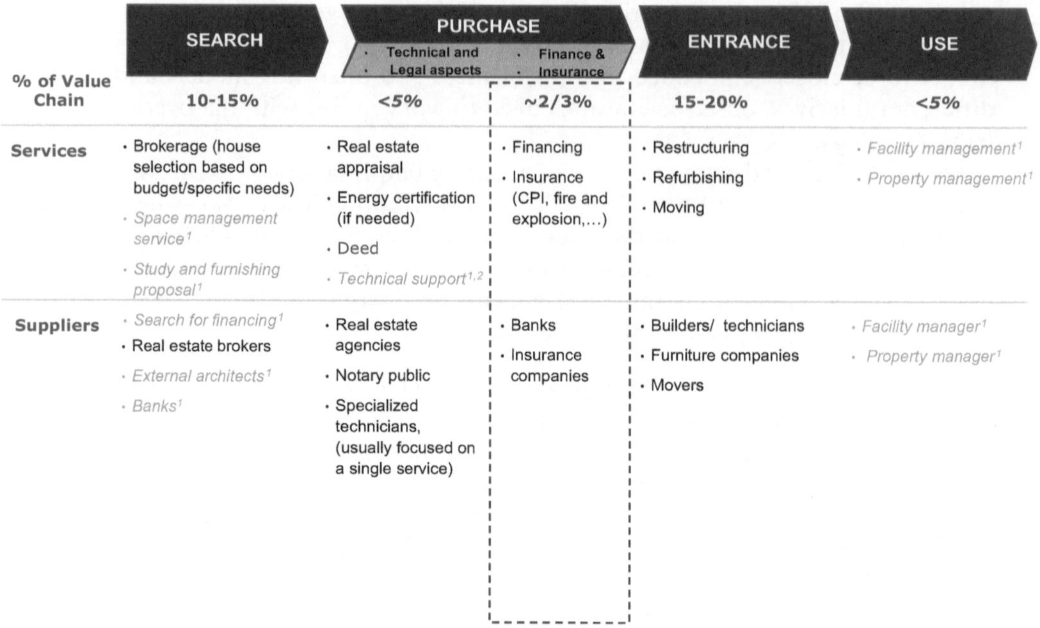

Figure 2.14 Real estate value chain: owning and renting.
Source: AlixPartners estimates.

the required competitive moves of the bank as it looks to deleverage and de-risk, or to take a new long position on an emerging benign cycle, but hedging its risks in multiple ways, whilst accreting the potential returns attainable by (e.g.) cross-selling and new service offerings. A simplified version of the main real estate value chains is shown in Figures 2.13 and 2.14.

Once a targeted positioning is defined, and a set of initiatives is designed and activated, banks need to address and overcome all the potential dis-synergies coming from their inconsistent development. Banks need then to craft an integrated banking and real estate business strategy that contextualise their real estate risks and opportunities and related competitive positioning along the value chains in the context of their overarching mission and competitive market dynamics. On this basis, they must then build the governance and organisational structures required to execute the selected strategy – sitting consistently within the framework of a regulated financial institutions.

2.4 Defining a real estate governance and organisation

By achieving this integration of activities, all informed by a consistent strategy that tackles the real estate trade-off in a proactive and holistic way, banks gain important competitive advantages. For one thing, they can better address their real estate–related risk exposure and potential diversification from an ex ante perspective (asset allocation and related underwriting and pricing on new loans) and from an ex post angle (NPEs and NPLs). They can also boost the productivity and the net margin of their REO assets and improve the yield on repossessed assets, hence heightening their exit value. Finally, they can unlock new sources of revenue (such as commissions).

They might do this, e.g., by capitalising on banking and insurance cross-selling opportunities (from mortgages, to payments, to P&C and even life insurance policies) that come from completing real estate development projects that were part of its "unlikely to pay" (UTP) or "grey area" portfolios. These achievements can all help banks pursue other strategic objectives as well. Examples include generating regulatory capital, reducing VaR and economic capital, and defining lending prices that better reflect and therefore optimise their real estate risk exposure. Actually, a different set of objectives could inform different overarching strategies for banks at different stages of their economic and real estate cycles – from "rundown" to "business transformation" to position for a new set of revenues growth opportunities.

Table 2.1 Strategic approach and objectives of REIS

Approach to setting a "Real Estate Integrated Services"	*Critical objectives pursued by "Real Estate Integrated Services"*

• Start with **"holistic" diagnostic of the real estate (RE) exposures** and **understand the main potential risks** and **opportunities** and how to address them using different levers in the specific context of the relevant RE market
• Define a **business case to create a dedicated business unit** or **service company** and related operating model **with the right set of governance, organisation, processes** and **targets**, including:
  • Regulatory capital generation and reduction of "value at risk"/ economic capital
  • Better risk-based pricing on lending and better monitoring driven by underlying valuation
  • Lower and less volatile cost of risk coming from the lending portfolio, across all its life stages
  • Increased productivity/lower operating costs of the owned assets (including repossessed ones)
  • Increased commissions and net margin from core business driven by "unlocked" situations
  • New sources of revenues, mostly commission-based, driven by new REIS
	• **Better address the risk exposure** and **potential diversification coming from RE** both from an ex ante (asset allocation and related underwriting/ pricing on new loans) and ex post (NPE/NPL) point of view
	  • Also considering future volatility of cost of risk
	• Better address the productivity and net margin of "owned" RE assets, and the yield on repossessed ones, hence increasing their exit value
	• Develop new revenue/commission-based opportunities for the bank P&L, unlocking the cross-selling opportunities coming from the completion of RE developments or restart of trading activities
	• Banks at different stages of their (and of the relevant country's) RE cycle could focus on these objectives in sequence. However, some parallel pursuit could be suggested and synergic (from "rundown," to "industrialisation," to "transformation" as new profit-seeking, adjacent business)

A summary of the strategic approach and related critical objectives pursued by a "real estate integrated strategy" is provided in Table 2.1.

However, in order to execute this "integration" in a consistent and flawless way, proper governance and organisational approaches need to be defined and implemented – defining "ad hoc" solutions that, apart from the overall business strategy and competitive positioning of the specific bank, need also to take into account the specific context of the real estate market and its overall exposure.

Bank' executives can then start addressing the right governance and organisation by diagnosing its real estate–related exposure – in the most holistic way. They can start identifying the biggest potential risks and the most promising opportunities and determining how best to address these using levers available in their market, given the specific phase of the real estate sector economic cycle in the relevant bank's geographies. It is a very local market, after all, and where location is king.

They also need to define and aggregate, based on the selected approach and critical objectives, the most relevant activities that the "integrated strategy" needs to execute, in order to pursue its aimed targets. In Table 2.2, presenting a bank in a "rundown" and then progressively "business transformation" mood, key priority activities are still largely driven by its goal of real estate (mostly coming from NPL/NPE) deleveraging and de-risking and they could be grouped into two larger blocs. It is then worth focussing on these two broader set of services and activities that need to be performed for the bank, that we could aggregate into strategy, risk, monitoring and controlling (as a staff function) and advisory, asset management services and commercialisation, with focus on the sale of assets (potentially also as a staff function, but that could become a line function, with profit and loss responsibility and a full business unit through time).

The first set of services and activities, encompassing strategy, risk, monitoring and controlling should aim at setting the overall target risk/return profile of the bank on real estate and related capital allocation: supporting the definition of the future lending policies (hence identifying the target loans portfolio allocation); providing inputs to the chief lending officer (CLO) on best allocation/diversification on real estate collaterals; defining and monitoring current direct and indirect real estate exposure risks, eventually moving towards a mark-to-market approach; defining the fair IFRS 9 compliant value of real estate assets as input to accounting and internal transfer price for incentive system settings; defining and vetting the valuation approaches of any new or existing real estate collateral, setting the golden standard of appraisals; defining and managing internal service-level agreements (SLAs) for owned assets and for the property facility management services offered; developing and owning the overall real estate dashboard, to get to a net yield (net of Capex, Opex and considering the opportunity cost) of the REO assets; and setting the overall top-down real estate strategy and helping to coordinate, from a planning perspective, the cross-selling of other products and services.

The second set of services and activities, encompassing advisory, asset management services and commercialisation could be facilitated by the set-up of a dedicated special purpose vehicle, or fully fledged company owning the real estate collaterals repossessed, and the equity stakes – mostly coming from debt conversion – of development projects at greenfield and brownfield stage.

In more detail, the services and activities carried over by this dedicated company or unit could regard the development and execution of active management strategies for the property owned, with contributions of experts from the real estate sector able to lead complex projects; the design and management of a rundown, sale strategy, working along third-party brokers and agencies, or leveraging the bank's branches (in partnership with the retail SME/distribution division of the bank) to operate its own REA; and the creation and promotion and sponsorship of other, ad hoc initiatives such as the REIT, that could be developed jointly with insurance and asset manager partners for distribution to retail and institutional clients as an investment opportunity and creating a need channel to tap new sources of capital.

Also, at a more sophisticated stage, this dedicated company could develop capabilities in-house and via an ecosystem of dedicated partnerships to accelerate the implementation of the various initiatives – fast employing skills that are not currently available in-house and that would require significant time to introduce, nurture and replicate. Finally, at a later stage of development, this dedicated company, focussing its services and activities on advisory, asset management and transaction services, could also extend its reach to the extra captive world, addressing one or few open markets, following a country-by-country strategy (as real estate markets are mostly local, and with specific characteristics varying across different jurisdictions) to address the clients of the bank, other smaller banks and else, to create a stable stream of fee-based revenues.

On this basis, the bank's management could start elaborating and developing the business case for creating a new organisational function or a proper service unit, or even a business unit that is also going to be tasked as a profit centre, according to the different kind of current positioning, development strategy and set ambitions as previously described. Whatever the option considered, a critical task is the definition of the governance, the organisational structures and the key processes the bank will need to adopt to make this consistent with its overall business and operating model – with significant variances from the "new function" to the "new business unit" extremes.

Governance, organisation and processes – as mentioned earlier – should be articulated considering the key objectives that this new structure or model will be responsible for attaining. To execute the integrated banking and real estate strategy a bank has defined, we recommend creating new types of governance and organisational structures. In the following paragraph, we take a closer look at two such structures, with a first hypothesis related to the creation a new, centrally integrated service unit, and a second one that is considering its evolution into a profit-seeking business unit, with a service "agent" left to basically monitor and control its working and ensure consistency with the overall bank's strategy. We specifically refer to these as Real Estate Integrated Services (REIS) company (whether as a service unit or business one) and as chief real estate officer (CREO).

Table 2.2 Key real estate management activities: two main categories

Risk/Strategy/ Monitoring	• **Setting the overall target risk/return profile** of the bank on real estate (RE) and related capital allocation • **Supporting** the **definition of the future lending policies** (target loans portfolio allocation), providing inputs to the CLO on best allocation/diversification on RE collaterals • **Defining** and **monitoring current direct** and **indirect RE exposure risk**, eventually moving towards a quasi-mark-to-market perspective • **Defining fair IFRS 9 value of RE assets** as input to accounting and internal transfer price for incentive system settings: • Defining and vetting the valuation approaches of any new or existing real estate collateral, setting the golden standard of appraisals • Defining/managing internal SLAs for owned assets and property facility management services offered • Developing and owning the overall RE dashboard, to get to a net yield (net of Capex, Opex and considering the opportunity cost) of the REO assets • Setting the overall top-down RE strategy • Helping to coordinate cross-selling of other products and services with the REIS

Commercialisation/ Transactions (REIS)	• Owning the RE collaterals repossessed, and the equity stakes of property companies/projects (coming from debt conversion)
	• Developing and executing:
	    • An **active management strategy**, with experts from the RE industry able to lead a development project
	    • A **sale strategy**, **working with B2B brokers**, or **leveraging the bank's branch network** (paying to the retail division a share of the commissions)
	    • **Ad hoc initiatives like the REIT** jointly with insurance or asset manager partners
	• **Developing capacity in-house** and/or **developing an ecosystem of partnerships in the relevant markets** to accelerate implementation and to fast employ skills not currently available (e.g. in-house vs. outsourced asset management)
	• **Potentially, in the longer term, providing asset**, **property** and **facility management services to the open market** and to the bank's clients (acts as a profit centre), including **negotiating JVs** with the other BUs of the bank or setting a JV with an international operator

2.5 The CREO and the REIS in the context of different strategies

From a strategic options standpoint, two main scenarios could be considered for the governance and organisation of the real estate integrated strategy of a bank. In a first scenario, a central unit (an REIS led by CREO) can be set up and act as a centre of excellence for real estate at group level. It will operate as a service centre, on a cost basis and be incentivised via multiple KPI, but with no prescriptive aim to develop and become a profit centre. In a second scenario, instead, a separate real estate unit managing all the integrated service offerings can be set as a separate business unit with P&L responsibility (REIS – usually incorporated into a company) and with an internal CREO that runs as a service centre and provide check-and-balance vis-à-vis the activities developed by profit-seeking REIS. Having clarified these two macro areas of services and activities, it now becomes easier to explain their different contextualisation for the two strategic scenarios considered.

Our first scenario (see Figure 2.15) involves the set-up of an integrated real estate unit (or dedicated company) as a service centre, where both the macro areas previously described are covered as part of its mandate. This REIS (unit or dedicated company) is chaired by a CREO that is incentivised as a non-profit-seeking decision maker and evaluated on several well-structured quantitative and qualitative KPI. This unit, and its CREO, may have (or not) direct ownership of the properties managed and is accountable for them, but it has a direct reporting line to the chief executive officer (CEO) or the executive committee of the bank, that ultimately take the final decision on investments and divestitures, hence owning the ultimate responsibility of their P&L impact.

The REIS and the CREO act as a centre of excellence for real estate, supporting and managing the processes leading to all strategic decisions that are ultimately owned by the CEO and by the executive committee – they cover and manage all the end-to-end information and promote and facilitate

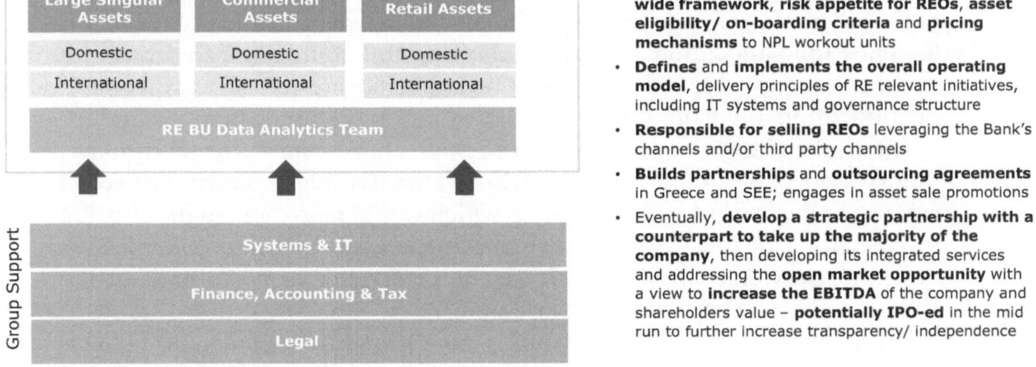

Figure 2.15 Setting up an integrated real estate unit as a service centre.

the internal alignment required to get to the final decision of the senior management. In order to achieve this, the REIS and its CREO can define and communicate the overall bank-wide framework, its risk appetite for real estate assets and exposure, the rules for asset eligibility, the on-boarding criteria and the pricing mechanisms to consider for the internal working of the overall integrated strategy – they lead from a strategic and technical perspective, potentially allocating the workload to other internal actors or managing the work of supplier and business partner.

They could also share a view to progressively promote and extend the service offerings of the bank to generate revenue opportunities coming from its real estate exposure – but that would again be promoted and executed as part of an internal service with no ultimate P&L responsibility, as much as a strategic planning, marketing, innovation and business development function would do.

Still, the REIS and its CREO would be in charge of defining and implementing the operating model and delivery principles of the most relevant real estate initiatives, including the information technology (IT) systems and governance structure needed to support them. They would also cover the transactional and commercialisation side, and they would likely be tasked on building partnerships and outsourcing agreements – driving, stirring or engaging directly into asset sale initiatives – leveraging the bank's channels and/or third-party channels to ensure the quickest and most effective wind down.

Our second scenario (depicted in Figure 2.16) would involve the creation of a business unit and (potentially) dedicated legal entity (the REIS) clearly identified as a profit centre and tasked with targets of revenues growth and profitability. The REIS will be supported (and checked and balanced) by a separate service centre, ideally defined as a staff function and headed by the CREO. This CREO – ideally reporting to the CEO or, as second best, to the chief financial officer (CFO), would be mandated to set the overall risk/return profile targeted for the bank on the real estate sector.

It would also support the definition, along with the CLO and/or the CRO of the bank, of the future lending policies, and the identification of the target loan portfolio allocation, defining, analysing and monitoring all direct and indirect risk exposures of the bank. It would then be responsible for its risks' quantification and would set the standard for real estate valuations and for its internal and external SLA related to the management of the (eventually) repossessed assets. Typically, the CREO would develop and own the overall real estate dashboard and set of KPI, which would help them in monitoring the execution of the REIS strategy and in coordinating multiple business units and service centres to promote the cross-selling on the back of the overall real estate exposure underwritten.

On the other end, the REIS would typically end up owning and managing the real estate collaterals repossessed by the bank and the equity stakes of property companies coming from the restructuring and debt-to-equity conversion of sub-performing positions. The REIS would then manage such

Figure 2.16 A business unit (REIS) supported by a service centre (CREO).

assets, on the basis of the high-level mandate assigned by the CREO, but with a degree of independence on the more granular levels of execution: defining, e.g., an active management strategy for the development for the main clusters and main assets of the portfolio, with the support of experts from the real estate industry; and a sale strategy, again working with brokers or with the internal REA of the bank, but with a clear "skin in the game" for the REIS, driven by the performance achieved in terms of exit price versus the fair price and the target realisation price assigned to this by the CREO and as part of its incentive system.

Several other "ad hoc" strategies, developed in partnership with third parties, could be thought off to augment the service offering of the REIS aimed at the open market. An REIS could, e.g., offer new, dedicated asset management products (e.g. via REIT) or services (e.g. property management) that clearly pursue the objective of growing its commission revenues, on top of the return achieved on the capital invested and at interesting levels of profitability. Ultimately, the set of objectives of the REIS, even if mandated top-down by the CREO, will tend to progressively de-correlate from those of the bank (in terms of managing at best its real estate risk exposure) with an increasing relevance, through time, of the profit-seeking activities of the REIS.

A well-known market example is shown by BNP Paribas, a global SIFI and one of the largest financial services group in Europe, that creates a quite profitable business out of a set of internal and fully captive capabilities, in less than ten years, as shown in Figure 2.17. BNP Paribas Real Estate, now

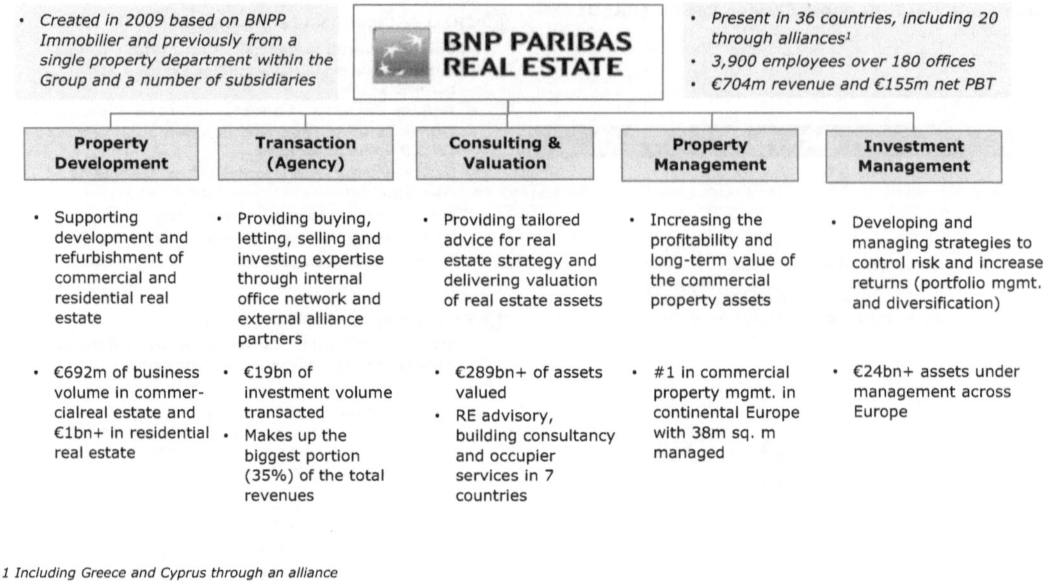

Figure 2.17 BNP Paribas Real Estate has a full range of REIS.
Source: BNP Paribas Real Estate website; financial figures based on 2016 results.

a dedicated business division, is covering most of the critical phases of the real estate value chain, from property development, to agency and brokerage, valuation and other property-related consulting services, to property management and real estate investment management.

3 Credit workout and real estate management – in the digital age

Claudio Scardovi

3.1 The two storms – financial and digital

The global financial system is being taken by two storms. The first one, the storm of digital innovation – some critics have recently argued – is really driving an "Industrial Revolution 4.0" in many sectors and notably in banking, introducing severe disruptions and discontinuities. This digital transformational is mainly driven by the unprecedented amount of data now made available and ready for use (the "new oil," according to *The Economist*) and by a new generation of applied analytics (mainly driven by ML/AI techniques).

Big data and ML/AI are now leaving the realm of R&D and truly hitting the ground, introducing new critical challenges for "traditional" banks and unleashing the new competitive forces of non-banking (or shadow banking) players – most likely digital start-ups playing their cards at FinTech. Banks are getting "robotised," with entire processes that will be progressively managed by machines: routines and AI applications – with heavy losses in terms of head counts. Even lending, banks' core business, could, one day, become the home turf of cyborgs if not of a super machine.

This first storm, already visible at the horizon but not yet fully clear in its timing and sizing, is starting to hit the top and bottom lines of banks and is following a second, older storm, that started in 2007, more than ten years ago. We are obviously referring at the storm of the global financial crisis that started with the prick of the real estate bubble and with the related mortgage sub-prime crisis in the USA and then led to the demise of Lehman Brothers and of few others regional banks and to the freezing of the interbank international markets, before spreading rapidly across most of the developed world, driving the banking industry towards a near-death experience.

This older storm, the global financial crisis, saw the unleashing of the brutal market forces coming from excessive leverage, unchecked duration mismatch, uncontrolled risk-taking – all multiplied by the increased "intensity" and "velocity" in the usage of the bank's equity capital allowed by derivatives and securitisation… almost bringing the banking system to its knees, with the required intervention of the all too visible "public hand" of the state (still the largest shareholder at a number of systemic banks in the UK, Ireland, Italy and Greece and main shareholder of "bad banks").

Governments, in the USA and in Europe, had to intervene to avoid the final meltdown of the global financial system – at the cost of taxpayers and of its public debt underwriters – given the shift in risk experienced on public debt. In some cases, as in the USA, or even in Ireland, or in Switzerland, the state intervention worked well, recapitalising the most ailing banks and supporting the creation of "bad banks" where and when needed. In most of these cases, most of the state monies have been recovered and the banking system, sufficiently cleaned, has restarted working in an almost proper and stable way. Actually, in the USA, investment banks have recently hit record earnings, surpassing any previous record as registered in 2006, just before the burst of the real estate bubble.

In other countries, the late, limited or badly designed state intervention has not yet been fully delivered on its promises, with few regional markets (say, Italy or Greece) still clogged by the excessive weight of sub-performing loans and NPL, and with the real estate market – representing the main collateral to these loans – still pretty much in a position of illiquidity and well below its over-the-cycle average valuations (a weak real estate market acts in turn negatively on the NPL cycle). It is also worth mentioning that other international markets, like Canada, Australia or the Nordics in Europe, that went through the global crisis mostly unscathed, are now most likely experiencing a real estate bubble, with potential issues to come on their banks' asset quality.

Following one of the most typical "market failures" (the "adverse selection" one), the asymmetric information characterising the NPE/NPL market in continental Europe has led to further issues for the banks with a significant and certainly unwelcome exposure to both loans and real estate collaterals. In fact, these banks have been unable to tap effectively new private funding and are therefore themselves wary of extending new credit.

As they have avoided a clear-cut separation and recognition, on a mark-to-market basis, of the "good" and of the "bad apples" in their portfolio, they still discount the scepticism of credit agencies and equity investors alike, with "market-to-book" ratios well below one. As they are unclear on "how many" resources they need to support their "bad bank" portion, they have also been remarkably uncommitted on the origination of new business, let alone on investments in designing and executing innovation in their business and operating model to address the digital innovation storm. Troubled NPE/NPL heavy banks risk then losing the boat of the digital revolution, with even more worrying consequences – as they are caught in a vicious circle that is difficult to break.

3.2 The "many" transformations of the banking sector

The most recent storm of "digital innovation," hitting hard the international and local players in better shape, is becoming something of a perfect storm for some of the most traditional banks operating in continental Europe, which are still dominated by their focus on getting rid of their NPE/NPL exposure. They have dedicated little attention, and almost no capital budgeting, to undertake their digital transformation journey, for the lack of financial resources and management focus.

The exemplification may be crude, but observing these banks effort to get out of their past mistakes and postponing their worries about their future is a little like seeing a patient being treated for the amputation of a hand or an arm, with the surgery doctor not paying much attention and postponing his treatments for the patient's open heart surgery that would also need to be undertaken in parallel (and maybe with even more urgency). In a way, banks cannot cure their ailing past if they are not addressing their worrying future as well – and manage to get through their present times alive.

Transformations are needed, and several of them – all different – are required to get banks out of these storms and off the woods of the crisis factors (financial and digital) specifically. A first wave of "transformations 1.0" was mostly pursued by banks in the aftermath of the global financial crisis, with its zenith usually epitomised by the failure of Lehman Brothers, on September 15, 2008.

These "transformations 1.0" were usually focused at fighting for survival in the short run, de-risking and deleveraging aggressively the banks' balance sheet, and reducing the "intensity" and velocity" of its capital usage: e.g. reducing their exposure to risky lending like sub-primes and emerging markets and alt-A financial trading instruments, limiting their total assets-to-equity ratio and duration mismatch, and almost stopping any activity on the derivatives and securitisation side.

After these, a new wave of "transformations 2.0" was then aimed at redesigning the cost structure of banks and of other financial intermediaries on the basis of the "new normal" sustainable revenues – to put it bluntly, focusing on cost takeout: firing people and closing branches, amongst other things. Some players have taken inspiration on this from other industries, introducing principles of "industrialisation," to increase not only their efficiency but also the efficacy of their operating model (hence its productivity): taking ideas and experiences from other sectors (e.g. automotive) that already went through several "near-death experiences" and learned to survive in a world of ultra-thin margins – where standardisation, lean processes, pooling of shared resources and Six Sigma quality become the basis (the qualifiers) to compete, but by no means the winners.

A new-new wave of "transformation 3.0" is now required to address the digital innovation challenge, fostered by changes in regulation (e.g. the PSD2 and new "open data" requirements), the increased competition coming from

FinTech start-ups (such as The Lending Club), non-banks (such as the telecom provider Safaricom) and big digital (such as Apple, Google, Facebook and Amazon, or Ten Cents, Alibaba and Baidu in China) and the evolving demand of generation Y and Z customers.

Some global SIFI have announced investment plans for billions of Euro, planning the re-platforming of most of their core IT systems and applications, the redesign, end-to-end and in a more digitally savvy way, of some of their most critical customers' journeys and the definition of entirely new, more disruptive "use cases" that leverage data, ML/AI, but also new business models and solutions that are more stakeholders-encompassing and able to create new value in the ecosystem.

How can then traditional NPE/NPL sandbagged banks – most of them based in continental Europe (but not only as other negative credit cycles hit other geographies and markets) – get this right? Have these banks still very involved with the heavy lifting remaining from the "transformation 1.0" and with the less than sufficient earlier results from the "transformation 2.0" (addressing efficiency, not to mention efficacy) a chance to do the "transformation 3.0" well and in a timely manner?

Ultimately, can these banks avoid the "risk of the frog" (i.e. of getting cooked as the water temperature reaches quickly the boiling point and the frog waits too much before jumping out of this (truly) burning platform)? Can they leap frog, and in which way? Can they come up, out of their own weaknesses, with some unexpected strength and competitive advantage?

3.3 A chance to leap frog – you have to start from somewhere

How can these NPL clogged banks (most of them based in continental Europe, but not only as other negative credit cycles hit other geographies) get this right? There are a couple of good news to the benefit of traditional banks that are still long on NPE, NPL and real estate exposure.

On one side, much of the talk and hype on digital transformation is actually... just that, as multiple transformation plans and big budgeted investments in new technologies have failed to concretely materialise as yet – for the combination of several factors, including too big and too ambitious plan, too unclear on what to do and deliver, and given the almost inevitable internal cultural resistance to change of banks that are already in better shape and that, having make it well through the first storm, are just feeling in a safe harbour again, and taking some time before changing path, with the urgency of the FinTech challenge not yet hitting their financials in a relevant way as well.

On the other side, if we buy the idea that digital transformation should not be a "grand plan" to revolutionise the bank from A to Z (with Z being maybe the right end target, but not a practical ambition to start with) but something more of a pragmatic plan to do "something about something," then any point of the starting journey is as good as others, if it fulfils a set of clear criteria.

Such criteria are as following: it's a data/information critical business/service; with great opportunities to create transparency and intelligence by leveraging on new applied analytics techniques (the more "traditional" are the metrics and analytics currently used by the bank, the greater the opportunity to do better); in very traditional, underlying economic sector; that is urgent and critical for the bank to address and solve – looking not just at targets of efficiency but also efficacy and time to market; and, finally, that is also potentially introducing new governance and organisational models (and related processes) as a way to really change the paradigm and create new incremental value at the level of its overall ecosystem and for multiple stakeholders.

The credit workout (CWO) and real estate, as businesses and services, are just about fitting in the best possible way across all these multiple criteria. And the combination of the two could stand as the ideal issue/solution construct to start with – to change things in a holistic way, truly revolutionising their workings and expectations of transformation – getting them digital to create real value added.

As a start, value creation in contemporary "traditional" banking is today, particularly in mature markets such as continental Europe but in emerging markets like China, India, Russia and even the Middle East as well, as much as about "new" value creation as it is (or should be) about value preservation and recovery. And what about the UK, or the USA, if we consider what has already been moved to "shadow banking" players. What about then future volatilities in the real estate sectors of Canada and Australia, France and the UK, China and the Nordics etc.? Aren't banks and other financial players mostly focused on how to migrate in their favour the remaining value of these assets anyway and not focused as much on new value creation endeavours?

The amount of NPE and NPL left as remaining of the global financial crisis on the balance sheet of international banks and of other financial investors is just staggering, with official numbers probably underweighting the phenomenon, as other loans are still being treated with "intensive care" and classified as "grey area" (with variations in different shades so numerous so as to recollect the eponymous book) and UTP, whilst others are just being kicked (as the proverbial can) down the road – with banks still extending and pretending that everything will be good again, in a not so near future (technically, you just have to wait long enough and hope for a high inflation).

Banks, we have said, are not the only interested counterpart in this "workout" challenge, as we cannot forget the NPE and NPL that have already left their books as they were sold, via securitisation or straight sale, to professional investors or to the state (in the case of the creation of "bad banks" recapitalised with public, taxpayers-funded, money). No matter who the current owner is, all these financial and underlying real assets are still there and are still waiting to be "worked out" – with most of their chances of a good recovery resting on the active management of their underlying collaterals, first and foremost real estate assets that need to be "holistically" and "actively" managed.

If such a big opportunity to recover huge amounts of value exists, and if the creation of new economic value in banking is proving so hard anyway, why has the effort of best banks and bankers been so limited so far? And why have the approaches and methodologies to CWO and proactive, holistic and integrated real estate management remained so basic, sometimes confined to the realm (and to the related privileges) of few practitioners happy to work in opaque and less than efficient settings? Why, in other words, a proper "science" has not developed for this most "alternative asset management" subsector, given its vast opportunities to create "alpha" (defined as sustainable and uncorrelated excess returns that a CWO and real estate servicers could get on top of the market performance) through technology, process excellence, and the likes?

The opportunity is large and even larger if banks, professional investors and recovery services players as well move quickly and straight to a digital end game (something we could end up dubbing "credit workout and real estate app") that is capitalising and managing vast amounts of data (both structured and unstructured), to be analysed by advanced analytical capabilities leveraging ML/AI, to produce intelligence on the best way to work out and recovery, building an end-to-end excellence embedded in the process and organisation of a digital organisation that truly aims to deliver alpha, in a transparent way, to the benefit of the owners of the loans, but of the other related stakeholders as well – starting from the "customer-debtor" and encompassing the real estate and economic cycles. This will be discussed in the coming chapters.

3.4 The day of reckoning in continental Europe – the new European Central Bank rules

The day of reckoning for the paramount NPE and NPL exposure inherited by banks from the past global financial crisis has been invoked many times in the past years and usually with limited effect. Still, the tipping point could be now truly approaching in continental Europe, and this time for good.

Not only has the European Central Bank (ECB) published recently (spring 2017) a new set of guidelines to set straight the current governance, organisational and processes-based approaches of CWO units owned by banks. But also its new recommended guidelines are "suggesting" provision policies that require the full accounting and depreciation of unsecured NPL within two years, and within seven years for the secured ones, therefore almost forcing banks to "recover or sell" (they capital will be hit anyway) as their incentives to kick the can down the road are brought to a minimum.

Following the ECB governance, organisational and process-based guidelines, banks will be incentivised to accelerate the path to final recovery, with a greater focus on the optimisation of their NPV (ideally connected with the IFRS 9 value representation that is already in place from January 2018 – shifting the valuation approach from "losses incurred" to "expected losses").

Following the accounting guidelines, banks could instead decide to sell whilst retaining some "earn-out" optionality on future, higher recovery rates, and the end investor will, however, need to find its way to "create alpha" out of that portfolio, even if it flips this through multiple counterparts, stripping collaterals aside as a quick way to start realising cash flow, if not "real" economic value.

The challenge for them all is to realise the "optimal value preservation and recovery" on the NPL/NPE – as a mix of optimal workout on the loans and active, holistic and integrated management on the repossessed real estate collaterals. Indeed, CWO and collection and real estate management – traditionally one of the most opaque and underinvested components of the banking lending value chain – are now one of the most critical play at stake for the banking sector.

An optimal approach to both, as commented earlier, could allow banks to recover their asset quality faster, generate regulatory capital, smooth volatility in provisions and hence earnings and dividends and – potentially – provide further sources of fee-income growth. These same advocated proactive, holistic and integrated approaches would also support the overall economy, helping the new, positive credit cycle restart, sustaining the growth of the construction industry and, in turn, of further investments and consumption cycles in the overall economy – for retail and corporates alike.

In a "day of reckoning scenario," CWO and real estate management need to be considered, de facto, as "vertical" components of the larger alternative asset management industry, where higher, above-market, uncorrelated, sustainable gains ("alpha") are attainable, given large the volumes at stake, the opaque and underinvested starting points and the opportunities brought about by the industrialisation and digitalisation of this "business" (as opposed to mere "service").

Interesting "alpha" could be created not only by leveraging robotisation, automation, standardisation on one side (what we have sometimes defined as "industrialisation" of the banking sector) but also by harnessing the disruptive power of structured and unstructured information, ML/AI applications and the end-to-end electronification of new, breakthrough use cases on the other (digitalisation – what we also referred as "synapsezation"[1]).

Eventually, the return on investment opportunities (coming more from value preservation than from value creation) from such a "business" could be amongst the highest attainablse at industry level and an exciting opportunity to attract, grow and retain talents. Should the bank decide to pursue the digitalisation angle (and not only the industrialisation one) and target aggressively the Nirvana "credit workout and real estate management app," if successful, it could also provide a first case of full digital transformation in banking – the "something about something" delivered against a pot of very sizeable value to be attained, as opposed to the many fads and consultants' talks on "digitisation."

In order to design and execute at best such opportunities, the CWO unit and their heir-apparent (along the value chain of recovery and optimisation), the real estate integrated services unit (or "REIS" unit), whether "bank owned" or "financial investors" owned, or independent, addressing a captive client or the open market, must embrace an holistic, active and integrated approach and invest as much in new governance and organisational and HR management models, as much as in data management, ML/AI and new digitisation use cases that start from the value end games and redraw the relevant processes front-to-back, end-to-end, superimposing a new way of working on the organisation as a result.

3.5 Back to the future: from bad to good assets

The end game of a CWO and real estate management functions or companies "getting digital" is larger than that, potentially aiming at creating new value and not just preserving the existing one, defending it from mere destruction or from unjustified migrations and misappropriations along its way. In fact, as best practice CWO units get "digital," they may consider further discontinuous moves, introducing new, breakthrough functionalities, starting from IFRS 9 industrialised and fully automated valuation tools, aggregation and other portfolio management tools, cluster and dossier-level optimisation tools (built on self-learning technologies powered by ML/AI) and even getting to the mark-to-market of collaterals and loans driven by digital intelligence.

The mark-to-market scenario for a real estate collateral, specifically, may look like a "fiction," as banks would need to start from a base case of real estate appraisals done once in a while, following disputable and often inconsistent methodologies and by independent advisors that are all too often prey to their "client's capture" phenomenon (with the advisor ending up expressing the value expected and hoped for by the client, that is actually hiring them and footing the bill).

Still, the very lateness in the "state of the art" of this industry, and the renewed regulatory focus, could provide the perfect ground for quick and brutal accelerations that do not need to integrate and syndicate new technologies and scientific methods with the existing ones – as not much is there to be capitalised anyway. Not to mention the potential money at play – if we think of the potential applications of the perfect algorithm able to set best recovery strategies, or the mark-to-market valuation (and related mean, variance and distribution of frequency) of any real estate collateral…

They would create the basis for huge efficiency and efficacy opportunities for banks and investors. The case for getting workout and active real estate digital could become a case to deliver substantial real value on a two-fold perspective: (1) on the NPE/NPL recovery side (as already commented) and (potentially) on the underwriting of new loans one, for the banks; and (2) on the investment side for hedge and private equity investors. Starting from the many mistakes of the past, and applying advanced data management and ML/AI-based applied analytics, banks or investors could derive an incredibly powerful new intelligence to do better lending (or better investments) in the future, applying the lessons learned in the commercial origination, risk-based pricing, collateral and covenant structuring, and final underwriting of new loans (not to mention their later collection).

We have already discussed (for reference, see Figures 3.1 and 3.2) how the mark-to-market valuation of real estate assets could be developed as a combination of macro- and microeconomic "traditional," statistically conjoint analysis, based on structured information, and of further ML/AI analysis mostly based on unstructured information, including social, subjective information, that could be gathered on the Internet in real time, via crawler (scrapping information from websites as they appear) and application program interfaces (API). These "unstructured" data would then be analysed via ML/AI applications, informing the bank's (or investor's) information system to support final decision-making and support a final course of action – driven by the real-time valuation of properties.

More specifically, these complementary unstructured data set would include all kind of social information that contribute to make a location particularly looked for, or vice versa. It would then include (as shown in

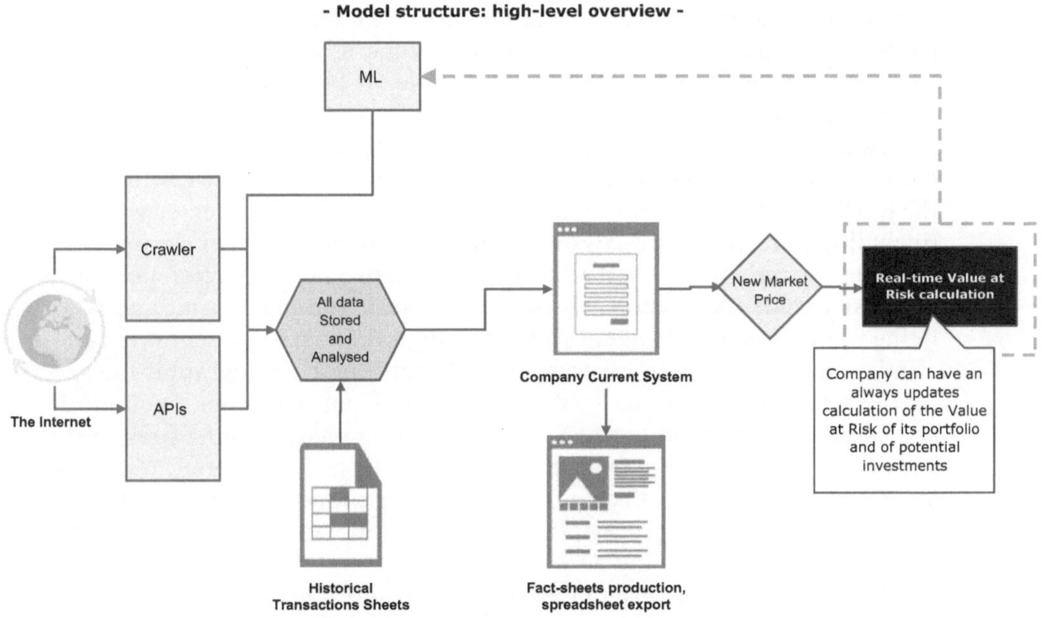

Figure 3.1 Capturing big data to get to a mark-to-market price.

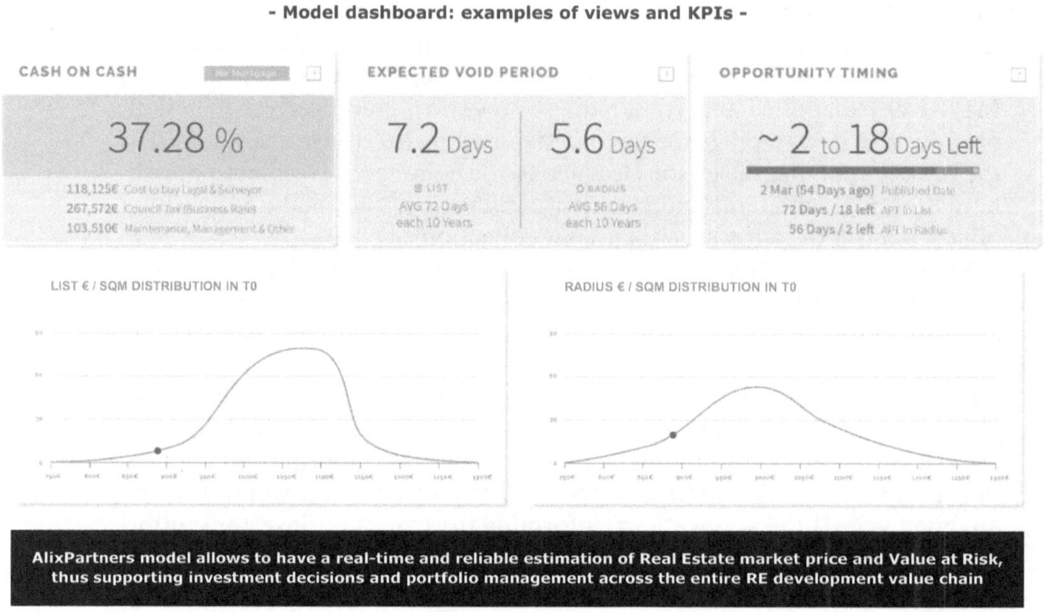

Figure 3.2 Market information on interactive, real-time dashboard.

Table 3.1) information on how people like the place, or its nightlife and restaurants, and it would make predictions on how their expectations and perceived happiness could change through time if, e.g., traffic or weather conditions are changing, or the criminality rate is increasing, or new stores are opened, and entertainment options are offered.

New approaches to credit scoring based on structured and unstructured data and ML/AI applications are also getting more and more common in the FinTech space, usually mixing behavioural analysis of the end customer (including psychometric analysis to gauge how much risk taker she or he is) and other social information relating to the main cohorts of reference (say, university students in their early twenties, born in the countryside and now living in London, multilingual and native digital, pursuing a degree in economics and business administration) and traditional, demographic ones.

On this front, leveraging past data coming from bad loans to support analysis and predictions on the new underwriting phases, whilst stress testing earlier results coming from behavioural analysis with more traditional statistical analysis, can become an interesting proposition for banks, as their risk management proceeds like a salmon – moving from the bad loans to the UTP and performing ones.

On another front, an even more interesting and potentially complementary approach would consider starting from the analysis of the collateral, to gauge the risk of the loan, as it is certainly not only dependent on the counterpart but also driven by the volatility in the value of the underlying.

Table 3.1 Captured "big data" should include unstructured data

Information	*Description*	*Source*
Real sale price	Price + Sqm + Distribution + Time evolution	Public repositories
Centrality	Value + Time evolution	Google Maps API
Neighbourhood type	Value	Google Maps API
Number of transactions per area	Value + Time evolution	RE agents, RE groups, public repositories
Avg. listed days	Value + Average time evolution	RE agents, RE groups
Change in labour dynamics	Time evolution	JOB online indexes
Job postings	Value + Time evolution	JOB online indexes
Tourism activity	Value + Time evolution	Tourism websites (e.g. Booking, Trivago, Airbnb)
Night life	Value + Time evolution	Nightlife & tourism sources
Cultural life	Value + Time evolution	Tourism & cultural sources
Traffic	Value + Time evolution	Google Maps API
Travel/transport connectivity	Value + Time evolution	Google Maps API
Presence of parking spaces	Value + Time evolution	Google Maps API
Surrounding relevant points (e.g. airport)	Value + Time evolution	Google Maps API
Green areas proximity	Value + Time evolution	Google Maps API
Commerce proximity	Value + Time evolution	Google Maps API, Tripadvisor, Yelp
Services proximity	Value + Time evolution	Google Maps API, Tripadvisor, Yelp
Seismic risk	Value + Time evolution	Emidius, Ingv
Flood risk	Value + Time evolution	Emidius, Ingv
Life quality rate	Cost of living, business freedom, safety	Teleport.org API
Interest ratio per asset	Number of likes, number of questions, number of clicks	Public screening & matching app – social media
Profiling social media clusters per asset	Education, job, career, mobility, location, brands	Public screening & matching app – social media

Take, e.g., a real estate asset, on a leasing or banking loan to a retail or corporate client and consider (assuming an economically rational behaviour of the borrower) how so much of the loan PD and LGD are driven by volatility and expected return on that asset, as if it were a financial one, that could be fully described by its frequency distribution. Interactive dashboards could be designed to offer an integrated view of all structured and unstructured information collected, with selected KPI used to monitor its behaviour.

Ultimately, the unintended consequence of doing CWO and real estate management in a more scientific, digitally savvy way could imply that a larger digital transformation of the entire lending value chain becomes attainable, changing the banking business at its core, with relevant implications at the level of its overall lending supply, on the real estate sector and on the overall economic cycle – hence on the sustainable rate of growth of the economy. In this way, new value creation opportunities could surpass the value preservation ones and change the dimension of this profession and of its practitioners – making whole and seamless the "digital" lending value chain.

3.6 Towards a real estate value at risk

If we take a look at the most well-known "risk management" handbooks for banks, we will likely find a long list of potential risk taxonomies and related risk factor. Most likely, we will not find a "real estate risk" in this list, as if it were something of no interest for financial services intermediaries. Still, most of the recent (and historical) bank failures have been driven by a collapse in the value of the real estate sector, then heavily impacting on the asset quality of the banks (loans mostly) via the collateral to those loans, the properties directly owned and their exposure to development projects.

It is then critical, as part of this shift towards a proactive, holistic and integrated approach to the management of CWO activities and real estate services, to define what could be the framework for monitoring and analysing such a "real estate risk." If we take the perspective of a real estate developments (or of a real estate development company), several macro risk areas could be logically identified, as shown in Table 3.2 – from financial to real estate and operational, to financial, to regulatory and compliance, to environmental etc.. For each of these categories, several sub-drivers could then be defined (e.g. market price, city planning, development).

For each macro area and sub-risk drivers, it is then possible to define an appropriate methodology to quantify, monitor and eventually predict their future behaviour and how they would negatively impact across the main phases of the real estate value chain (Figure 3.3). Of critical importance, the market price (the exit value of a long development project) remains a key risk factor to try and measure, as it also captures other risk factors as they could be included in the expectations of the demand side and influence negatively the value of properties as marketed as, e.g., any environmental risk, or potential changes in the city planning impacting the timing and end use of the development could be discounted by institutional investors looking to but to let.

As we have argued before, the market price for properties that we also dub as the almost unavoidable "intrinsic risk" of the real estate sector is one of the key challenges for the evolution of risk management in both real estate and banking (as banks are a major underwriter of real estate risk). A challenge is that both real estate companies and banks could try to address

Table 3.2 Key risks of the real estate development value chain

Areas	*Risks*	*Description*
Real estate and operational	Market price	Significant divergences in assets market value due to high volatility of real estate assets due to fluctuations in final, exit market price by specific location and end use
	City planning	Sudden changes in urbanistic requirements (e.g. height of buildings, energy-saving requirements, social housing) and significant delays/stops in projects approvals
	Development	Unexpected land structural weaknesses (e.g. presence of water, gas, toxic deposits), engineering failures (e.g. structure, materials) and design flaws
Financial	Capital markets	Unexpected changes to basic interest rates, foreign exchange and currencies values and basic inflation rates, including changes in price of commodities needed to build
	Credit	Sudden credit difficulties due to termination of credit lines (e.g. breach of warranty) or for suppliers and/or customers difficulties (e.g. bankruptcy or liquidation)
	Liquidity	Cash shortage due to significant increase in working capital levels and/or required investments or larger than expected go to market of first developed "plots"
Regulatory and compliance	Regulatory	Unforeseen changes in corporate (e.g. reporting, accounting) and/or real estate development and management regulation (e.g. records keeping, statements)
	Compliance	Unexpected reports or whistleblowing on company or suppliers compliance breaches (e.g. AML, KYC) with specific reference to corruption and money laundering cases
	Legal	Claims due to labour incidents or deaths, delays in project deliveries or payments and disputes with suppliers – associated potential delays, liabilities, bad reputation
Environmental	Macroeconomic	Economic growth stop or recession (country-specific or general), lower access to credit and rise in unemployment, hence drop in rents and available income
	Macroeconomic	Earthquakes and volcanoes, floods and tsunamis, and other unexpected and unpredicted natural disasters, including act of terrorisms
	Others	Changes in political situations and/or population sentiment, country-specific risks (e.g. nationalisation of projects), country-level corruption and other scandals

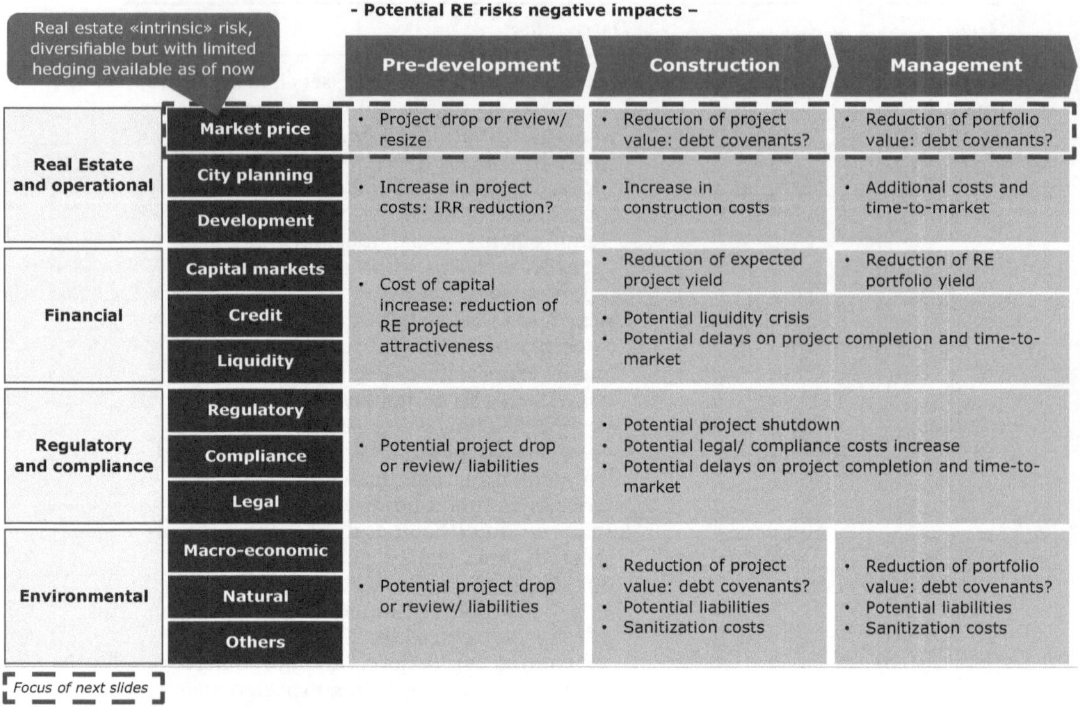

Figure 3.3 Potential impacts across the real estate value chain.

leveraging a mix of structured and unstructured "big data" pools and both traditional statistical and more innovative ML/AI analysis. Once a mark-to-market valuation of properties is achieved, it will then be possible to calculate their set of variances and covariances and, from that basis, get to a VaR quantification for the real estate risk, similarly to what has been done for market or credit risk.

This RE VaR would then provide the basis for a new generation of much more advanced enterprise-wide risk management systems, where risk/return profitability analysis can be done at the single asset level or at the portfolio level, for internationally diversified real estate development companies and for banks with a sufficiently large and heterogeneous loan book with properties as a collateral.

Note

1 "Digital transformation in financial services", Claudio Scardovi, Springer 2017.

Reference

Scardovi, C., 2017, Banks should practice active, holistic, and integrated real estate management – and they should do it now, AlixPartners.

4 Data management

NPL assessment in a digital world

Claudio Scardovi

4.1 Lending and real estate valuation: fifty shades of grey

Stable, objective value assessments, in the lending and real estate businesses, has been for decades more of a myth than reality. The value of a loan, or of a real estate asset (and of a loan whose main collateral is a real estate asset) is, by definition, something extremely "volatile" and "subjective." It is "volatile," as it is dependent from many endogenous and exogenous factors, from the credit quality and behaviour of the borrower, to the quality and performance of the underlying property to the loan, to the state of the overall economy – anything from its rate of growth, prevailing interest rate and money and lending supply, inflation, unemployment, available income and many others.

Value is also "subjective," as it is dependent from the expected asset end utilisation (ideally the highest and best available use) of the current or targeted final owner – his or her investment strategy, approach to recovery, restructuring and liquidation (in the case of an NPE or NPL) or final end use (in the case of a real estate property: for owning and direct use or renting).

The idea of having lending portfolios, and portfolios made up of their related real estate collaterals, or hard properties already repossessed and directly owned by the bank, showing limited volatility through time, with the occasional write-off as the bank is approaching the end of a bad cycle, is just a myth, or actually an accounting objective. It is based on a static view of values, subject to limited testing of their real, mark-to-market creditworthiness, and untested vis-à-vis their exposure on performance risk (the risk that a loan extended at, say 3% – given prevailing market forces at the time, could have been extended at 4% or 5%–6%, at similar counterparts and with the same given collaterals, as market conditions change; a similar example could be applied to a property, rented at 3%, with rents going then to 4% or 5%–6%). A mark-to-market view would reflect a heavy loss for both.

In fact, as argued in previous chapters, loans and real estate assets could be (at least in theory, as we are mindful of the many practical difficulties) marketed to market and, indeed, we have discussed, they should be, initially via proxy and adopting more and more sophisticated approaches, by embracing the digital revolution brought about by the use of structured and unstructured (qualitative, also coming from social sources) "big data" and the more and more powerful applied analytics connected to ML/AI applications.

A mark-to-market approach to loans and real estate would allow banks to better manage their underwriting policies and risk-based pricing and their restructuring, recovery and liquidation strategies as well, managing at best their exposure during the critical "limbo," between the performing and non-performing stages (i.e. when the loan and its related property is moving towards a near-performing or sub-performing stage, also commonly called, by bankers and regulators alike, "grey area" – indeed, as for the eponymous main character of the bestselling book, there are many shades of grey that are difficult to qualify and quantify, but nonetheless worth the trial).

These many "shades" of grey are determined by the interplay of multiple risk factors. We have mentioned the "solvency risk" and the "performance risk" of a loan, but we should not forget other critical ones such as the "real estate risk" as we discussed in the previous chapter. A real estate risk mostly determined by negative swings in the real estate cycle impacting on the value of the collateral and hence of the loan, by influencing its PD, LGD and EAD (and term to maturity).

Banks should also avoid forgetting the "operational risk" – the downside in value related to many factors such as the operational failure of the IT system supporting the management of the loan and their related properties. They should also consider the conduct risk on the side of the bank employees and counterparts to the loan, or other catastrophic events like terrorism or natural disasters that could affect the willingness or ability of the borrower to perform, or the value of the collateralised properties etc. The value of loans backed by real estate and of properties are also influenced by the interplay of a multitude of micro- and macroeconomic factors, some of them of a behavioural nature (also impacting on the risk factors above) – anything from the perceived attractiveness of a certain location – its traffic, development of shopping or residential areas, exposure to sun or pollution, criminality rate, the monetary policies and related lending supply, the purchasing power given swings in unemployment, the available income and foreign exchange rate are just few examples of factors that should be considered when assessing the value of a property.

This "fifty shades of grey" in loan and real estate valuation is also determined by the subjectivity inherent in the valuation process; this should always start with the question "which value for whom?," as the value of a flat situated near an office area and primary school will be higher for a white-collar person working there and with a family and sons approaching school age (and less so for a single, soccer player, looking for a more mundane lifestyle, and travelling all the time anyway).

As it would be impractical to keep working on the analysis of a multitude of values related to a number of potential counterparts, the valuation process should then answer to the question "who is the highest and best available user for that property?" – willing and capable to pay the price that is matching the NPV of its highest and best (subjective) future use, in a transparent, liquid and competitive market. Following is an optimal allocation of scarce resources.

We can define the target optimal valuation process for a real estate backed loan or for a property as the one that is offering a "mark-to-market" approach, based on multiple, relevant risk factors and on their related micro and macro influencing factors. The optimal process should also have a subjective view that is considering who the target end buyer and owner is (and who would be the best available as of now). On this basis, we can then work backward, looking at what is done today in the banking space and identifying the gap to get to the optimal solution. We will then be able to discuss and address the key components of the target end state, from data and analytics, to models and methods, and see what impacts on a holistic, active and integrated value management it could have.

4.2 Moving towards a "fair value" approach

Under current accounting regime (i.e. before the introduction of the IFRS 9 principle, with its first adoption that happened in January 2018), the valuation approach used to assess a lending portfolio, whether performing, near-performing or sub-performing (including into this the "grey area") or non-performing, has been grounded on a backward-looking, historical-based approach – a nice way to say that performing loans are never re-valued till maturity (hence their fictitiously low, or "zero" volatility) and NPL are written off just on their post-mortem, with a few zombies still going around freely.

Real estate properties used as collaterals to loans have also been assessed mostly on the basis of comparables (proxy like "price per square/cubic meter" or "price per bedroom") that are also grounded on historical data and very rough in the way they can discriminate a good or bad quality asset ("new," "need refurbishment" or "rundown" being the typical categories) or their location ("city centre," "rural," or "industrial area" – "prime location," the most segmented approaches).

Also, real estate appraisals have suffered from their limited frequency (usually done at underwriting and then rarely reassessed through the life of the mortgage) and by "independent" appraisal professionals that have tended to fall short of minimal methodological standards and subject to "client capture" (as they are hired and paid by the bank, they tend to express the valuation that is hoped for by the bankers – i.e. the one that is supporting their P&L and regulatory capital targets).

According to current "best practices," the revaluation approach done by banks on existing lending portfolios is then based on the available historical information (usually in need of heavy lifting into a more structured, cleaned up, dedicated data base) and subject to stratification analysis carried out in terms of loans distribution by gross book value (GBV) size; level of collateralisation (unsecured vs. secured – of which, how much from real estate, equipment, personal guarantees or else); vintage (average life for each stage) and status analysis (the fifty shades of grey, reduced to a few: performing, UTP, doubtful); concentration analysis (Pareto analysis showing how many borrower groups are explaining a 50%, 80% or 90% of the overall exposure of the bank); loan distribution by net book value (NBV) and related coverage by typology; and status of legal procedures or indication of stage in its potential restructuring or extrajudicial ones.

Based on most historical information and this "stratification" analysis, best practice banks are then deriving target recovery rates following a segmentation approach – observing internal and (where available) market recovery benchmarks of achieved workout performances for similar "loan buckets." These "buckets" are defined out of the possible permutations that can be obtained selecting some of the key drivers used for the stratification analysis. As an example, permutations can be obtained using the different stratifications observed by superimposing on the loan portfolio the segmentational criteria of size of the dossier (by GBV), vintage of the dossier, presence of a collateral and legal status (e.g. initiated bankruptcy or advance extrajudicial negotiation) (Figure 4.1).

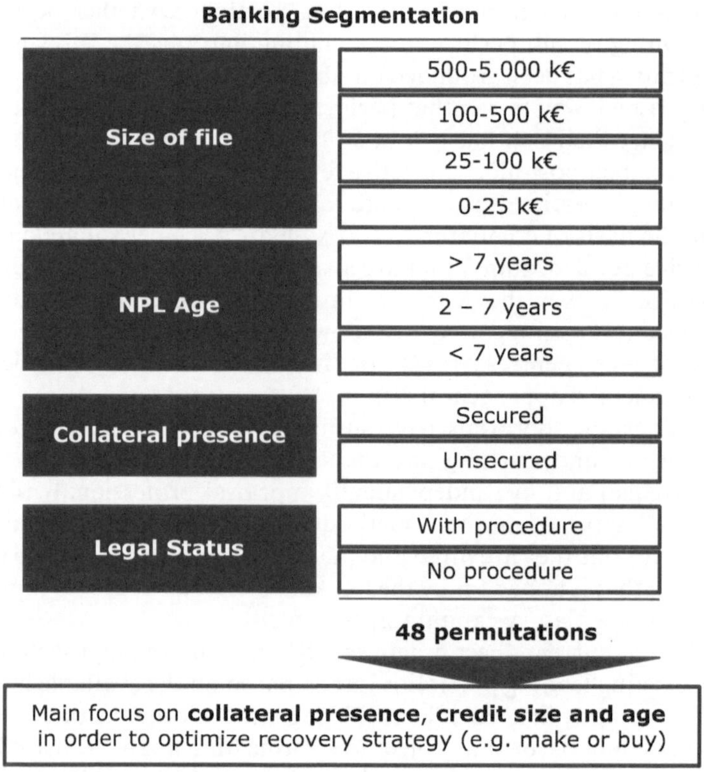

Figure 4.1 Segmentational approach to NPL.

As "best practice" this can be, this "historical stratification" approach falls short on many instances that should already be obvious vis-à-vis the description of the "optimal" target end state of a valuation that is "marketed to market" and subjectively defined according to the best available and willing end user or investor. On one side, the use of internal and external benchmarks is factoring in a previous "market era" that is simply not relevant anymore – and for a few potential reasons.

Different macroeconomic scenarios could have significantly changed the ability of borrowers to repay their obligations (e.g. with a significant rise in unemployment); or the changes in transparency, liquidity and competitiveness of the real estate market (no matter what the "fundamental" value of the collateralised properties) could simply prevent or constraint the open and full monetisation of those assets – e.g. discount on auctions and their feasible frequency can dramatically increase/decrease (respectively) during periods of lending and real estate market dislocation, making a "fire sale" almost impossible to execute in reasonably economic terms; and the same reasoning could apply to private placements of NPE/NPL portfolios to private equity funds.

Other external factors, exogenous to the bank, are also related to regulatory and accounting treatment – with weaker regulatory guidelines (on their derived capital absorption) that may imply more "flexibility" in NPE/NPL management; or more stringent accounting guidelines working the other way around, as it should be the case for the new, suggested guiding principles proposed by the ECB to fully write-off unsecured loans after two years and secured ones after seven. Not to mention the biased perspectives offered by independent credit rating agencies and by equity analysts and institutional investors – usually asking for higher quality balance sheets (i.e. with lower NPL ratios) at the trough of economic cycles, when banks can least afford to take P&L hits.

Also, internal (or endogenous) factors are driving significantly the full re-valuation exercise, no matter what the micro, macro and regulatory and accounting changing scenarios are. Ultimately, as we have repeatedly written, credit workout (CWO) is as much a science as it is an art, as it is a sub-sector of the alternative asset management industry in all forms and factors, with a beta "passive – market driven" approach that can drive its industrialisation and super-efficiency, and with an "alpha" one that can potentially lead to sustainable, sizeable, uncorrelated "over-recovery" performances. Following this reasoning, a newly "optimised" CWO unit, or the creation of a dedicated "real estate integrated services" unit (described in a previous chapter) could allow higher future recoveries versus past historical performances and peers' benchmarks, hence beating the market.

It is now easy to understand how the potential mix-up of wrong internal and external benchmarks (as irreflective of prevailing micro, macro, regulatory and accounting and internal workout/real estate capability factors) may drive to the incorrect targeting of future recovery rates. And how the very strategy, organisational and business-operating set-up of CWO and real estate units could be designed in the wrong way: building, e.g., the too rigid (or too flexible) cost structure; selecting IT infrastructure and application systems that are not adequate to get to the real targets; or defining processes and procedures that are built on go to market liquidation and commercialisation timing and approaches that are simply unsustainable given market conditions.

Finally, almost obvious to say, no matter what the exogenous and endogenous factors analysed and addressed, the loan and real estate portfolio analysis and the resulting valuation vary a lot in quality according to the quantity and completeness of provided data tapes ("garbage in-out").

Lack of information could, e.g., limit the extent of the segmentational approach and the resulting number of statistically relevant attainable permutations (or "buckets"), or the bank may need to resort to a judgmental approach (highly subjective, and for the wrong reasons – it could be based on workout experts' inputs that typically have "skin in the game" and are partial to the baseline obtained) to complete its stratification analysis internal work.

All in all, all these shortcomings are calling for a new approach to the valuation of loans (irrespective of their status, ideally covering also the performing and "grey area" ones). An approach more "grounded" in the future, also as a way to address potential issues of quality and completeness on past data, and certainly more consistent with prevailing state of key influencing variables. A valuation approach that is now, luckily enough, called for by new accounting and regulatory principles and that, more importantly, can lead to the better (if not best) holistic and active management of the lending and real estate portfolio of the bank.

4.3 An IFRS 9/ECB compliant approach to portfolio assessment

A new portfolios' evaluation approach is required to overcome most of the issues of the traditional backward-looking approach now in use at "best practice" banks. It will lead, if not, to an absolute "fair value" analysis of the lending and real estate portfolios – moving from its current "historical value" one – rectified for losses just as incurred – to at least a "fairer" value analysis that is still a far cry from the target end state of a "marketed to market," "best user/investor" one. Nonetheless, it will represent a much better baseline on which to inform the banks' holistic, active and integrated management strategies that could allow it to optimise the value of its NPE/NPL portfolios.

A new portfolios' evaluation approach is also required to be compliant with the new (from January 2018, already enforced) IFRS 9 accounting principle and with the new (still only "suggested") guidelines issued by the ECB, as they both require forward-looking evaluations, based on expected losses instead of the incurred ones, and need taking into consideration the potential evolution of micro and macro scenarios and most relevant markets – the real estate one being obviously "key."

First of all, traditional backward-looking assessment approaches may be improved through the implementation of specific digital enablers that could allow to the bank the creation of an interconnected and enhanced ecosystem of data that could be easily transformed into a more forward-looking, sufficiently accurate, future recovery rates and in a related sensitivity/stress testing model. In order to achieve the above-mentioned target, the key major elements influencing the recovery (including the underlying asset evaluation) may be listed and linked in a proper and unique evaluation template aimed at the digital acquisition and storage of relevant data.

On this basis, a series of mandatory and interlinked fields related to both loans and real estate key features could allow the automatic assessment of the portfolio's key dynamics (e.g. the incidence of loans distribution by GBV size, its secured vs. unsecured composition, its vintage and related status of work-out activities), whilst paying the utmost attention to the completeness, consistency and overall quality of the information. In such an interlinked, automatic model, the change of each of the fields (e.g. to simulate evolving market trends and stress test results) will result in a "bottom-up" sensitivity of the related loan recovery values (e.g. lowering the expected asset liquidity will decrease the expected auction sale and the final monetary recovery of the related loan).

This approach to progressively move towards a more forward-looking approach looks feasible and sounds certainly very appealing, without requiring major transformational efforts and discontinuities in the IT infrastructure and application systems of banks. However, there are a number of questions that are born out of banks' real-life experience, and these need to be addressed and solved to ensure the implementation feasibility of such an incremental approach: have, e.g., banks, or independent CWO units, been accumulating – or have they a plan in place to gather and store – the target data, with the required level of depth and accuracy to start testing and then implementing such digitally enhanced approaches? Have they then proceeded to integrate such data with historical ones, to make sure that past investments are capitalised and fully leveraged? Have they further clarified which required unique fields are key for the loan and real estate valuation, and the way they are getting interconnected to ensure a holistic, comprehensive and consistent view? And finally, have they developed an appropriate set of tools to connect these "augmented" data with enhanced applied analytics for the creation of relevant intelligence not previously available?

As already anticipated, we strongly believe that a key driver of this incremental approach towards the digitisation of the CWO activities of the bank should address the critical interrelations between the loan portfolios and the real estate ones (either as collateral or as already repossessed and "bank-owned" assets). Missing this holistic perspective would impair the overall effort and limit the forward-looking effectiveness of the incremental transformation programme highlighted.

4.4 A "crash programme" approach

No matter what the strategic objectives pursued by the bank and the mid-term transformation timeline implied by this incremental digitisation programme, a more tactical "crash programme" could also be run in parallel, with more hybrid approaches meant to get the most out of current available data and of easy-to-use and quick-to-deliver new applied analytic solutions. In a recent case, we worked on to support a global SIFI, key positions where initially selected, given time and resources constraints – focusing on the larger groups driving most of the GBV of the overall NPL portfolio.

These positions were then individually reassessed by a mix of internal asset managers and external independent servicers, all using a new digital "data acquisition template" designed to be receptive of all the most critical fields that would have then allowed us (acting as leading independent advisor) to pressure test some of the key positions, screening them by both relevance and statistical significance (ensuring some representation of all main categories involved).

The remaining smaller positions (numbering in the tens of thousands) were then assessed following a purely statistical approach, given certain target of (limited) volatility and (high) level of confidence in the analysis – translating in a high probability to get the valuation numbers right. The selected sample was then analysed, with its results being projected on the remaining population of loans.

In parallel, an extended re-run of the real estate collaterals was performed, following a uniform methodology and approach as designed by the bank and us and then outsourced to third-party appraisal professionals. Also these appraisals, following shared and "closed" standards, were fed into digital templates to ensure a consistent and complete data acquisition and a quicker and more flexible manipulation of data, to run the overall business plan and valuation of the portfolio and, on top of this, the simulations and stress test scenarios that are contributing, albeit partially, an initial forward-looking perspective into the analysis, for IFRS 9 and other active management purposes.

Whilst clearly representing a suboptimal solution vis-à-vis the target end state highlighted in the beginning of this chapter, this "crash programme" approach can deliver good results in a relatively short time frame, if the bank is observing few key success factors, such as ensuring it selects the most efficient and effective data integration approach – i.e. defining the target number of positions to be analytically reviewed "ad hoc" and the "optimum" sample of positions to consider, in order to run the inferential statistical analysis for the remaining positions; to integrate/enhance portfolio information; leveraging specific digital assessment tools – i.e. building up evaluations templates to assure key input homogeneity and data flexibility (forward-looking) for both NPL and RE dossiers; setting up an automated assessment control process – i.e. designing and enforcing structured control mechanisms to verify data consistency and accuracy; and, finally, ensuring that a common standard and a minimum quality to the revaluation efforts are pressure tested and signed off by a central, "content heavy" programme management office, also in charge to main a tight timeline. An approach to pressure testing and sensitivity analysis is highlighted in Figure 4.2. A full re-underwriting process for real estate is instead described, across its main stages and activities, in Figure 4.3.

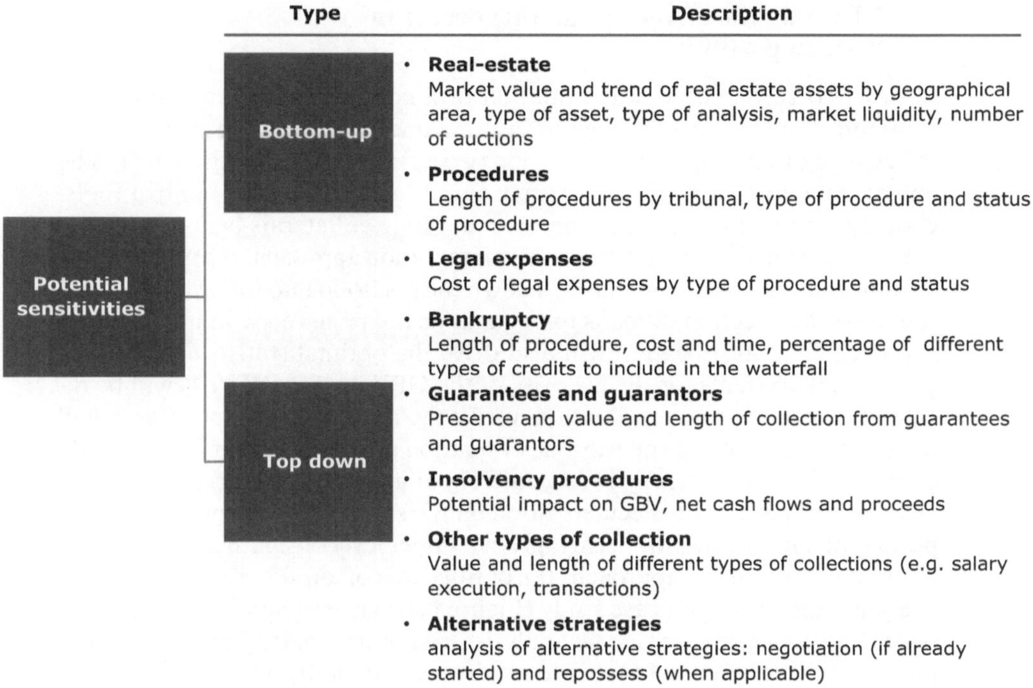

Figure 4.2 Approach to pressure testing and sensitivity analysis.

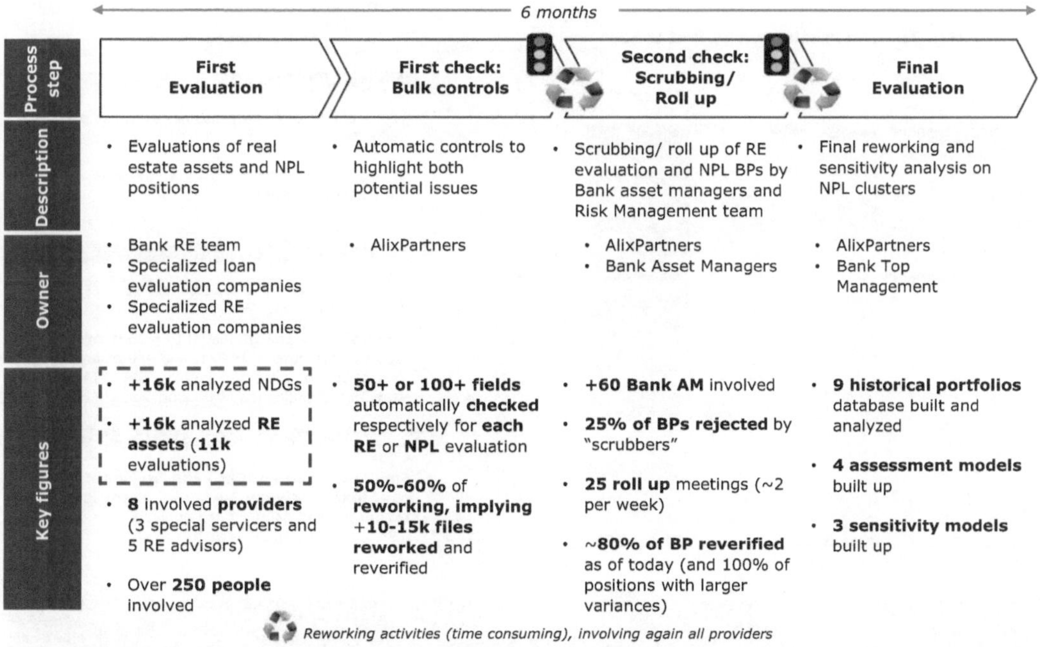

Figure 4.3 Re-underwriting process for collaterals and real estate.

4.5 NPL valuation analysis: getting deeper in the loan portfolio

In order to run a successful valuation of a complex NPL portfolio, some common standards with a given minimum quality need to be ensured. It is then worth discussing, in the following two paragraphs, what these would be on data integration, digital assessment tools and automated control tools, with regard to both the loans and the real estate collaterals being reviewed.

Starting from the loan portfolio data integration approach, the initial stratification analysis has already broken down the portfolio into different tiers that can drive the selection of loans to be analytically reviewed with a bottom-up approach. The stratification will also drive the optimal statistical sampling: groups that accounts for the majority of the GBV in scope (Tier 1) will be reviewed with a one-to-one valuation, whilst the remaining groups (Tier 2) will be assessed based on the one-to-one evaluation of dossiers in similar portfolio clusters using a statistically based, inferential analysis approach. This Tier 2 analysis will need to be executed based on the selection of the optimum sample that defines the overall tiering, given a target level of significance.

The portfolio tiering approach is an optimal mix of top-down and bottom-up analysis from an Italian case study (Figure 4.4). The exemplifications of templates (for loans and real estate analysis, see Figure 4.5; for bulk control and pressure test, see Figure 4.6) should ideally be all digitally integrated and consistent with the main processes and workflows of the CWO unit and related real estate services – whether or not played by an IRES (for real estate valuation, addressing the collaterals of the secured loans, see Figure 4.7).

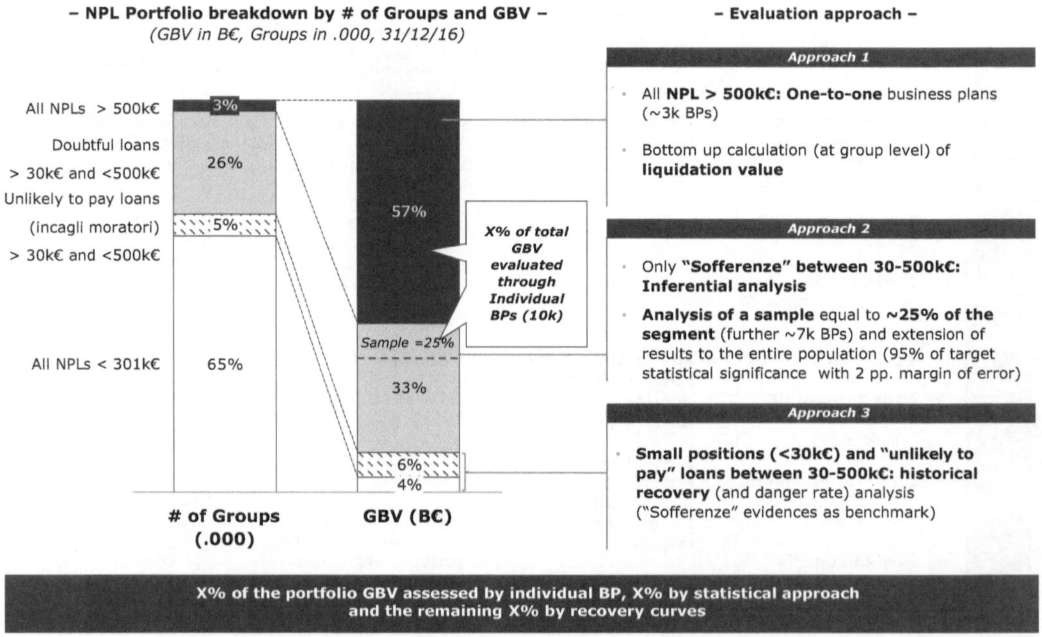

Figure 4.4 Portfolio tiering: top-up versus bottom-up.

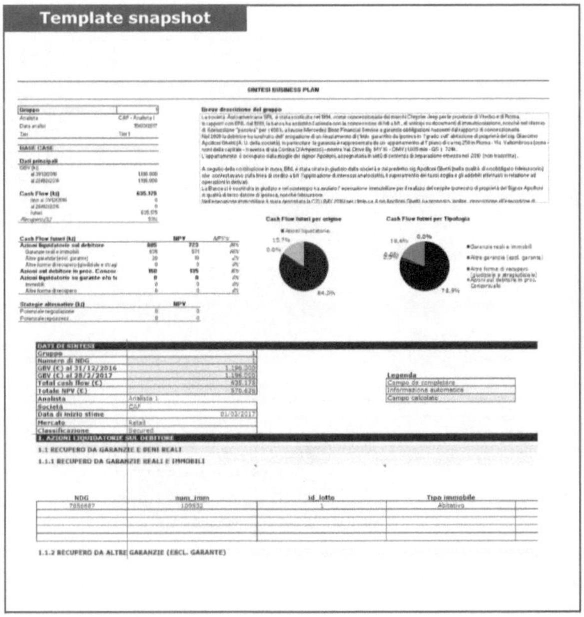

- Template rationale -

- **Sensitivities - ready**
  Template is built to allow for sensitivities once all information is received; thus
  - Analysts' considerations are split to "atomic" level, in order to understand key analysis factors
  - All assumptions are parametric, in order to already allow for sensitivities
- **Group level vs. NDG level analysis**
  Portfolio analysis is performed both at group level and at NDG level
  - The group is the main object of analysis, thus each template will be focused on just one group (1 group - 1 template)
  - The NDGs (debtors) composing the group will be analyzed individually in the template, in order to maximize group level returns
- **Source of cash focus**
  Template is focused on clearly and individually identifying all sources of cash for each NDG and group; in this way, the template can be stripped of non-value added information, allowing analysts to focus their time on "what is really important"

Figure 4.5 Digital template for loan and real estate analysis.

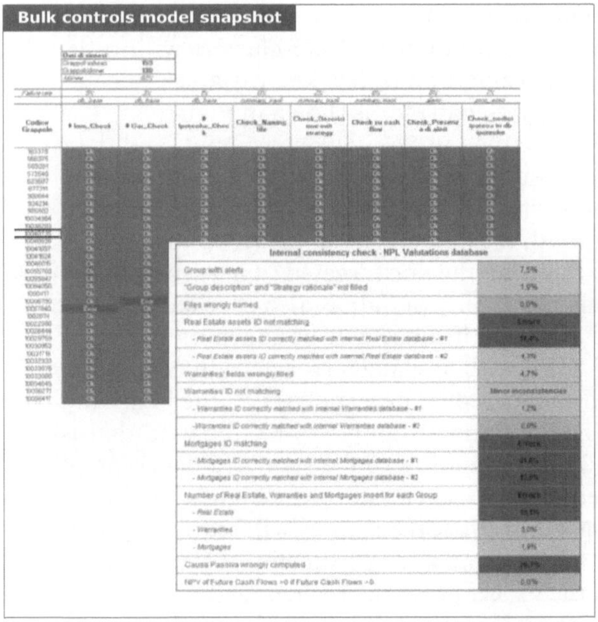

- All evaluations received weekly are run through a "bulk controls" model, which automatically highlights for all evaluations:
  - Sections not filled-in appropriately
  - Identification numbers not indicated properly (e.g. typos)
  - Assets not included in the analysis (e.g. guarantees not evaluated)
  - Discrepancies between key variables (e.g. cash flow value)
  - Missing key fields for the overall evaluation
- Once the model presents the summary output, the bank can quickly analyse individual error messages to evaluate the pass or fail test:
  - "Passed" evaluations can proceed to the next step of the second-level controls process
  - "Failed" evaluations are rejected and sent back to the outsourcers (with details on the specific errors) in order to be sanitized and uploaded again on the following week

Figure 4.6 Bulk control model for review and pressure test.

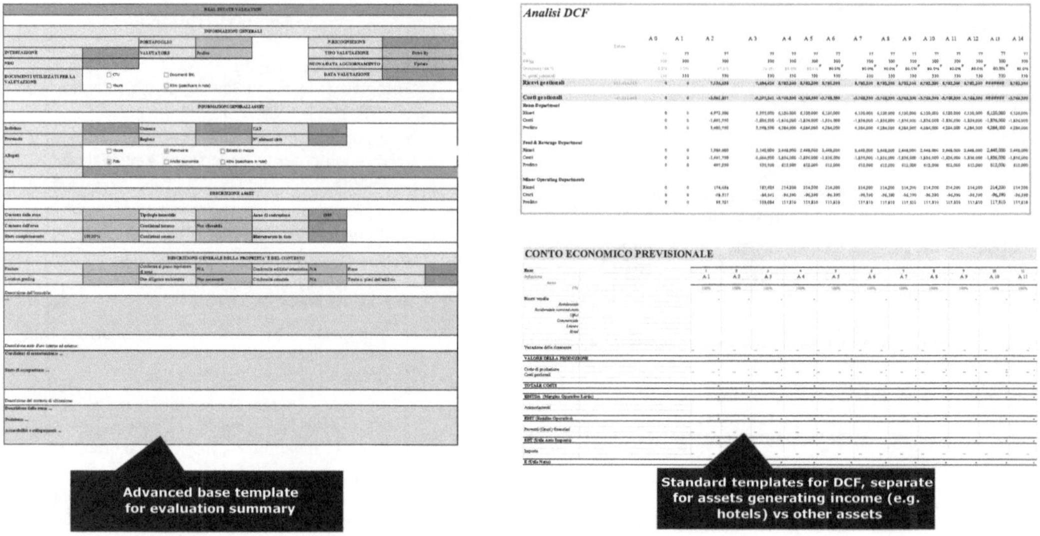

Figure 4.7 Digital templates for real estate valuation.

Going back to the tiering and sampling approach, it is important to understand that these processes are usually driven by a target level of confidence, or "statistical significance." The targeting of a certain statistical significance (and its related margin error) can be addressed as follows. The bank can initially define a certain number of sub-clusters within the Tier 2 groups, as derived by the permutation of few key variables, such as the GBV size, NPL ageing, typology of loan etc. as shown in Figure 4.1. The statistical targets of the analysis are then initially taken as input, and their feasibility is checked – given the required workload to be done to meet them. Through a process of "trial and error," a certain level of statistical significance, given the workload required, the numerosity of the sampling and the time/expenses associated with that, can then be targeted (it may require few changes through the process, as the quality of data is also checked).

Typically, a 90%–95% statistical significance can be taken as the "best practice" targeted by a global SIFI, with a related error margin of 2%–3%, but it requires a significant workload and related analysis on the loans and collaterals. These targets define the optimal sample to be analysed that is also going to be selected based on the analysis of the standard deviation of main sub-clusters as above identified. As a general rule, a higher number of permutations and a higher target of statistical accuracy will require a larger sample basis, hence a higher workload and a longer timeline to execute (and higher associated costs to run the process with independent advisors).

In fact, in parallel, one-to-one evaluations will have to be carried out by a panel on internal and external asset managers to assure a balanced and timely workload management and an overall evaluation effectiveness, as it will involve multiple counterparts, but all working on a consistent methodology and based on a homogeneous and exhaustive digital acquisition template.

These digital acquisition templates will form a key component of the digital assessment tools that the bank will need, in order to manage the overall first-time process, also with a view of ensuring it can be repeated consistently and with a more limited effort through time. To do this, these digital templates need to bear a number of unique and relevant characteristics.

They need to be "complete," as portfolio analysis is performed at debtor group level (1 debtor – 1 template to be filled up) and then broken down at the single product lines level, to identify all potential sources of cash. They then need to be "granular," as analysts' considerations are broken down to an almost "atomic" level, in order to understand target recovery key elements and related dynamics, should some of these hypothesis change (e.g. foreclosures are "automatically" linked to auction values that are linked to open market values). They also need to be "consistent," as all assumptions are parametric and managed at "central level," to ensure that a consistent recovery rationale is used by different analysts (e.g. auction average discount, court timeline). Finally, they need to be "sensitivity analysis ready," as their template is built to allow for sensitivities that are derived by changing "pivot" hypothesis (e.g. the increase in the value of a specific real estate typology will cause a corresponding change in value in the loans with such collaterals).

Other exemplifications of the valuation (or re-underwriting) process are also offered. The approach to sampling, as driven by a certain target level of statistical significance and working on the basis of the main segmentational variables identified (and related numerical buckets: e.g. for GBV, 3–5 sub-segmentational based on tickets' nominal outstanding), is shown in Figure 4.8. A summary of the required elements of a re-underwriting

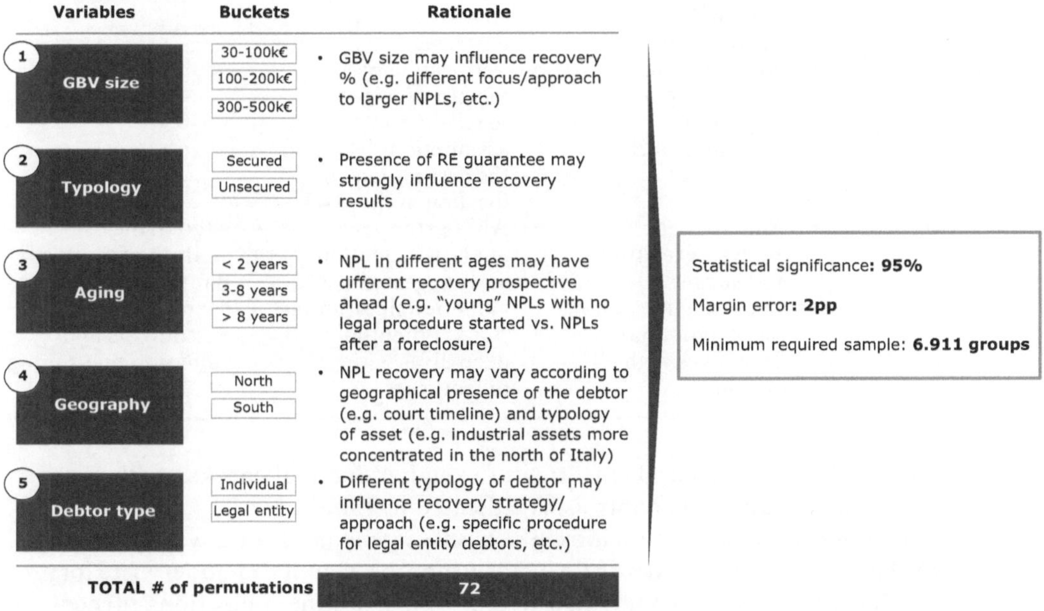

Figure 4.8 Sampling is driven by target statistical confidence.

Table 4.1 Valuation process to ensure robustness/consistency

	1 Individual check	*2 Consistency checks*	*3 Bulk controls*
Target	• ~100 RE assets • Selected priority assets: • Top assets by asset size and complexity in Tier 1 (~50) • Selected assets in Tiers 1 and 2 based on results of "consistency checks" (~50)	• ~1,000 RE assets • Selected assets in Tiers 1 and 2: • Based on asset size and complexity • Detailed criteria for selection based on operational guidelines	• ~12,000–15,000 RE assets • All RE assets not otherwise included in second-level checks
Objective	• Double-check the individual evaluation by: • Verify the approach and the overall logic of the valuation • Confirm the main assumptions for the specific asset	• Make sure that evaluations for priority positions use consistent assumptions • Identify potential outliers in evaluation outcomes	• Identify potential outliers in evaluation outcomes
Methodology	• Review of the RE form ("Scheda immobile") • Review of the relevant attachments (e.g. DCF calculations) • Potential double-check/integration with external sources when appropriate	• ine by line" check of the consistency a subset of priority assets, based on selected data structured in a database • Verification of inconsistencies in results and assumptions based on the destination and location of the asset	• Aggregated controls of consistency of valuations results, i.e. identification of outliers
Resp.	• AlixPartners: analysis execution and suggested valuation fine-tuning • Bank: potential deep dives with outsourcers	• AlixPartners: analysis execution and suggested valuation fine-tuning • Bank: potential deep dives with outsourcers	• AlixPartners: analysis execution • Bank: potential deep dives with outsourcers and valuation fine-tuning

process that is robust and consistent, through individual checks, methodological checks and bulk controls, is indicated in Table 4.1.

The overall process may look like cumbersome (and, in a way, it is) as the bank needs to re-underwrite in a few months what it did underwrite for the first time – and allegedly in a wrong way, as all these positions turned into non-performing ones – over the course of many years. The solution to this heavy workload rests in the industrialisation of the process that needs to be well designed, standard, automated and smooth and lean as it can be. And it rests in its digitalisation. Critical to this, the digital data acquisition templates need to assure standardised data inputs and guide and help the enforcement of structured and homogeneous guidelines for the evaluations.

Ideally, digital data verification tools should already be in place and checking automatically each evaluation template field to find potential issues, whilst human-based, manual controls (either played internally or offered by professional and independent external advisors) should be limited to large files and for the smaller ones only when showing larger variations from previous assessments.

4.6 Real estate valuation analysis: from the end investor point of view

The common standards required to run the valuation need to apply to real estate collaterals as well, as most of the recoverable value will come out of them and the approach to their valuation (first) and active management and commercialisation (later) can drive a significant volatility in the value of the portfolio being reviewed. We have discussed at length how the banking and real estate relationship is a critical and potentially risky one. This is true at inception, when new lending decisions are taken by the bank, and even more later on as wrong lending decisions are addressed and a significant value can be recovered (or lost forever) based on the real estate management.

Starting from the valuation and re-underwriting process, as for the case of loans, the common standards should be applied to the real estate data integration's effort and digital assessment tools should be used to support the automated assessment control process. As a start, the real estate assets being selected for the analysis and the approach to run their valuation effort should be based on their previous known (and ideally recent) asset value coming from independent appraisals.

Ideally, a reassessment of all real estate properties should be run every year, covering single names one-to-one approaches and other statistical sampling, and their valuation should consider, at least once in their lifetime, a "drive by" analysis and not just a desktop one. These assessments will need to be carried out by specialised real estate appraisal companies, selected based on their specialisation on specific asset typologies and/or geographies. We have already shown (in Table 4.1) how the real estate valuation approach should ideally be driven by their potential buyers and, on this basis, an appropriate analytical approach should then be consistently selected.

As for the loans, the real estate valuation carried out by the professional third parties involved in the process (ideally, more than one, to ensure limited biases, and with an international coverage and reputation to limit the "client capture" already commented) should then feed into specific digital assessment templates that should be differentiated according to the final end user/investor.

For example, an initial differentiation could cover the assets to be potentially sold to final users (e.g. apartments sold to individuals and families) that could be evaluated on the basis of comparable transactions to derive their "open market value"; the assets to be potentially sold to financial investors could instead be assessed using either an "asset sale DCF" (estimating the NPV of the revenues and costs related to future asset sales), or an "asset rental DCF" (estimating the NPV of future rents and costs derived from the renting of the asset to either retail or corporate clients), or an "asset earning DCF" (representing the NPV of the potential earnings derived from the business and operating company as end user of the asset – i.e. in the case of hotels, the earnings derived from the hospitality business).

Finally, from the point of view of the automated assessment control process, the real estate digital data acquisition template needs to assure the standardisation of the information in input and a structured, homogeneous approach to the valuation, based on theoretically correct guidelines. Digital data verification tools could then automatically check the completeness of each evaluation template field, the use of the right evaluation methodology (according to the typology of assets and potential investor identified) and, finally, the "pressure testing" of the valuation results, given real estate benchmarks segmented by geographical area (e.g. city – urban/sub-urban) and typology of assets (residential, industrial, commercial etc.) with automatic alerts on the outliers. Following this approach, manual controls could be limited to larger assets and to smaller assets that are however showing large variations versus the most proper real estate assets identified.

Once the loans and real estate collaterals valuation analysis is completed and digitally integrated into dedicated data bases and via standard templates, an automated (or semi-automated) sensitivity model can be developed to enrich the forward-looking content of the model. This database, aggregating both loans and real estate information, can be uploaded by the bank into proprietary tools that have modelled the recovery curve by asset typology and can therefore show the portfolio recovery dynamics and their potential deviations around the mean, and for different scenarios.

A "best practice" sensitivity tool could, e.g., allow the following, forward-looking views, analysing: the overall recovery curves by NPL clusters and/or by single positions; the total expected cash-in by years and broken down by key loans/recovery features (e.g. recovery by loan typology, by procedures, by geography); the real estate market evolution – a real-time sensitivity of the impact on total recovery driven by the expected evolution of the real estate sector, by geographical area, type of asset, city – country location etc.; the legal procedure length – a real-time sensitivity of the impact on the recovery NPV due to the expected evolution of the length of procedure typologies by tribunal; the legal expenses – a real-time sensitivity of the impact of potential changes in legal expenses, by type of procedure and status; the passive lawsuits – a real-time sensitivity of the impact on GBV, net cash flows and proceeds driven by the probability of winning passive or active lawsuits; the guarantees and guarantors – a real-time sensitivity of the impact of the exclusion of selected typologies of guarantees and guarantors etc.

In this way, the portfolio assessment and sensitivity tools can show different recovery scenarios and be broken down by year, given selected sensitivity analysis performed on both loans and real estate. As more forward-looking as this can appear, this approach still stands as incremental and not truly "breakthrough" in nature, and quite far from the target model where the mark-to-market approach is applied to all kind of loans and real estate properties to get to a real-time view of the single asset and aggregated volatility of the portfolios. In order to further progress this, banks need to address several other questions related to the best possible use of available and captured data.

Apart from defining the right set of relevant data to target and aggregate, banks will need to clearly specify the way in which they could leverage them at best, enhancing the intelligence that could be derived from them with the use of more sophisticated applied analytics techniques. Also, a more structured approach could allow banks to capitalise on their earlier data "crash programme" approaches, to make the exercise more easily repeatable through time, for the same portfolios and for new ones, and more granular, moving progressively away from a top-down segmentation approach towards a name by name, bottom-up–specific review. If this looks like science fiction when considered in the context of current IT systems and traditional analytics, it does not, if reconsidered at the light of the new use cases, now made available by ML/AI techniques.

4.7 Value targeting: ML/AL-based applications

As previously commented, a number of common pitfalls can be observed in the day-to-day management of CWO activities that are based on established technologies and traditional applied analytics techniques. For example, in setting the preferred asset strategy and related potential recovery, a high level of subjectivity is introduced in the system, as most of the decision-making is almost uniquely grounded on management experience. Therefore, not only the value targeted could appear disputable, but also its actual achievement may become closely dependent on the retention of the key managers that defined this in the first place. It would all lead to further endogenous volatility being added up to the already high exogenous one.

The more extensive and intensive usage of proprietary big data algorithms can come handy on this, helping to reduce the intrinsic level of subjectivity and smooth the future level of volatility in performances, as targets are continuously revised and adjusted, as new information comes available. Using "big data," banks can calculate best asset strategies and related expected potential recovered value following a two steps ML process (with ML usually referred as one potential application amongst the vaster realm of AI ones). A summary of an ML/AI-driven approach is shown in Figure 4.9, following

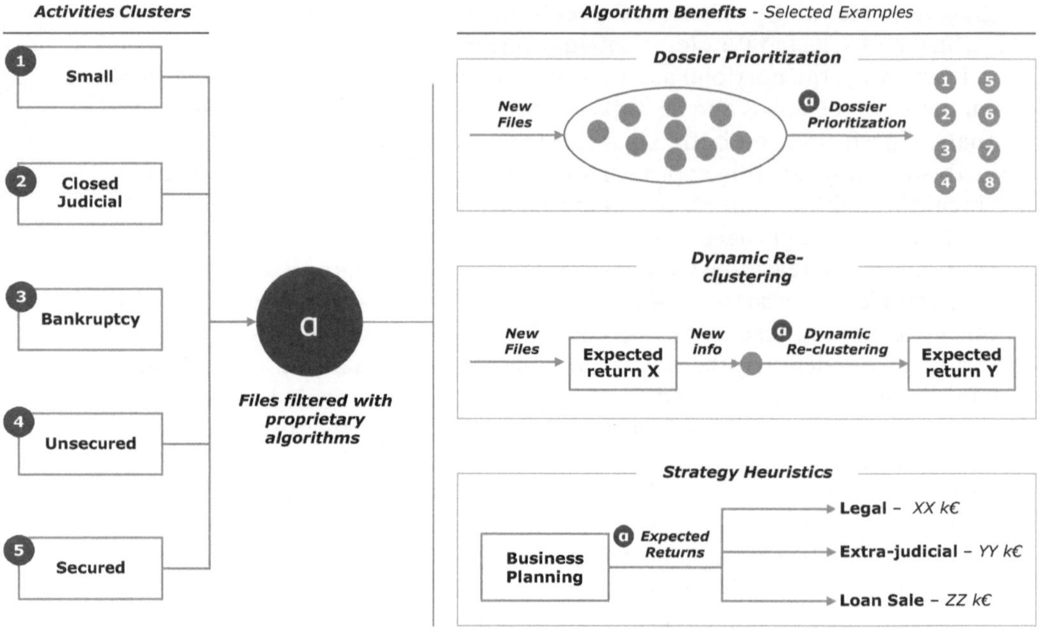

Figure 4.9 Digitization opportunities in valuation and recovery strategy.

an approach that we dubbed "alpha algorithms" and driving dossier prioritisation, dynamic re-clustering and related business planning – other useful considerations can also focus on internal workload allocation and selection of third parties that could be better supporting for each and every set of dossiers.

In a first step, a "big data" set-up is pursued, collecting, aggregating and structuring data coming from credible historical collection series – encompassing both the data owned by the bank and other data that can come from third parties. In a second step, ML techniques are then employed and trained and fine-tuned to provide an optimal navigation through the relevant decision tree that the CWO needs to consider, with a view of optimising the value recovered. Basically, for each potential scenario along the issue tree, an expected value recovered is predicted and, on this basis, the "algorithm" suggests the best way forward as the one maximising this.

In practice, predictive algorithms are employing a mix of the latest available ML techniques, including, e.g. the Long Short Term Memory (LSTM) – a deep learning technique designed to recognise time patterns by portfolio sub-segment characteristics (these patterns can then be used for estimating upcoming repayments); the Extreme Gradient Boosted Model (XGBoost) – a most performing decision tree technique, where the "algorithm" chooses, in a "white box" manner, the most significant portfolio characteristics that are used to estimate the overall recovery amount and time horizon; and many others, with different level of "black box" characteristics. The main phases of work are described in Figure 4.10, across modelling developments,

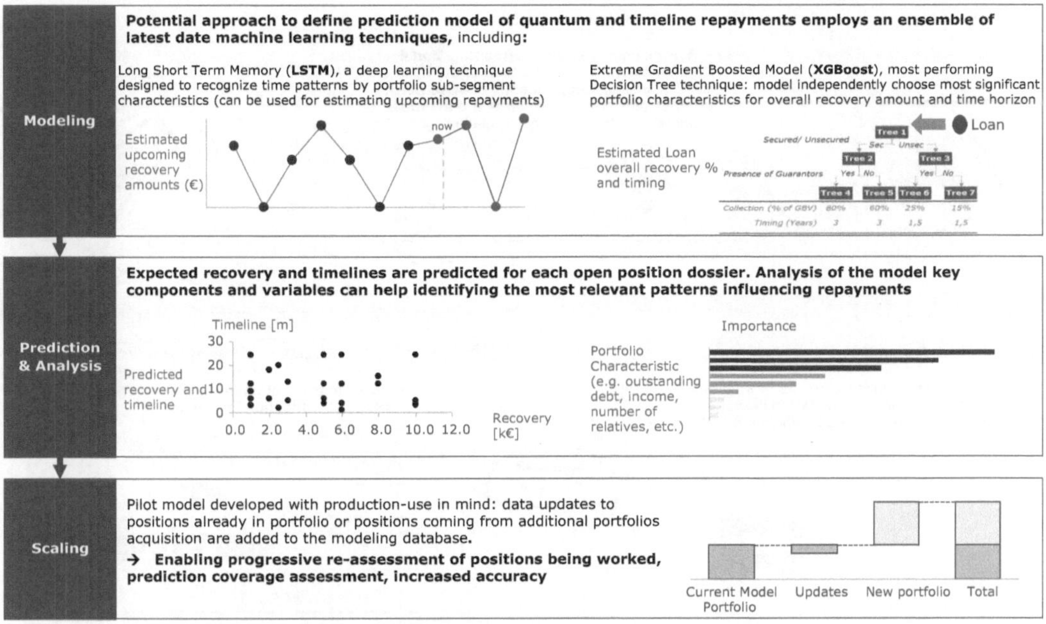

Figure 4.10 Valuation and recovery strategy with ML/AI.

analysis and prediction and then scaling the findings obtained at the level of the larger portfolios being assessed.

Once the ML technique is selected, the model independently analyses clustered dossiers and draws expected collection and timing for each position. The beauty of this technique sits in its "self-training" and "self-improving" characteristics – as the algorithm develops by continuously choosing new and better variables that are stronger predictors of the attainable recovery rate and hence leading to better decision-making on value recovered maximisation.

The algorithm keeps changing as new data are coming available and therefore it ends up influencing itself – the more it works out better, the better it can predict and therefore work out in future. The implications of this approach are almost revolutionary, as new NPL flows, or new portfolios acquired by investors, can become now automatically assessed with a new, more digital approach that addresses most of the issues related to the backward-looking nature of data and valuation models.

Whilst internal and external benchmarks are inevitably factoring in a previous "market era," as the predictive algorithm is based on a data structure capable to simulate future market trends, it follows that its assessment of future recovery flows will be forward-looking as well, regardless of the initial benchmarks data used. In fact, even if the starting mix-up of internal and external benchmarks may drive to an initial, partially incorrect, targeting of future recovery, the algorithm can train itself on the basis of the achieved performance as realised day by day, hence building a strong baseline.

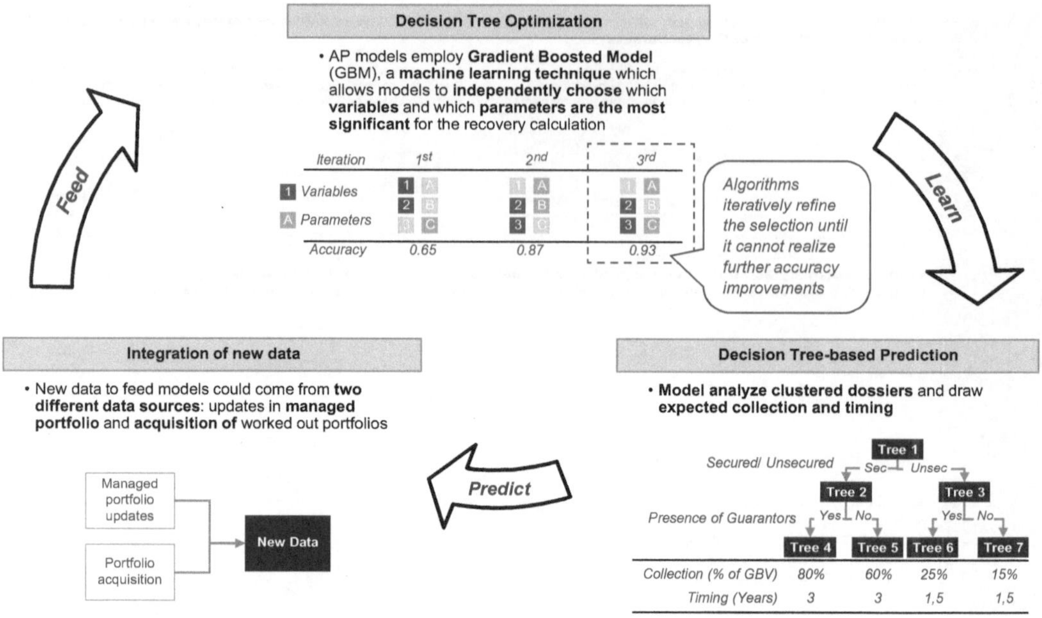

Figure 4.11 Valuation process using ML/AI.

NPL portfolio analysis performed by ML/AI applications is still, of course, heavily dependent on the quality of provided data tapes. Therefore, the critical "holistic data management review" we described initially remains as such, even if the choice of the variables influencing the recovery rate will be independently performed by the algorithm and by the ML techniques, hence limiting radically any further degree of subjectivity supplied by the management. The iterative nature of the way of working of this approach is described in Figure 4.11.

The iterative approach starts with a decision tree optimisation phase, with the independent selection of relevant variables that will be used as parameters to drive predictions and perform the calculation of the recovery curve. In the prediction phase, the model analyses the clustered dossier to draw the expected collection and timing. Then, the model keeps learning, developing as new data are captured, integrated and analysed, then feeding in turn the decision tree optimisation.

4.8 Digital real estate: fast forward?

The world of global finance stands out for its intrinsic intangibility, as money is ultimately immaterial, and the information that underpins the core intermediation business of banking is also intangible. Banks have in the management, transformation and trade of risks its key production factor. Given this intangibility, real estate has been traditionally called upon to confer some degree of materiality to it. Real estate, as the traditional view goes, is a very concrete business, actually made of bricks and unmovable stuff that preserve their value through time, no matter what.

Following this reasoning, it may appear almost an oxymoron to discuss the future of the real estate as also becoming "digital." On the contrary, the potential implications of the digital revolution on real estate are very little understood and most likely oversighted by common people and real estate experts alike, not to mention banks and other financial investors. The way digital is getting under the skin of the sector is, however, multiple, and the implications could in fact become far reaching.

In the construction sector, e.g., new digital technologies are certainly being employed to design and realise new developments, to ensure more efficiency and efficacy to the overall structure of the building or infrastructure being built, and better risk management on many perspectives. And the "smart home" – where several digital applications are making the use of our home appliances easier, cheaper, more convenient and safer – is also becoming a well-known concept.

Also, the development and success of digital platforms promoting social networks and alternative ways to trade goods and services are also promoting the "shared economy," which can lead to an entirely new fungibility of residential, commercial and industrial assets, as they are rented either as substitute to hotels or as temporary shops by the week or for a production or marketing cycle. This has huge implications on the relative value of different locations. Internet-of-things applications can also produce new use cases for the day-to-day management and utilisation of real estate assets.

All these examples, and many others, are all good and interesting to observe. However, they are still far from that revolution in the real estate sector that we mentioned in the beginning. If not for the further, almost unlimited flow of new and richer, augmented data and information that all these new things keep producing, in real time, leveraging other data sources coming from satellites, video cameras, our smartphone taking snapshots of our social life in the city or in the country, not to mention the sharing of views, on social network, regarding our preferences on locations and places.

Hence, the potential "digital revolution" to come on the real estate sector is one built out of new sets of unlimited data and information, most of them "unstructured" (as coming from social sources and mostly qualitative in nature). They can, however, generate, with the help of new ML/AI applications, new intelligence on the behaviour of the very material, unmovable asset, i.e. increasing its immateriality, as its value relies more and more on intangible data and information, and its behaviour through time can be analysed and predicted towards the dream of a mark-to-market approach realised in real time also for the most intractable asset, i.e. the real estate one. If we follow this reasoning, digital means that new information and new intelligence, multiplied by the new use cases made possible by the new technologies (as for the example of the shared economy) are making real estate not only more intangible but also observable and predictable.

In the context of a banking strategy on real estate, this means that mark-to-market valuations could be developed for single assets and for asset clusters, and for their related lending portfolios – either performing, sub-performing or non-performing. Unstructured information on traffic, the level of pollution, the average weather and exposure to sun, the trend in criminality, or nightlife at fashionable restaurants and theatres could also give extra intelligence to predict trends in prices. And the data feeding the analysis would change every second, allowing the readjustment of the predictions. Open market prices could then be derived to express all this and offered with continuous updates and fine-tunings, following the self-learning principle, hence supporting the transparency of the asset values and their potential liquidity. Homes and offices and industrial building would all become data rich.

It would also mean that new market indexes could be objectively developed and used as reference benchmarks and leveraged as the basis of new derivatives trades and of financial guarantees. Hence, the real estate risk could be separated from its physical assets and traded over digital markets, allowing for hedging, swaps or highly leveraged, speculative investment strategies. These new, real-time measurements would generate a lot of volatility on real estate prices (it was there, always present, but not observable and not observed as properties assets were re-valued very rarely through their lifetime and with a lot of opacity, subjectivity and client capture in the process).

This real estate volatility would then stand as the basis for modelling the sector distribution of frequency, in that it would then help in predicting the future value on a statistical basis and in defining PD and LGD components as driven by such distribution and by its tail risk. It would then put the real estate sector in an even more central role – more well-known and better understood, regarding banking, to its lending business and insurance and asset management ones as well.

Far from being an oxymoron, real estate could become and is already becoming more digital in nature. Given its centrality in banking, and its key role in the lending business – from underwriting to collection, to work out – and its likely bottom ranking in terms of current level of sophistication, the digitalisation of real estate could become the single, most disruptive component in the digitalisation of the lending business and CWO management as well. It is, therefore, critical to consider how real estate could get digital to understand how to turn the credit business into a digital one.

5 Optimal value management

Strategy, governance and organisation

Claudio Scardovi

5.1 Not done yet: the new European Central Bank principles for credit workout

Following the perfect storm of the global financial crisis, and possibly in anticipation of the new "digital storm" to come, several international and local banks have strived to upgrade their credit workout (CWO) and real estate management capabilities. Certainly, the sponsorship and moral suasion of the European Central Bank (ECB) has contributed a lot on the interest paid now by European banks, and – even if so far limited at offering suggested and non-binding "guidelines" – it has certainly raised the level of awareness of "what it takes" to manage in an optimal way the workout of NPL and the active management of their underlying real estate assets.

More specifically, the guidelines issued by the ECB in the spring of 2017 are aimed not only at defining the best strategy to maximise the recovery value of NPL (and setting consistently related quantitative targets – given NPL root causes and current capabilities) but also at implementing the most appropriate operating model to enable an effective execution of such a strategy and ensure the achievement of related targets, including deleveraging, de-risking and overall recoveries.

Starting from the strategy, the ECB guidelines are suggesting a two-step approach to define an overall "industrial plan" for the CWO unit and hence its recovery targets coming from loan workout and collateral (mostly real estate) active management. In a first step, a diagnostic should provide an independent and objective assessment of the relevant operating environment, focusing on the bank's internal workout and asset management capabilities and on the external factors impacting the NPL recovery and related capital implications. On this basis, the industrial plan should present a more granular approach to then develop the NPL strategy, with specific actions planned to strengthen its operational capabilities – on a mostly qualitative basis – and projected NPL reduction targets – quantitatively – planned over the time horizon (from short-term to long-term).

On the implementation side, the industrial plan should focus on what it takes to implement the most appropriate operating model, including any necessary changes in the governance and organisational structure of the bank. Whilst the guidelines are not as specific to suggest a given governance or organisational option, they set the stage for establishing a clear and transparent accountability, ensuring that appropriate means are aligned to the bank's ambitions and driving a correct allocation of responsibilities to the key people and to the most critical functions.

In a way, the option of developing a strategic partnership or an ecosystem of alliances is also left open, as the form should follow the strategy. And strategy here is really focusing on getting the NPL issue under control, as we have seen, recovering as much as possible, with a clear alignment of objectives and a new mindset, closer to the private equity business one than to traditional banking (Figure 5.1).

Once the governance and the organisation are set, the NPL strategy needs to get "embedded" into the CWO and active asset management unit (or "units"), by means of consistently redesigned key processes, then broken down into a number of subprocesses. These processes need then to be as seamless and efficient/effective as possible, with workflows that are designed to be able to leverage as much as possible on all kind of opportunities of automation and robotisation now made available by the technological innovation. Also, the efficiency/efficacy of such processes should be augmented by the utilisation of the "big data" captured, stored and analysed, to bring new "intelligence" into them, to ensure that the best recovery strategy, at the macro level as well as at the micro level, is pursued and put into action, following an almost self-pilot, driver-less approach.

Finally, the execution of the selected strategy should be subject to a periodic, regular and independent review and continuous monitoring, to ensure that what it's in the plan gets realised in a tightly consistent way. Moreover,

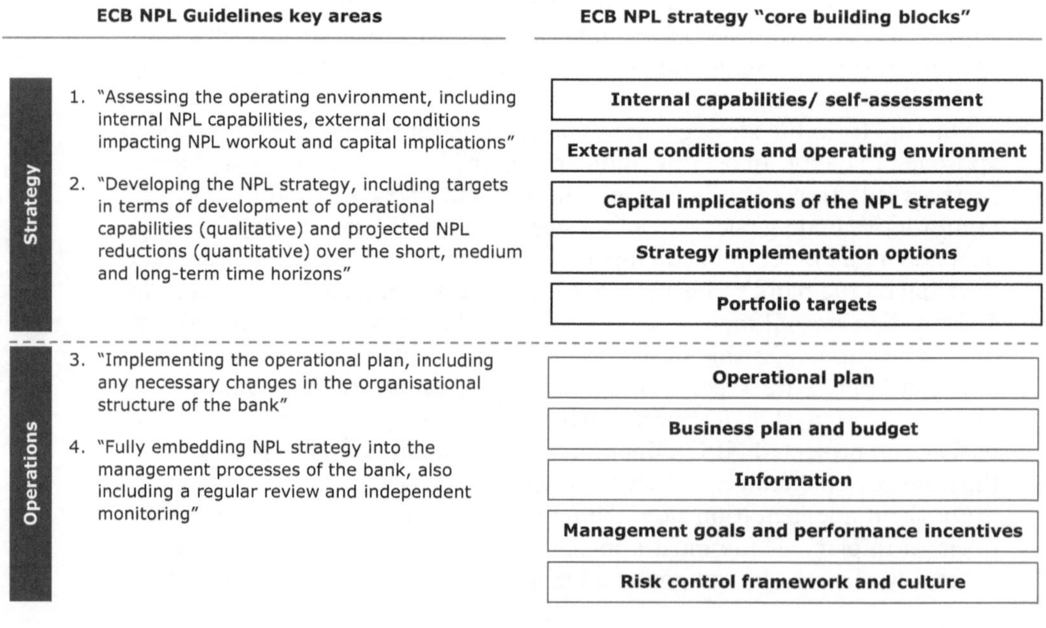

Figure 5.1 ECB NPL guidelines on strategy: a summary.

strategy and execution should not be considered as individual and separate tasks, as they stand like the two sides of the same coin, i.e. the overall industrial plan of the CWO and asset management unit (units) (and related financial targets).

This continuous control and monitoring phases are then becoming even more important in a digital world where business and operations come as strictly interconnected and interloped because of the big data applied analytics that are now allowing more frequent updates and "mark-to-markets." In other words, the quasi "real-time" analysis of the performances obtained in the NPL recovery activities should back feed continuously on the business and operational choices made by the servicer and confirm selected path forward or suggest fine-tunings or changes "in flight."

This is indeed a critical point of the overall digitalisation of the recovery process and for the active management of repossessed real estate assets. Its transformation is, in fact, ultimately driven by the new "ideas" made available by a better and richer use of data as they come available and by smarter applied analytics, leveraging machine learning (ML) and artificial intelligence (AI). Their net effect is to create better "row" intelligence in the system. But it is the mission of the governance and organisation of the workout unit (or units) that needs to ensure that business and operating models are changed accordingly, to ensure that this extra power in the central processing unit gets translated into an optimised "synapsis model" that can use this extra intelligence and synapsis capacity at best.

5.2 The "synapsis" CWO – digitally minded

As we discussed in the previous chapter, the overall recovery strategy should be driven by the target of the maximisation of the economic value attainable; it may seem an obvious statement, but in reality, most of the workout activities are still driven by strategies informed by accounting or "cash flow" approaches, aimed at minimising the accounting loss in the short time, or in maximising the cash flow generated on the overall GBV also in the short run, regardless of the overall economic value recovered (both are typically leading to losses in the portfolio's NPV).

If the economic value attainable is set as the overarching target, then the strategy set by the industrial plan must be defined as value driven and each and every decision-making component has to be pursued on a quantitative basis so that each resulting output is maximising the NPV of the NPL portfolio. The operating model needs then to be data driven as well, to ensure that objectivity and independence of the analysis can offer the proper basis for the development of such decision-making. This data-driven approach can be developed by planning two specifically independent and separated functions in charge of the overall portfolio analysis and of the definition of the strategic guidelines for the workout and asset management unit (or units).

The strategic targets should then be consistently mirrored at the operating level by more granular quantitative targets – i.e. where an overall recovery target is defined top-down for the overall NPL portfolio, the clusters of such portfolio should also reflect a bottom "sum of the part," which is consistent with that, and that can be further broken down to get assigned to portfolio managers – they will be responsible for the execution of the strategy and its related performance.

Both strategic (and, more importantly) operating targets should then be monitored to analyse the trends in performance and how this could change given a different set of operational choices, e.g. assessing how a redesigned, quicker collection process may impact the overall NPV. The value-driven approach to CWO and active asset management is, therefore, driven by data and its progressive digitisation. Digital gest everywhere, in a way, from the organisation to the processes and from strategy to execution – becoming an almost paramount driver of excellence.

Even the ECB guidelines are suggesting as much, with considerations related to the operating model that should include specific arrangements at the level of the governance, such as the creation of a specific "value recovery intelligence function" that sets the strategies and quantify the targets; specific reporting mechanisms, based on quantitative targets linked to the "holistic" data assessment that should include more efficient and faster "digital" approval processes if possible; and specific requirements at the level of the resources, where dossiers get optimally allocated to portfolio managers and teams, based on the analysis of past performances and inferred expected recoveries – segmented by groups, assets to repossess, specific recovery strategies and the like.

Other specific requirements could also relate to the technical infrastructure of the CWO and asset management units, where the indication is to plan any future change and development to address specific and pragmatic "digitisation targets." Other specific requirements could then relate to the overall budget at granular and consolidated level, e.g. structuring the cost plan and future investments as a function of the extra expected recovery to ensure that any extra layer is justified by an expected return on investment (driven by the incremental collection).

Ultimately, other specific requirements should also be considered for the overall external and internal communication functions of the CWO and asset management unit, to ensure that it is all driven by this value maximisation approach and well understood by interested counterparts, including all kind of stakeholders (such as regulators and potential buyers), leveraging again all potential digital innovation that could make this as seamless and timeless as possible.

5.3 Alpha and beta strategies in CWO

Our view that CWO and active real estate management should be informed by an overarching economic value maximisation objective is also consistent with our previous statement regarding the NPL workout business as, effectively, a specific branch of the alternative asset management industry, where opacity is higher and liquidity is lower and hence the opportunity to obtain higher and "abnormal" returns should be higher and potentially sustainable through time.

As noted previously, the asset management industry is in its turn currently dominated by an increasing polarisation between "alpha players" – players that are able to outperform the market over the cycle – and "beta trackers" – asset managers that are instead just trying to replicate the market, reaching an almost perfect correlation in performances, whilst focusing on delivering the best efficiency: squeezing costs, building economies of scale and industrialising and standardising the operating model as much as possible (as in a mass-production assembly line – Figure 5.2).

Digitisation can get to their help, fostering their industrialisation and standardisation processes towards quicker and more effective ways, and helping these "beta platforms" in building and managing scale through technology (e.g. robotising and automatising workflows). As the success of this model is driven by the prevalence of the efficiency factor and the achievement of economies of scale, it is hard to think of this as the best one for banks that are overburdened by huge amounts of NPL but are still operating for their own captive business only.

Given the very limited value of the cost structure of such CWO platforms, compared to the huge volumes of loans managed and their market value, efficacy, but not efficiency, should be the primary value driver pursued. Consistently, the main focus should be in managing the bank's portfolio, before distracting the limited resources available and the top management attention to embark in consolidation games with third-parties' portfolios that may yield economies of scale only in the mid-long term and (given the relative value of the cost structure) with a limited impact.

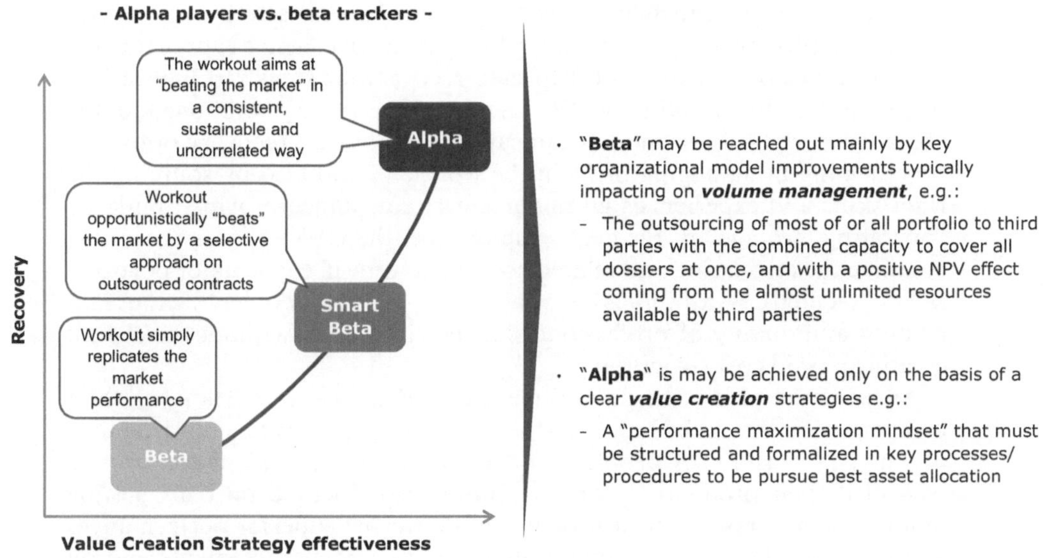

Figure 5.2 Alpha and Beta strategies in credit workout.

"Beta platforms" could be a good business model to pursue only when an independent servicer is focusing on managing large stocks of NPL made up by a very large number of dossier that are individually "low ticket," typically unsecured or "exhausted" and hence can lead to NPV of recoveries of few cents on the dollar. Just in this case, an extra cent of recovery gets comparable with the extra costs required to attain this and the profitability could then benefit significantly from the scale up of the business, even if the consolidation plan is forced to give up to some efficacy.

For traditional, "long-on-NPL" banks, a "beta" strategy can then more logically executed with the outsourcing of most of its low ticket, unsecured, exhausted portfolios to large, industrial, super-efficient BPO platforms that are able to aggregate and manage huge scales, with a lot of flexibility on resources (BPO typically use high numbers of "internal contractors" to manage picks in volumes and can optimise the labour cost of employees that are not required to be hired with a banking contract).

Leaving aside such very specific taxonomy, the opportunity for optimising value in the CWO and real estate business is mostly driven by the creation of "alpha" – i.e. the realisation of extra performances vis-à-vis the market that are almost perfectly uncorrelated with it and sustainable through time. As we said, this "alpha" could be achieved only on the basis of clear value creation strategies and following a "value maximisation mindset" that must be structured and formalised in key processes and procedures to ensure that best NPL allocations and best recovery strategies are always pursued and at all levels of the organisation and no matter what the economic cycle is.

5.4 The seven pillars to create "alpha"

In our approach, we can define seven "key pillars" potentially driving the creation of "alpha" from an operating model perspective, hence supporting the value optimisation of the NPL expected recovery (as shown in Figure 5.3). As first pillar, the flexibility of HR (also mentioned as key component of the "beta tracker" business model) can support the overall recovery optimisation, helping in managing picks in the workload and also by sourcing the right skills and experiences given current circumstances – whilst building "operating leverage" in the cost structure (i.e. the CWO platform can discontinue the resourcing and related costs in no time if, e.g. a major portfolio sale is executed). Flexibility is hence about the possibility of having the right amount and quality of professionals at the right time (without the risk of creating a rigid cost structure).

As a second pillar, the commitment of HR is also important, as their compensation should be linked to the recovery targets and be rewarded accordingly, to ensure key people have "skin in the game" and an appropriate pay-off if their productivity and commitment is focused on truly getting more value and faster and if it turns out delivering superior performances versus the market, e.g. focusing more on extrajudicial agreements and on execution velocity.

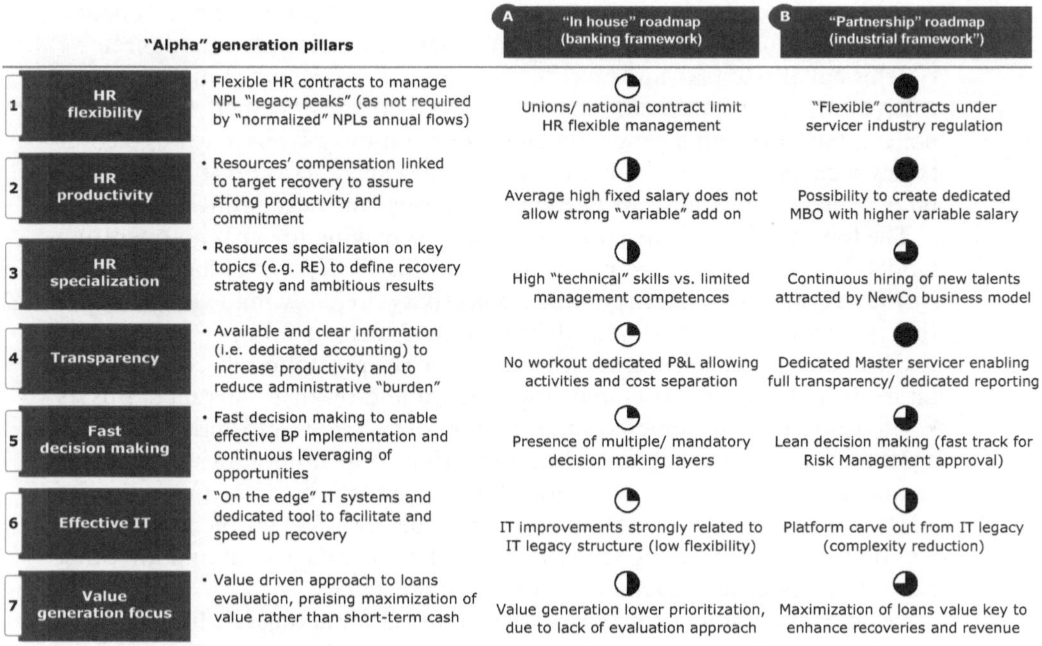

Figure 5.3 Alpha generation key pillars.

As mentioned, CWO and the active management of repossessed assets should be considered almost like a private equity business, where the equity invested by the professionals and their teams is their "sweat" they effectively "sweat for equity" in the hope of sharing some of the extra returns delivered. Having a greatly incentivised "standard" professional is, in this business, often better than having a "standard" incentivised great professional. Of course, the bank should strive to have the best of both worlds, focusing the greatly incentivised packages on the great professionals (and outsourcing everything else to the most efficient BPO "beta trackers").

As a third pillar, the focalisation and specialisation of resources is also key in a field increasingly characterised by a required greater holistic and proactive focus on the underlying collateral (vis-à-vis a traditional approach where legal skills were making up and supporting most of the work). Not only it is critical that a CWO unit has professionals with background in real estate active asset management, but they also have to master a broader mix of functional expertise, from valuation and M&A, to corporate finance and structuring to – in the case of real estate assets – asset strategy and development, property management, marketing and commercialisation – not to mention knowledge of the urbanistic components, and of any relevant legal and fiscal constraint or requirement.

As the skill set of these people is significantly changing, along with their mindset (a la "private equity") and approach (from legal procedures – driven in an almost bureaucratic way, to extrajudicial procedure, requiring a much more commercial mindset and negotiating skills to match), the HR support function becomes even more critical, not only to design new hiring plans and incentive systems but also to plan and execute (often jointly with leading universities) extensive training programmes – not only with a theoretical/methodological component, but also with a pragmatic, hands-on, on-the-job approach – to cover topics such as real estate valuation and management, corporate finance, liability management and securitisation structuring, and negotiating techniques.

The fourth pillar of our approach, which is driving towards an operating model that nurtures and supports the creation of "alpha," is then made up by the overall "transparency" and "objectivity" reliably made available on the status and on the key value drivers of the NPL portfolio.

Clear, complete, consistent information on the portfolio sub-components, on its past recovery curves and track record and on their current status, is key to lead the management to the right set of decisions and actions. Hence, a dedicated data management and reporting/controlling unit could be instrumental in increasing the overall CWO productivity and in reducing its administrative burden. Not to mention that better information and the control of it are also reducing the risk of fraud, mismanagement and anything else related to misconduct and compliance breaches.

Velocity and the related decisiveness in decision-making is a fifth pillar to create "alpha" in CWO and active asset management. As time is of the essence in the maximisation of the NPV of the recovery strategies, and typically banks suffer of decision-making failures driven by their excessive internal syndication, overextended bureaucratic approach and highly regulated set-up, in many cases a suboptimal decision is often much better than no decision at all.

The CWO manager will have to decide on the basis of a limited set of information anyway and, in some cases, the time and costs to recover the right information could just not be worth it. In fact, the trade-off is not just about the decrease in the NPV driven by the "time value of money" effect: certain collaterals could just get stolen, or lose value, as they are left unmanaged or made obsolete by new technologies or product developments (think of a car as a collateral, with an expected decrease in its value of 10%–20% per year just driven by new releases and innovation).

IT and the overall technological ecosystem of the CWO and real estate platform (or platforms) is the sixth pillar of our approach. Leading hedge IT systems and dedicated tools (e.g. big data, ML/AI-based algorithms) may support, accelerate and maximise the recovery expected (e.g. suggesting recovery strategies by cluster, prioritisation of dossiers to be worked out, third parties to be used for each and every single dossier) and build an intelligence in the operating model (embedded in semi-automated processes and robotised workflows) that can lead to better decision-making – done by the machine, in a more independent and objective way.

Finally, as seventh and last pillar, it is worth to consider the "cash flow." Whilst we stated that the overarching target should be the portfolio's economic value maximisation and not just its nominal cash flow (the CWO could easily maximise the cash flow in the short run, by pruning ineffectively the most promising positions, or maximise this in the long run on a nominal basis, running negotiations lasting decades and counting on the help of inflation), it is important to embed the cash flow culture and metric in the governance and organisation of the CWO unit.

These should lead to a re-basement of fair values that are simply too theoretical to achieve (e.g. in some asset, there is value, but no liquidity; hence, cash flow attainable is much lower) and of many accounting treatments that cold just lead the CWO to use the wrong set of assumptions and hence to the wrong selection and execution of certain recovery strategies. Ultimately, many dossiers will just present negative expected cash flows; hence, they would be better left untouched, of course managing with care the potential "moral hazard" side effects that this strategy could bear.

5.5 Embedding the "alpha" pillars: a strategic perspective

Looking back at the seventh pillars introduced, a simple question may arise: is, in fact, the bank the best holder of such a unit to ensure that these seven dimensions are pursued at their best? Is the "captive" CWO and real estate active management unit (or units) best owned by a bank? On a totalitarian or majoritarian basis? Or, should they become minority-owned operating assets, jointly with other financial or industrial counterparts? With which partnership objectives and strategies and which governance and organisation? In a nutshell, who is best placed to become a market leader in CWO and real estate active management, all other things being equal?

It is rather intuitive to state that, on one side, whilst there is no assurance that a private, third party will be able to deliver a better job (if not the best job), a traditional, highly regulated and structurally bureaucratised bank is not in a good starting position to build an "alpha" alternative asset management business – across all asset class and even more so with regard to NPL and repossessed real estate assets. A private equity mentality is simply not for banks, and it should not be theirs.

On the other side, a strategy based on the full outsourcing of these bank's activities could also be suboptimal, as the bank could lose the strategic control and direction setting of such a critical component of its lending value chain and it would be difficult to get the counterpart to have sufficient "skin in the game" so as to behave and perform as it was a principal along with the bank (it is obviously an agent as it does not own the NPL portfolio – hence the typical information failure related to the "principal agent" potential contractualisation and management).

It is important to remember that, in our view, the bank should, however, retain some control of the CWO and active real estate management unit (units) because they are critical not only for what they mean financially (in terms of their potential impact on its P&L and capital position) but also for their implications on the future underwriting activities of the bank – the bank learn from past mistakes to design better risk underwriting tools and create intelligence

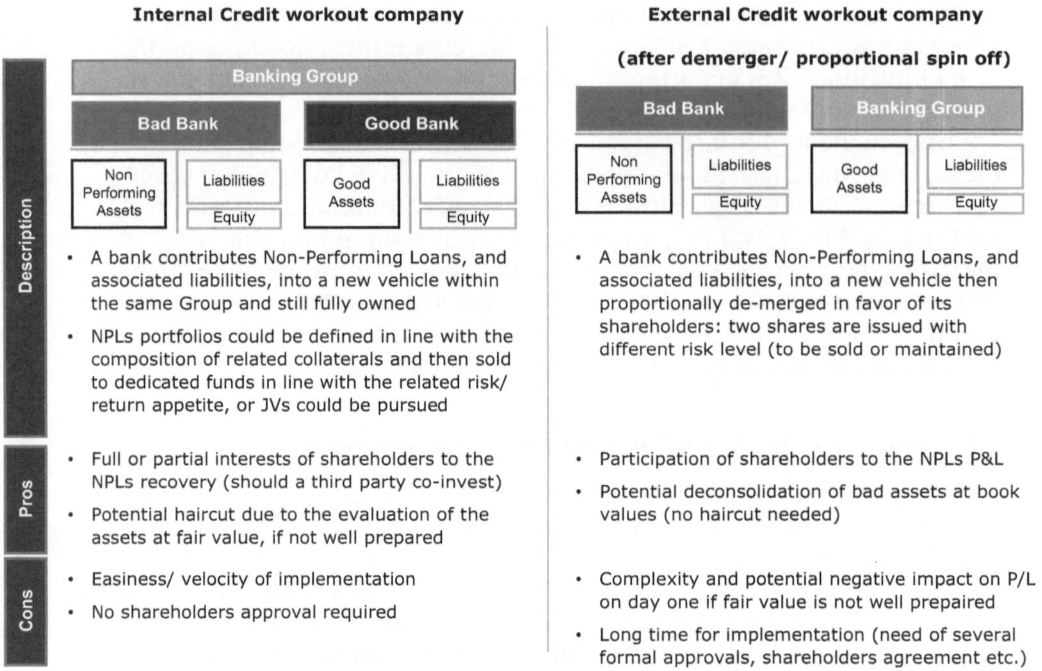

Figure 5.4 Internal versus external credit workout.

out of the big data coming from the recoveries. Also, as the real estate exposure is and will remain a fundamental one, the bank should benefit from the know-how created in any active asset management activity, also regarding their remaining direct or indirect (i.e. via collateral – but still performing) exposures.

As multiple strategic set-ups are available (from the bank creating its own fully owned, but still partially independent legal entity hosting the CWO activities, to the JV of this legal vehicle with some financial or industrial counterparts, with the bank retaining a majority, or a relevant to marginal minority stake), it is important to address these options on the basis of a structured way of reasoning and considering all relevant pros and cons. Also, in case a decision regarding the creation of a bad bank is taken, the options to achieve this should be considered, including the ones regarding a potential demerger and proportional spin-off (Figure 5.4).

5.6 Strategic options: JV and alliances

As a start, in order to fully embed the seven key "alpha" pillars, the workout set-up should be designed and optimised considering two key dimensions of analysis. On one side, the governance model has to address the most appropriate set-up based on two critical dimensions: the NPL and real estate collaterals ownership and the asset management ownership and related decision-making.

The bank could, e.g. decide to securitise its NPL portfolio and sell part of its junior notes (in order to de-risk and de-consolidate) or of its senior ones (to reduce overall financial exposure and create liquidity) or a mix of the two financial investors. It could, at the same time, decide to retain full ownership of the management of the assets, with some selective outsourcing. This solution would address the de-risking/ deleveraging issue and increase the pressure (from the new "principals") to have more transparency and stronger recovery performances from the CWO unit – but it is unclear what would change in the governance, organisation and incentive system that could not be achieved by other means and without necessarily having to sell the portfolio.

Alternatively, the bank could retain the full ownership of the portfolio and sell a majority stake of its workout to a third-party industrial player. This solution would have the benefit of leaving all the potential pay-off in the bank's hands, with the industrial partner incentivised via a "carried interest" and other incentives linked to his contribution of knowledge (people, processes, data, applications etc.) into the new shared platform – but still far from putting this in a position of principal investor.

Or, the bank could just sell – as it has happened several times in Europe in the recent past – the junior tranches of its NPL portfolio to a financial partner (i.e. a private equity fund) that is also a majority owner of its own carve-out workout and keen to contribute its distinctive industrial capabilities on recovery management. It would, in this way, have a clear skin in the "alpha" game.

Whatever the strategic and legal/financial set-up, the CWO should then be focused on developing and delivering a competitive operating model – designing the most suitable organisation given key portfolio features, and with a view to maximise the overall effectiveness and efficiency – enhancing, as we said, its value creation activities via their digitisation and industrialising its back-office activities – leveraging all kind of standardisation and robotisation opportunities.

5.7 A governance perspective: which reporting line?

As mentioned, different strategic options are available, to define the best governance of the CWO unit, as defined by the best mix of choices regarding the assets' ownership and their management responsibility, but not only. Other choices need to be considered even before these two, as the bank should initially consider whether to build up a CWO company internally or via a separate legal entity or a special purpose vehicle, with direct ownership or not of the asset. Also, the bank should define the relevant reporting line, as the CWO could report to the CLO, the chief operating officer (COO), the chief risk officer (CRO) or even the CFO, or it could directly report to the CEO.

Different reporting lines could influence heavily the set-up and working of the workout unit. A CWO reporting to the CLO would offer less transparency on the "cut-off" and passages between different life-cycle phases, with the potential risk that the CLO would wait longer before recognising his or her mistakes, hence waiting too much marking the loans as UTP and then non-performing – this, apart from the potential breach on the accounting rules and related regulatory capital implications, would have negative effects on the overall NPV of the loan.

The CLO could also have a softer incentive to play hard with the borrower, as it could have multiple lending relationships with the stakeholders of the counterpart (say, a company has defaulted, but the entrepreneur and many of its top managers are still clients of the bank). Still, a unique reporting line to the CLO it would ensure that a more seamless sharing of all relevant information across the different stages of the credit life cycle and the CLO and its team would have the full story of that loan, since it is original underwriting (mistake). They would also capture more effectively all the relevant "post-mortem" data that would then be incorporated in future underwriting decisions.

A CWO reporting to the COO would instead be likely very focused on efficiency and quite careful on its contribution to the overall cost structure of the bank, hence potentially sub-optimising the efficacy of the recovery and the overall net effect for the bank, especially in case of very large loan portfolios and with multiple, small ticket portfolios.

The COO would, however, have a stronger sensibility on the relevance of the IT system in this business and likely be ready to invest accordingly. Should the chief technology officer (CTO) report to him, further synergies could be achieved, specifically on the implementation of a digitalisation plan focused on data management, applied analytics and the automation/robotisation of the unit.

In case the CWO reports to the CRO, it could then end up being heavily influenced by the portfolios' valuations done for regulatory and reporting reasons, with may be a stronger approach to the definition of the methodologies and statistical approaches used, but with a softer sensibility on the "real" set of actions to be pursued to maximise the recovery's NPV.

Likewise, the chief financial officer would influence the design and management of the CWO unit and likely focusing mostly on its capital implications, with a more aggressive stance on NPL sales, that could quickly reduce the Texas ratio even if at the cost of some economic value for the bank. It could, however, have a stronger experience in the structuring of financial solutions aimed at achieving de-risking and deleveraging, making the most of the potential financial investors interested in buying a slice. It would certainly contribute on the management of the overall financial risks and structuring, but may be missing out on key competencies on the real estate collaterals.

Finally, a CWO reporting directly to the CEO would certainly overcome most of these issues and ensure the proper level of sponsorship and strategic insight, but it would suffer of the likely limited attention paid by him or her and be justified only when the relevance of the NPL issue is critically important and for a limited period of time – for extraordinary circumstances as it is now the case for most of the Mediterranean countries in Europe, where the NPL "bad" bank is a bank within a bank, sometimes with an overall GBV that is approaching the one of the "good bank."

5.7 A governance perspective: setting an independent workout unit

Once the reporting line is defined, more strategic choices are due to the operating set-up of the platform and its internal versus external scope and scalability options – the two decisions are also intertwined, and these options are also influencing the reporting line. The degree of externalisation is a key input required to design the most appropriate target operating model. A workout unit could, e.g., be managed internally and in an integrated, end-to-end way, leveraging in a very marginal (and tactical) way external outsourcers. Its scope could then be focused exclusively on the bank's captive portfolio, or potentially be open-ended, and ready to serve other counterparts, to generate fees and leverage economies of scale (and information), to the benefit of the bank owner.

In contrast, it could leverage a lot on outsourcing, retaining the key planning, monitoring and performance reviewing functions and the "information-based intelligence" and relying on multiple third parties managed as in a "competitive horses' race" (the better the single parties perform, the greater volumes of NPL they get to serve, and the more performance fees they gain as well).

For this set-up, the dynamic reallocation of mandates would ensure a transparent and continuous competition, and the performance fees (set up on top of some "fixed fees" and paid on several KPI, including the overperformance realised on top of a certain interest rate threshold, the internal rate of return (IRR) on the portfolio – for portfolios owned by private equity funds, or the extra NPV realised above a given monetary value) would ensure a certain level of "skin in the game" of the outsourcers involved.

However, the risk from the suppliers' side would be mainly limited to the component of their cost structure not covered by the fixed fees, as they are not co-investors in the portfolios, and the accumulation and capitalisation of the information and intelligence produced would be more difficult for the bank to retain, with also a lower incentive on the outsourcer side in investing in new technologies and in better talents able to produce "alpha" (unless they are mostly paid by their client on the alpha produced). Also, a performance fee structured based on the cash flow recovered could promote the "pruning" of the "low-hanging fruits" of the NPL portfolio, with limited efforts on the "high-hanging fruits" – as they would require a lot of effort on the outsourcer's side.

The workout unit could then be developed as both "internal" and "external," if it gets externalised and contributed to an SPV or incorporated into a separate legal entity, as a first step to create even more transparency, greater accountability and then independency in its governance and management. It is important to stress how the attribute of "independency" is relevant, no matter what the internal or external option being pursued, as it is required to drive the value optimisation of the recovery activities, regardless of what other commercial interests could be found in the way and potentially influencing its decision-making. It is also certainly required to ensure that a professional, talented management can be more easily attracted, retained and incentivised.

We have already introduced alternative options related to "fully owned" servicers, with portfolios that are securitised and with different tranches sold to different investors. Other options introduced were then related to a development in JV, with third parties playing the industrial partner role and owning a super majority of it, with the NPL portfolio left as fully owned by the bank – and with many other options in between. The best decision on these governance options should be informed by the bank's targets and ambitions, and it should consider all kind of relevant regulatory guidelines and constraints. It could then change through time and given the specific life-cycle stage and the idiosyncratic composition of the loan portfolio managed. A more detailed discussion of selected, specific options is discussed in the following paragraph, with a focus on JVs.

5.8 The independent CWO as a JV

As mentioned, different governance options are available for the set-up and development of a CWO and active real estate management unit (or units). In practice, multiple servicer and asset models can be pursued, as owned by a banking group or by third parties, or as a mix of the two. Of the many options already introduced, it is worth to consider and further comment on few of them regarding the execution of a JV with a partner. In a first "all bundled" option, both the servicing capabilities and the assets of the bank (or parts of them, and associated liabilities) are contributed to a dedicated, separate legal entity, and usually requiring a "mark-to-market" for the transaction at day one – something like what in restructuring parlance is called "bad bank."

This "bad bank" could then be sold to a financial/industrial third party, in its entirety or as a minority or majority share to ideally reach regulatory and accounting deconsolidation, whilst still retaining some of the upside on the assets and fee income business of the servicer (and some access and control to the critical information and intelligence being produced by its ongoing management).

Alternatively, the bad bank could be deconsolidated whilst allowing the bank's shareholders to retain their full exposure on the asset and servicer business via a de-merger, usually realised via a stock split (the existing bank shareholders receive two stocks in exchange of the current one: a share representing their ownership into the newly created "bad bank" and a share representing their ownership in the remaining "good bank"). That would also allow to keep the bank stock (stocks) listed. Each shareholder will then could retain both shares or divest one of them (reinvesting the proceeds on the other) or else, allowing a better realignment between their risk appetites and the risk/return profiles of the invested assets (of the bad and good bank listed).

An "unbundled" model will instead consider the servicing business and asset portfolios as different and to be contributed to different legal vehicles, hence allowing a larger number of options, coming from the different possible permutations of the two, and a more segmented approach to the development and execution of alliances and partnerships with financial or industrial partners.

A specific case worth discussing further is considering an overall alliance with two counterparts (often with one – financial – controlling the other – industrial). For this case, the bank seeks a specific industrial partner for the servicing unit (units) (in case the bank is also considering a further split between the loan workout activities and the real estate active management ones), able to contribute experience, relevant technology and people and potentially facilitating the access to the open market, to develop the platform as a for-profit business.

This industrial partner is typically an existing, fully independent (i.e. not bank's owned) CWO unit (or a real estate service company, for the property active management component) that is committed to contribute relevant assets (most of them intangible). It will also need to have the strategic commitment to develop the platform in the reference market on exclusive terms: i.e. if the independent CWO has a "holding platform" in the country, and it develops a JV with the bank's one for the same market, it will have a strong incentive to treat this just as a way to capture another client and will keep developing the open market through the "holding platform" that fully controls, avoiding the potential cannibalisation coming from the one it just partially controls.

This industrial partner, ideally working in the relevant country on exclusive terms via the JV, and holding a controlling stake, so as to ensure any influence coming from the bank is managed in a detached, professional way, should be incentivised on (at least) three perspectives: on one side, as mentioned, it should be paid with a commission scheme that is highly skewed on the "alpha" generated from the workout management of the bank's portfolios, clearly distinguishing and incentivising what performance increases have matured since the partner took over.

Second, it should also be paid for the relevant, value adding services it offers to the bank that initially carved out its servicing unit and mandated the new JV on the management of its NPL portfolios. This is important as it becomes paramount for the bank to keep having access to the information and intelligence coming from the recovery and asset management activities – not just for the sake of its future NPL management but also of its future underwriting activities as – we have argued – it is true that NPL are born out of wrong underwriting decisions on day one, but it is also true that knowing how they have ended up, future, better underwriting decisions could be made. Finally, the industrial partner should be incentivised on the fee income derived from the open market business that it is now accessible to the non-bank–owned credit work, carved out platform.

To ensure that all these targets are rightly defined and incentivised, they need to be considered and included in the initial business plan of the JV and contractualised as relevant component of the transaction and related pricing structure (typically, such a transaction is contractualised on the basis of a long-term contract of servicing – e.g. for ten years and renewable – and of an accompanying, detailed SLA defining also the service quality expected).

Also, to make the overall incentives set on the right baseline, a full NPL portfolio revaluation should be considered before the start of the new partnership, with more reasonable potential haircuts to assets' value to be accounted before the JV starts running. A well-defined set of market and other (i.e. historical) external and internal benchmarks should also be contractualised and considered as integral part of the incentive system and be normed as a consequence.

Of course, the incentives' alignment on the value recovery targets is easier to set and more directly managed and monitored if the industrial partner chosen for the JV at the CWO and active real estate management levels is also investing directly in the financial assets being managed (directly or indirectly – the typical example being that the industrial partner is fully or majority owned by a private equity firm that is also investing – usually for amounts that are a multiple of the equity put into the workout platform) in the junior and mezzanine tranches of the securitised NPL portfolio being managed by the JV. In this case, however, it will become more difficult to align the new JV servicing platform with regard to other, more "holistic" objectives.

For example, if the platform is also managing other NPL portfolios (e.g. future new NPL flows coming from the same bank) where the partner and its financial shareholders are not directly invested in, the incentive system needs to make sure that it will do this with the same level of care, energy and passion – ensuring a "pari passu" prioritisation on the workout of the multiple dossiers and the homogeneous allocation of best recovery recourses available. Also, it will need to make sure that the right quantity and quality of information and intelligence is transferred back to the bank anyway, even if (in a more extreme case) most of the NPL portfolio is owned by the private equity fund.

Finally, it will need to make sure that no value maximisation strategy for the given NPL portfolio is eventually undermining the aggregated value of others (there may be cases where "to do nothing" on certain dossier or counterpart typologies is the best strategy – but that would increase the moral hazard on the bank's borrowers side; and other cases where the recovery on certain selected dossiers – say, a leasing on an equipment that is core for the production cycle of a manufacturing company – would almost paradoxically end up creating a much larger value destruction at the level of the aggregated, overall borrower's exposure as the company would stop producing).

5.9 The JV as a way to develop the seven pillars

No matter what the fine-tuning required in the set-up of the incentive model, the JV option could turn out as one of the most interesting for the bank, in situations of large amounts of distressed loans and with multiple constraints on resources, including management attention, and available strategies on the bank's side (as it is now the case for most Mediterranean banks).

In most of the observed cases, a JV-driven servicing approach has accelerated the development plans of the platforms, ensuring a more focused implementation of a flexible, dynamic and efficient/effective operating model. A discontinuity in the recovery strategy and its operating approach has also been instrumental in supporting higher levels of ambitions on the bank's side – sometimes reflected in accounting valuations that have revalued more aggressively the expected fair value of the portfolio and following an IFRS 9 accounting approach. Far from being accounting gimmick, this approach is sound and rational, as long as the targeted change in the "alpha" created by the JV can reasonably realise through time – and with the help of the industrial partner.

From an execution point of view, the JV approach at the level of the servicing company (or companies, should the bank decide to pursue a different alliance at the level of the real estate active management) is pursued via several subsequent, logical steps. First of all, a dedicated perimeter (addressing people, technologies, processes, data and contractual agreements to serve portfolios) should be identified as the target of the initial carve-out – with the key components of the workout unit selected for separation and contribution to a new, stand-alone legal entity, properly regulated and capitalised (it does not require a full banking license, but it is typically subject to some kind of lighter regulation and requires a license awarded and then monitored by the central bank).

Once the carve-out entity is contributed to the new legal entity, properly licensed by the regulators, the JV will then execute a business plan aimed at strengthening its recovery capabilities and touching upon all the seven key pillars we have already described as driving value maximisation.

On the side of the HR' flexibility dimension, the JV should be able to contribute with employment contracts (typically non-banking contracts) that allow more flexibility in the hiring/firing of people (to manage more promptly the picks in workloads) and in the working hours and habits (to follow more closely what is needed to, e.g., grow the rate of extrajudicial agreements). On the side of the commitment of these very resources, the JV should also allow the design of more aggressive management by objective (MBO) incentive systems, with compensation structures that are more highly skewed towards the variable component, to increase a productivity that can be measured in terms of NPV or cash flow per unit of cost.

Also, a JV-industrialised approach should help in the specialisation of HR and in fostering a meritocratic approach that can then cut across different organisational units and sub-units, and processes and procedures. More aligned responsibilities, with greater opportunities to make it into a fast-track career path, should also ensure a more effective proposition to attract and retain new talents (and vice versa, offer a one more reason to leave the company to bureaucrats). Everybody should have, at the end, some "skin in the game" of the CWO.

On the transparency dimension, a well-identified JV structure, with a master servicer mandate, with or without some special servicing capabilities, would also support better clarity and accountability and with a more easily readable reporting at legal entity level and for main areas of activities and portfolios managed. Having a third, interested counterpart in the CWO would then ensure that the transfer price and the contractual agreements are competitively agreed and reflect market values, as no accounting gimmick would be allowed by the new equity partner.

The dimension of decision-making (in terms of its velocity and ability to quickly run a process leading to some decisive management action) is also better supported by a JV structure, where an industrial partner is obviously keen to reduce its time to market and usually unencumbered by most of the regulatory, compliance and bureaucratic constraints affecting a regulated, fully licensed bank. A quicker decision-making will then speed up recovery process and reduce lead time, limiting the time value of money discount and increasing the optionality on certain opportunities.

The IT effectiveness dimension is also supported by the JV solution. Typically, JV platforms are born out of carve-outs from banks; hence, they already tend to reduce the complexity of the legacy systems as the carve-outs are typically partial. Also, on the basis of the newly ring-fenced entity, it becomes easier to develop new digital applications leveraging agile design, testing and full implementation approaches. It is also easier to allow the partner's contribution of dedicated digital applications and new co-developments, starting from a common understanding of the key role played by technology in making the platform distinctive, competitive and value accretive.

On the "cash flow" side, the JV solution is also instrumental in driving a new approach in the organisation – more pragmatically focused on the cash versus the accounting measures. Cash flow measure should, therefore, indicate which accounting values are potentially not worthy of any recovery activity (as they would be cash negative) and what prioritisation of efforts should be considered to increase cash flows and, given the underlying hypothesis on the discount rate, the overall net present value of the portfolio. Whilst it is important to manage the potentially arising "moral hazard" from the borrower's side, it is critical that zero recovery dossiers are not pursued or at least over-zealously pursued, with a negative net effect that depletes the overall cash flow.

Whilst the "seven pillars" are aiming at increasing the effectiveness (and, to a minor extent), the efficiency of the CWO activities and therefore the value recovered from the distressed credit assets, it is important to note how further value creation opportunities are available for the bank. On day one, the bank could realise an important transaction price from the sale of a stake in the CWO and active real estate management unit (or units) – mostly driven by the long-term commercial agreement that will mandate the JV platform for the servicing of its NPL portfolios.

This upfront capital gain will be equal, from a theoretical perspective, to the NPV of the future profits coming from the servicer – the higher the profits, the higher the commissions paid by the bank to it for the future services received, and the longer the contractual agreement for that services. But it should also include, on top of this NPV, a goodwill for accessing a CWO that is already up and running, with a given set of processes and technological applications, a license to operate and a team of professionals, not to mention a wealth of data on the reference NPL market.

The remaining stake that the bank will choose to retain could then appreciate a lot over a longer time frame, as the platform develops, with new investments and new people and – ideally – a better governance and organisation and potentially addressing also the open market as a profit-seeker entity. The capitalisation of the "seven pillars" being developed with the help of the partner should then be reflected in the remaining minority stake of the bank that would capture the pro quota stream of further commissions developed by the now independent CWO in the market.

A few, not exhaustive, case studies regarding recent JV between banks and industrial or financial partners (or both) in the CWO area are presented in Figures 5.5 and 5.6. Most of the examples are coming from those countries most heavily impacted by the NPL overhang, after the global financial

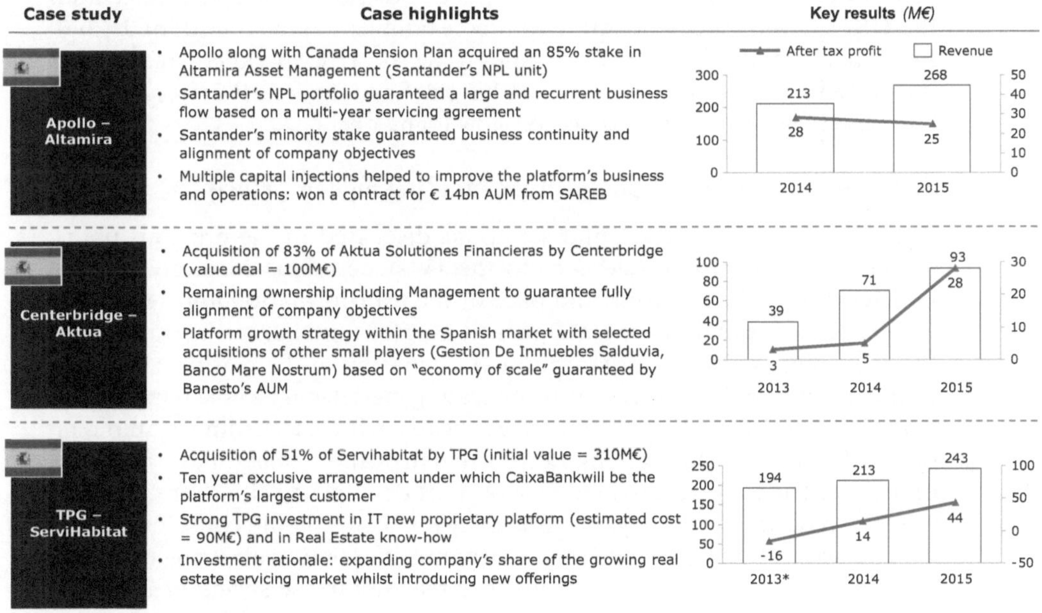

Figure 5.5 Joint venture case studies in credit workout (1/2).

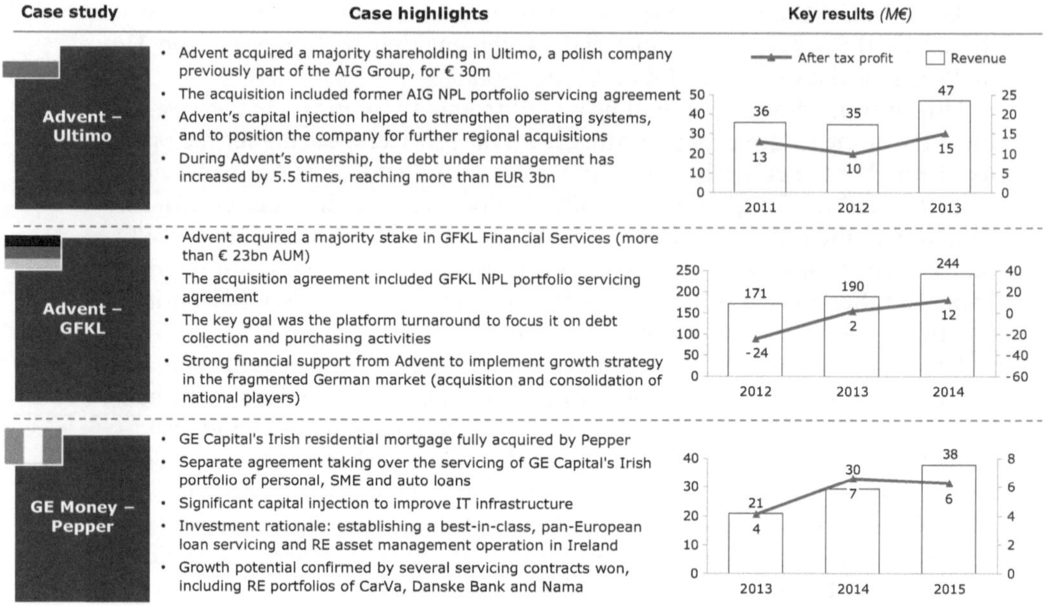

Figure 5.6 Joint venture case studies in credit workout (2/2).

crisis. Namely, Spain has been at the forefront of this trend, with Italy and more recently Greece to follow. However, other examples can be found across Europe, with other cases in Ireland, Poland, Germany, France and the UK. On the other side, more limited examples can be found for JV between banks and real estate companies to develop the so-called "real estate integrated service companies" (as we have defined them as REIS company), but with a few interesting discussion now going on.

5.10 An organisational perspective: building on new principles

The governance dimension and set-up, as discussed in the previous paragraph and with specific reference to the JV structure, is certainly critical in determining the direction and pace of the transformation journey of the CWO and active real estate management unit (or units). But is certainly not the only one, as also the organisational dimension of the platform will determine in a significant way how its operating model will be able to perform, at the light of the significant challenges ahead – with extraordinary amounts of NPE/NPL to be managed by European banks and – sometimes – new real estate markets to be reactivated from almost deadlocked situations.

When redesigning the organisational set-up, banks should consider a number of organisational principles that are aiming not only at ensuring the compliance vis-à-vis the new ECB guidelines released in the spring of 2017 but also at helping and supporting the progressive digitisation of the platform, as the future competitive challenge, as we stated, will be more and more fought at the level of aggregated data capture, capitalisation and management, for the creation of superior intelligence on the credit recovery targets and on the loan management and collection and real estate asset management (holistic, active) strategies that could be supporting the bank to that end.

The two "compliance" and "digital" dimensions are kind of complementary and actually allowing for a fast convergence, as the ECB – as many other international regulators – has started recognising the critical role played by data and information and has opened up to the potential value added coming from the adoption of new technologies and ML/AI techniques.

In practice, such an organisation should facilitate and support the fast and effective implementation of the identified portfolio strategy and the achievement of the related recovery quantitative targets. It should not do this in a rigid way but allow some dynamic adaptation of the workout – functionally to the continuously changing conditions in the NPL market environment (e.g. new regulations may change the readiness and convenience for banks to execute quick sales, or the investor risk appetite could change, or the underlying trends in key sectors such as the real estate one could also change).

The organisation of the CWO platform should react fast and be able to follow through with a quick decision-making, always based on quantitative data and objective information. The organisation should of course not only reflect the best practices in terms of compliance and regulator set-up but also be able to speed up the efficient and effective recovery key processes by embracing wholeheartedly whatever digitised and robotised uses cases could came useful to that end.

As a matter of fact, we can summarise six main key principles to be followed to allow for the pursuit of both the ECB compliance and digitisation objectives. As a first step, the organisation should be redesigned as driven by a clear value generation focus, and with clear separation of the two main value generation workout use cases (i.e. the credit recovery and the collaterals active asset management aimed at optimising their valorisation) to enhance the platform's performance and ensure a most proper management accountability, control and related incentive system.

Secondly, the organisation should ensure a clear-cut legacy segregation, with a full transparency and clear accountability of the results that may be generated in a heterogeneous way from quite different portfolios and recovery strategies. A distinction between a large "legacy" portfolio and the more "back to normal" new flows could, e.g., be a good way to start, with more sub-clustering to detail different recovery strategies and a further partition for the portfolios "ready for sale," that clearly need a different management and investments just focused on their short-term maximisation (e.g. to create fully loaded databases, ready for the buyers' due diligence).

As a third principle, the organisation should be focused on the maximisation of the value attainable from data and information and applied analytics. The strategies defined for the CWO platforms should be informed by all kind of new digital intelligence, and these in turn would perform better if the organisational set-up is consistently designed to that end. For example, the organisation should make the data/applied analytics based, continuous re-clustering easy to carry through and implement and should support the following reallocation of dossiers on a "best-fit" basis, to the many teams involved and also to the third parties for the portion of work being outsourced.

A fourth, suggested principle to follow when redesigning the organisation should then focus on the independence amongst who is doing the valuation, who is setting the targets and who is actually called to perform against those targets. It may look as common sense, but in most CWO and active asset management units now operating in Europe, the valuation of the real estate asset ends being done by the "front-line" people called to then manage them actively to close. As such, they could be incentivised to use higher cuts in valuation first, to show off their performance later.

And even the target setting may get influenced by either accounting information (most of them fairly disconnected from the fair value and market value of the loans or assets, and with a lot of volatility in terms of their gap vs. these values – with most of the undershooting being complemented by few overshooting in value) or by the same recovery teams that provide biased inputs at the beginning of the process that will then see them running judicial and extrajudicial processes.

Fifth, the organisation should selectively focus and invest on what to do internally, whilst pragmatically adopting other outsourcing solutions for what is non-core for the workout. The choice of what is core and what is less-core or non-core is a critical one, as it also influences the decision on the talents to hire and develop, the training programmes for the HR employed and on the HR investments allocation, given the limited resources available. This choice, far from being merely strategic, should also strive to maximise the industrialisation of the operating model of the bank as much as possible – applying the levers of process excellence, standardisation, consolidation pooling of resources for similar activities and much else – to increase the overall productivity – hence the level of output (NPV of recoveries) given inputs (the cost structure).

Finally, a sixth principle should focus on a value-based management approach, first making sure the definition of value creation is consistent with the expectation of the stakeholders of the CWO and real estate management unit (or units). Once set, and with a related set of KPI used as workable references for the top and middle management, the CWO should identify and monitor the most important "single tasks" and align the required specifics as needed. It should then keep measuring and controlling how the value creation is being performed at all times, revising strategies and set-ups as needed and incentivising people in a consistent way.

5.11 Transformation along the value chain

In our experience, the potential "alpha" attainable in CWO and active real estate asset management is justifying most of the high variance in the performances observed for different players. Differently from other segments of the alternative asset management industry, this one is likely much less sophisticated and surely less transparent – these combined two factors then allow the survival of many (mostly "captive") less players, dragging down the sector's performance.

As discussed, the disruptions introduced by digital transformation in the banking sector are also becoming evident in the CWO and real estate asset management, ideally leading to a redesign of the main processes end to end and with multiple applications of ML/AI (then driving robotisation and automation) along the way. The digital transformation, as shown in Figure 5.7, is then further widening the gaps between the best and the worst performers, with banks' captive services and businesses typically reacting more slowly to the innovation challenge. Wide variations in performance amongst players is certainly determined by their different levels of sophistication and stages of digital development, but also due to the many interlinkages present in this kind of service (or business) and involving multiple stakeholders.

In fact, credit recovery performances do depend on multiple external stakeholders that may directly influence the final outcome, e.g. the borrowers, the courts and lawyers. And their satisfaction and smooth management and coordination depend in turn on the smooth way of working across and along with multiple CWO's internal functions (from IT to finance, to purchasing) that can create synergies across the NPE/NPL value chains to maximise the NPV of the recovery. The workout is in fact a complex ecosystem that needs to be managed with care, with a strong focus on the management of cross-functional areas and of their many interrelationships. This is shown in Figure 5.8, depicting CWO as a concentric ecosystem.

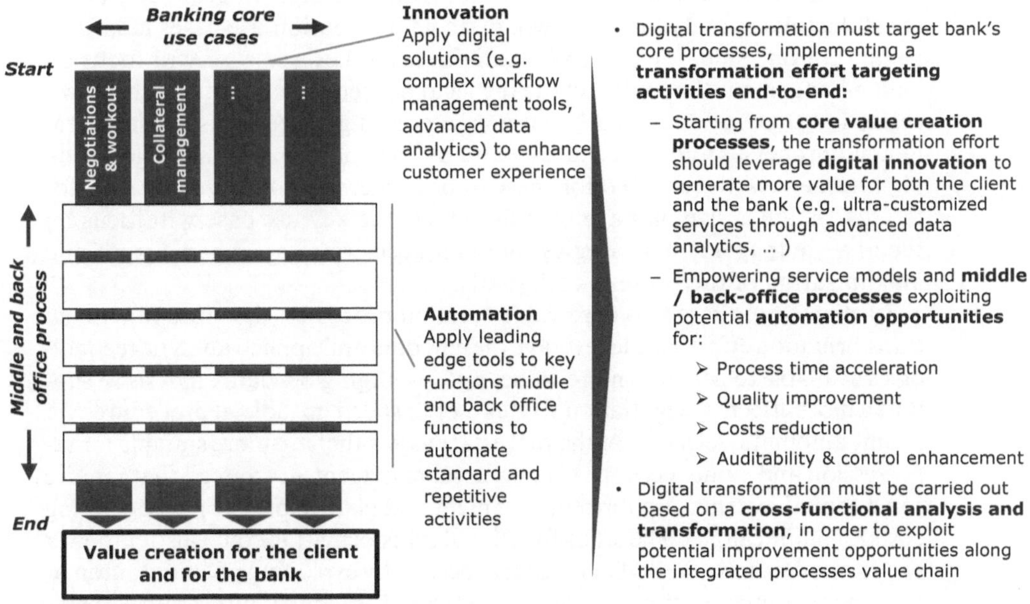

Figure 5.7 Digitalisation in credit workout management.

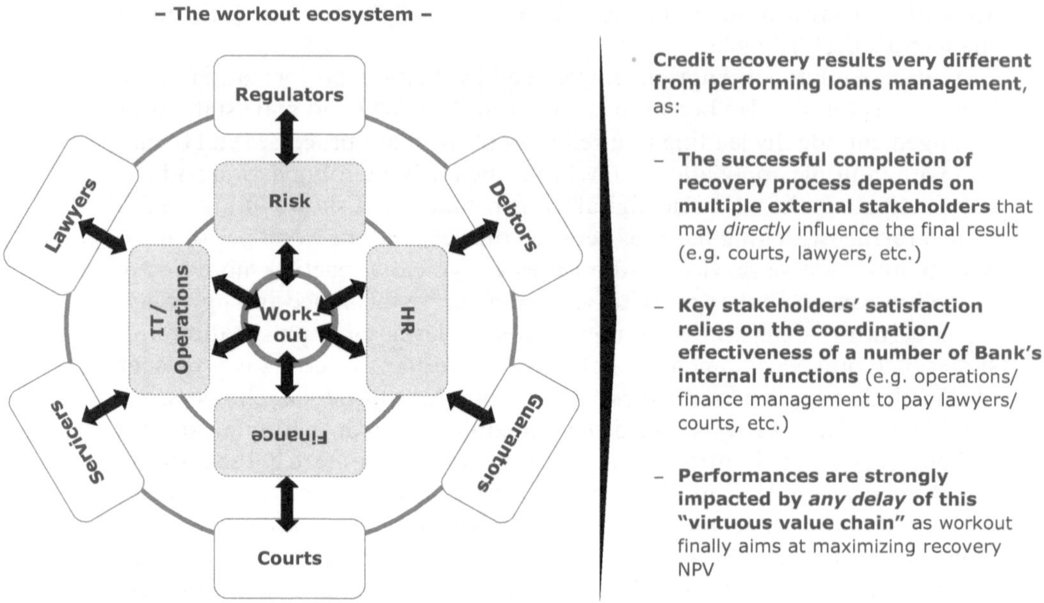

Figure 5.8 Credit workout ecosystem.

Because of these two factors, the implementation of an effective operating model requires the end-to-end digital transformation of the main cross-functional workout activities that involve multiple internal and external stakeholders and along the two, main value creation use cases identified so far. On one side, for the CWO activities, the key use case will focus on loan management that will include the legal procedures and the judicial processes but that will specifically put a greater and greater focus on the extra-judicial processes and procedures – and on the commercial and negotiation management skills required for these to be successful. On the other side, for the real estate active management activities, the key use case will focus on the asset management strategies that can accelerate the enhancement and maximisation of the value of collaterals.

Starting from these two core value creation processes, the cross-functional transformation effort should leverage the new data and applied analytic technologies available to generate more value, e.g., leveraging big data analysis to support a more effective negotiation strategy, or to speed up judicial procedures via a semi-automatic selection of the real estate assets that are more suitable for repossession and value recovery via new asset management strategy that require some capital expenditure for refurbishment and change of use, plus operating costs for maintenance. The cross-functional transformation could also empower service models and middle/back-office processes by exploiting potential automation opportunities for time to market acceleration, quality improvement, operational efficiency and cost reduction and control enhancement and auditability.

In all these examples, it is important to ensure that the digital transformation efforts are as much pervasive across the ecosystem and benefitting the highest number of internal and external stakeholders, without damaging none of them. These digital transformation efforts should also be carried out on the basis of a cross-functional analysis, to ensure that most of the potential improvement opportunities are addressed across the recovery value chain, front to back.

5.12 Management of recovery intelligence

Based on this framework of analysis, at high level, at least four, main workout cross-functional processes can be redesigned and streamlined leveraging on data-intensive, digitisation use cases. These "main four" processes, management of recovery intelligence, active asset management, operations management and real estate collaterals management, are further described and with reference to their main subprocesses. More specifically, we will look at the first one (the recovery intelligence unit) as a key driver and accelerator of the digitisation of the CWO and active asset management capabilities of the captive, JV-ed or independent unit (or units).

The process of developing and managing at best recovery intelligence via a dedicated unit could be, for a start, broken up into the subprocesses of the NPL portfolio recovery planning, the NPL recovery performance monitoring and the dynamic NPL dossiers' provisioning. The portfolio recovery planning would leverage data management as it can identify and digitise key information to automatically define possible portfolio business plans and hence optimal recovery strategies – defined as the ones that maximise the NPV of the recovery either by single dossier or by clusters.

The performance monitoring would then benefit from big data and applied analytics as it would link actual results to expected ones and review and improve the ongoing management of the portfolio on an objective, quantitative basis. Finally, automatic applied analytics could also allow to connect the provisioning of specific dossiers to the new data coming available from the recovery activities performed, potentially leading to the automatic, routines-based, generation of IFRS 9 compliant scenarios and final estimates with significant savings of time and costs for the workout unit.

The recovery intelligence management is a key component of the digitisation transformation of the CWO and active real estate asset management activities. It is, therefore, critical to address the relevant questions regarding who will take care of all the data-driven analysis, becoming the unique source of information for both internal and external shareholders and, finally, oversee the required continuous data update and the activities of quality enhancement of information required.

The creation of a dedicated "recovery intelligence unit" reporting directly to the head of the workout unit is a first step in the right direction. This unit should have a wide mandate that would include the responsibility for setting the methodology and for reviewing the real estate valuations, guarantying the required independence vis-à-vis the target recovery and asset management team dedicated to their workout and value optimisation activities and the performance monitoring that would encompass line asset managers and other staff functions (e.g. IT and operations).

The recovery intelligence unit should then be leveraged by "local" asset manager teams through dedicated data analysts that would support them in the day-to-day activities (reporting to them with a "dotted line"). In this way, the recovery intelligence unit would help the asset managers in all data-driven day-by-day activities (e.g. in the recovery plans reviews, based on credit life events), freeing up some of their time and assuring a continuous and correct flow of the information needed to effectively and efficiently pursue their targeted recovery strategy. The local data analysts would then support the central team to produce the information needed to carry out the planning and performance monitoring activities (i.e. the information on the cash generated by collection).

Finally, the recovery intelligence unit would also become the one responsible for identifying, designing and exploiting all kind of opportunities coming from ML/AI, and setting up the algorithms that could help in the optimisation of recovery activities. It could, e.g., set up and develop NPL and real estate aggregated indexes, used mark-to-market current exposure, or embed predictive algorithms to suggest the best recovery strategy per cluster, the best prioritisation of the dossiers to be worked out, or the best allocation of work between internal and external resources and the selection of the best third-party suppliers for each of cluster and main dossier – further digitising the workout and active asset management activities.

5.12 Active asset, operations and collaterals management

The process of actively managing assets to optimise their recovery value could also be transformed leveraging digital technologies and industrialisation techniques. A first subprocess, relating to the negotiation of single positions, could be significantly improved by assigning a quantitative, target NPV for each dossier and related friendly transaction. On this basis, the workload could be allocated to different teams given the required versus available skills and given the potential monetary pay-off – or the strategy could simply suggest as best option for the outsourcing of certain negotiations.

Also, the key decision-making, and related approvals, could be streamlined with the help of digital tools, as it would delegate decision power on the basis of the potential output variances in the closing of the dossiers and given the target NPV expected from their recoveries. The delegation would be larger, but with greater subjectivity and "quantitative control" throughout. It would also get embedded in each of the subprocess. Finally, the last phase relating to the closing of the dossier would also be enhanced by digital tools, as applied analytics could suggest when and how to strike a deal – consistently with the holistic assessment of the recovery rates of the portfolio.

From an operations point of view, significant improvements in efficiency and efficacy could be targeted by leveraging data and applied analytics.

The heavy workload related to documents management could specifically benefit greatly from the implementation of software based on ML application that can help in data capturing and image and semantic processing to support the acquisition and verification of paper-based documents (Figure 5.9).

Similar digital tools can also help in the optimal management of outsourcers, from their selection to contractualisation and monitoring. Data-intensive applied analytics could allow for a more effective periodic review of external structures and of their performances. This would in turn lead to the reallocation of workloads, to allow for the consolidation of volumes on the best performer per asset class. The workout performance would then benefit from the increased and dynamic level of competitiveness, based on the outsourcers actual productivity, and not just on their level of fees charges (usually, competitive auctions for outsourcing are driven by the minimisation of the fees paid – hardly associated with the expected outcome from their recovery activities).

Operations management could also benefit greatly from data management and applied analytics, and it would entail, e.g., the budgeting of future costs and the management of the accounts payable. Digital tools can now in fact link analytically the cost budgeting to the expected recovery flows distinguishing the asset-driven expenses and the servicing ones and hence increasing the accuracy and transparency of the NPV of recovery analysis and optimising the efforts of the platform as a consequence. Finally, the digitisation and streamlining of the accounts payable could allow to free up time for the asset managers, enhancing their control on costs and avoiding unnecessary delays in the collection process (e.g. for delays in paying lawyers and court specialists).

- Example of advanced software for data capture -

- Advanced software for data capture allow to **recognize all possible optical characters** (on paper)
- The software must be initially **customized** based on which **information must be "digitalized"**
- The character recognition is a **machine learning application**: the software continuously trains itself based on digitalized information **improving automation and accuracy**

- Semantic engine application and outcome -

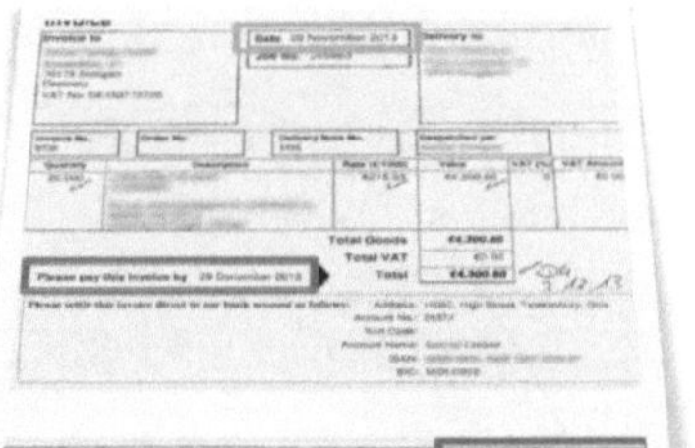

- The application **automatically understands where key information are** in the sheet and digitalizes the data (e.g. independently recognize prices/ payments, companies' logos, etc.)
- The advanced optical data capture allow to:
  - **Cross check information** between data tapes and original contract (minimizing efforts for contracts due diligence)
  - **Integrate missing information** in the data tape extracting them from original contracts

Figure 5.9 Advanced software and semantic engine apps.

The collaterals active management process could also benefit a lot from digitisation. Real estate valuations could, for a start, be set up on the basis of clearly identified and digitised information that would then be used to evaluate real estate collaterals, given certain key characteristics of the assets – from location to typology and end use. These valuations could then be refresh more frequently.

The definition and related approval of the real estate active management strategy could also be enhanced by ML applications that are able to suggest the most appropriate real estate enhancement strategies for each cluster and sizeable asset, based on their specific features. Once a real estate asset repossessing strategy is set, ML-based applications could then enlist the required activities for repossession and whatever else is needed to ensure that the relevant value creation process is optimised – from further asset development to targeted commercialisation.

Finally, once an auction is activated, the real estate collaterals active management platform could leverage digitisation to enhance the experience of the potential bidders attending the auction and ensure a more effective and profiled marketing – e.g. applications could suggest targeted advertising campaigns and automatic suggestions of real estate assets to buy, based on the social profile of the customers registered to this service. The benefits of using digital application tools to prioritise loans or collaterals to be worked out, in order to optimise the overall NPV and given the platform's constraints on available skilled resources and their related costs, is shown in Figure 5.10.

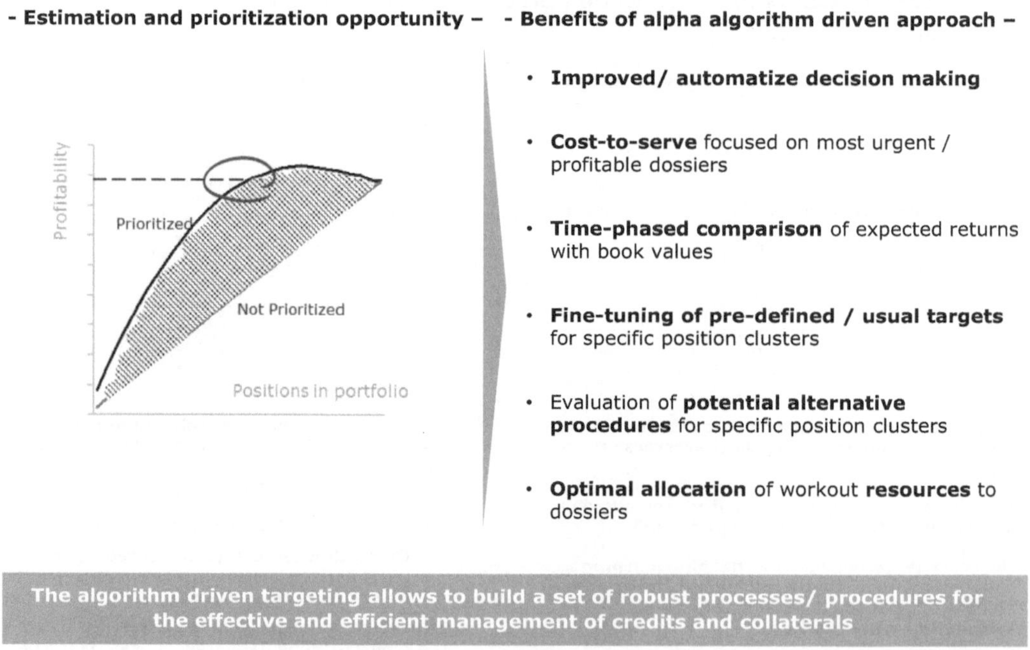

Figure 5.10 Dossier targeting and prioritisation.

5.13 Transformation in the organisation, leveraging digital tools and intelligence

Data management and applied analytics can also be useful not only in managing key processes and related subprocesses but also in driving the organisational transformation of the overall CWO and real estate active asset management unit (or units) and in optimising its set-up and HR management. In fact, the analysis of the organisational set-up and HR structure could be done following the typical hierarchical approach, or it could be developed following the mapping of the key processes and then set of most relevant subprocesses, till the level of detail that is useful to consider for the analysis. Dashboard, highly visual solutions, depicting the organisational set-up, could then define performance metrics across both dimensions and simulate improvement opportunities before their actual implementation is kicked off.

On a first level, the analysis should define the appropriate set of benchmarks at job family level and the required team alignment, considering multiple levers and the key drivers of performance to monitor. The sizing of the organisation should then try to optimise the trade-off between the current needs and the expected picks in the workload – that could be partially managed via outsourcing solutions. Also, some growth projections, in the case of independent CWO unit doing this for business, should be considered and optimised vis-à-vis the current workload and the attainable efficiency coming from the digitalisation and robotisation of the main activities – these "innovations" are potentially improving the productivity attained in a quick way and some flexibility in the technological capabilities should be considered as part of the simulation exercise.

Also, functional and geo-locational-based consolidation simulations should be run, to identify "shadow" sub-organisations that can imply organisational inefficiencies, or process fragmentation, across job families and organisational units. For example, geographical fragmentation could derive from the too extensive and unnecessary dispersions of units across multiple locations. Some decision could have been taken in the past based on offshoring consideration (to place less critical resources in low-cost countries) and need to be reversed as routine jobs are eliminated by automation and more critical activities need to be done near the borrowers' and collaterals' location. Or some functions that were deemed less relevant may become critical in the current environment, suggesting their consolidation and strengthening (e.g. for the real estate ones).

Other typical analysis that can be done using data and applied analytics could involve the "span of control," with the analysis of the direct reports and related levels of productivity and performance in credit recovery – to understand if some "alpha" is created by specific organisational and team set-ups, or to assess whether certain high performer should be given more (and vice versa) to enhance the overall productivity. The analysis on the number of "layers" should instead focus on how employees are distributed across the organisation and how different set-ups (e.g. planning a flatter organisation) could improve the performances at different point of the credit cycle. Also, teams and organisational units doing similar activities could be consolidated, to create scale and efficiency.

A data analysis of the organisation, leveraging digital applied analytics and visualisation techniques to build an integrated and interactive model, could also help the CWO in optimising its talent management and compensation system, focusing on critical activities such as the retention of key talents – identifying them and proactively trying to incentivise at best and building fidelisation and switching costs – or the management of structurally under-productive people – making sure they are not focused on the most value adding activities and on the higher potential files. The analysis of the performance in terms of "alpha" generated should then drive the design of the compensation, with the definition of appropriate salary bands and packages of cash and equity.

More broadly, applied analytics powered dashboard should be aiming at offering a dynamic analysis of all kind of make versus buy opportunities (with internal or external staff) – helping the CWO in selecting the best mix of permanent employees and temporary contractors. The dashboard should also support the CWO in assigning performance ratings to recovery teams and individuals, based on the analysis of data and relevant benchmark and correlations with market trends, assigning objective "alpha" financial contributions to each of them. And it could complement this "alpha" analysis with other KPI more focused on operational productivity and customer service, including the number of processed customer invoices, call centre interactions and sales force effectiveness. And it could support simulation analysis to review the implications on the "alpha" and on other operational and customer service indicators coming from the re-configuration of teams and people – to optimise the organisational set-up and the HR management leveraging digital innovation.

Whilst the typical approach of such a dashboard driven by and is following the typical hierarchical structure of the organisation, an alternative approach, more consistent with the overarching goal of digitising the CWO and real estate service unit (or units), could be driven and would follow the key processes and use cases of this business. Key processes and related subprocesses could be reinterpreted as "end use case" – e.g. reaching an extra-judicial agreement with the counterpart, accelerating the repossession of the collateral in good shape, optimising the end value of the repossessed asset via active management etc. and aggregated accordingly, to offer an alternative, and more end-user–driven view of the organisation and of its HR management.

The "end use case–driven" analysis would be more useful in spurring the digital transformation of the CWO and active real estate management activities, as it would offer the opportunity of rethinking traditional approaches anew, and – leveraging on data and applied analytics – offer new perspective

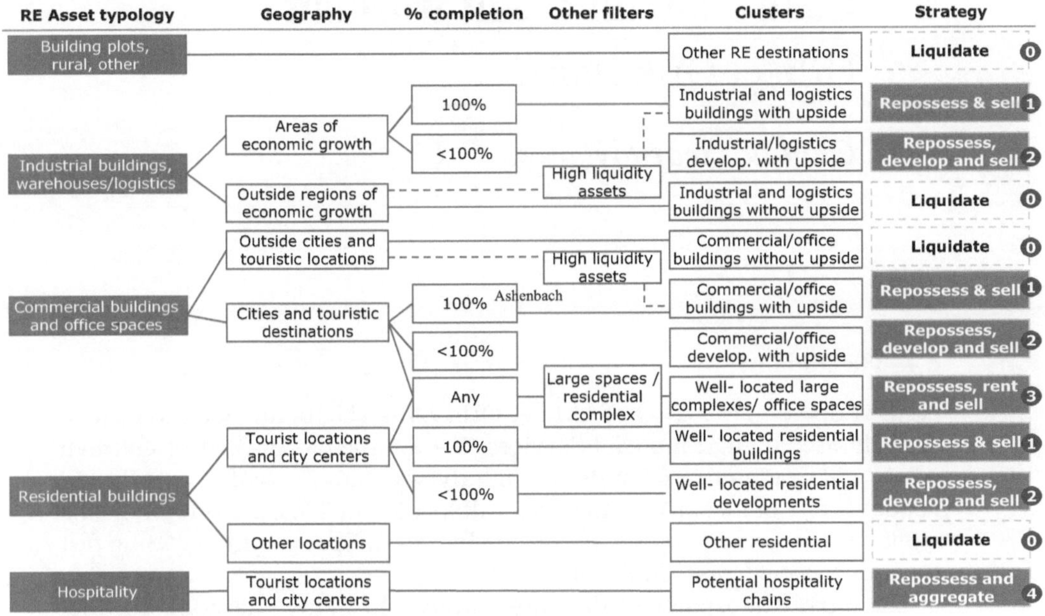

Figure 5.11 Top-down approach to real estate active management.

on how to transform them by digitisation, with the end uses driving the technological applications and not vice versa. Simulations would then need to be run to understand how processes and teams could be reorganised to optimise the use case (a mix of efficiency and effectiveness, and much more) and how the upgrading in critical capabilities (i.e. new technologies) could change the team resourcing and productivity and related cost structure, and the "alpha" attainable.

At a greater operational detail, simulations could be run on how to best structure the organisation and the HR capabilities around recovery strategies defined by clusters of loans and collaterals. In Figure 5.11, an exemplification of the asset management strategies that could be used to optimise the value of the real estate collaterals of an NPL portfolio of denounced loans is shown. Based on them, a consistent organisational strategy, defined at the level of the micro function of the organisation, and the required HR resourcing, could be defined to ensure the proper funding of such strategies, and for operating costs versus attainable uplift in the NPV of the portfolio considerations.

6 Case study in credit workout

Urbi et Orbi Bank

Claudio Scardovi

6.1 The good life

Andrea Sperelli, the CEO of Urbi et Orbi Bank (UOB) and Country Head of Weltanschauung Financial Services (WFS – the global SIFI of German origin and headquartered in Berlin) in Italy, was walking swiftly past the old headquarters of its bank, at the time still located in Via Condotti and just a stone's throw away from the notorious Piazza di Spagna, and heading fast towards Via del Corso, in Rome.

The warm atmosphere of that late March 2016 sunny afternoon, just before the approaching Eastern weekend, was incredibly reminiscent of the "good life" ("la dolce vita") that was what the eternal city of Rome (and Via Condotti specifically) had become known during the sixties and (of course) leaving aside the previous 2,000 years of epic history, ancient worldwide dominance, decay and renaissance till the late days of the Fascist regime and the early ones of the Republic of Italy.

Still, there was no "dolce vita" in his mind and no careless attitude towards life, as he was rushing to get a taxi for the Fiumicino Airport to fly to the still chilly and foggy Milan.

Andrea had joined just shy of six months earlier. He was now in his mid-fifties and had been a banker for over 30 years, most of which as an investment banker, as managing director and head of asset management at Impromptu Call (IC), the Bermuda-based hedge fund specialising in long – short trades on illiquid assets. He had then become the general manager of Nemesis Re, the record financial guarantees reinsurance unit of Monster Insurance Group (MIG), during the years of the Lehman Brothers default and of the ensuing global financial crisis that had hit hard all kind of insurance companies and their reinsurance business even more, but leaving Nemesis Re' one untouched.

More interestingly, Andrea had left Nemesis Re at the peak of its success and worked as CEO at Caronte Credit Management (CCM) just a few years earlier, to run the specialised lender and credit servicer after it was bought from IC by another former investment banker and Global Chairman for Bulge, Brackets and Brothers (BBB), Leonida Parassitallous – along with a few other co-investors including, in a second stage financing, the Activist Investor and Private Equity House Watch Your Back (WYB).

Andrea, who had also personally invested in the once rundown CCM as he joined it, was put in charge of the restructuring and relaunch of the bank, to be transformed in a specialised credit workout platform focused on the management of the ballooning stock of NPL (nonperforming stocks) now clogging the Italian banking system (see Figures 6.1–6.3) and on the related principal investing activities, where the company was actually betting its own money to buy other banks' NPL and recover them more efficiently and effectively, with a target of making two times the money put at work in a few years, at IRR of 15%–20% or higher.

Andrea had perceived the entrepreneurial opportunity just a few months earlier, as Nemesis Re was also getting involved in few NPL financial guarantee transactions for "small FIG" (small, mid-sized regional banks) and for international investors trying to enter into this space in Italy.

Andrea had perceived an opportunity related not just to the acquisition and reinsurance of those assets from banks, leveraging on their need to clean their balance sheet and increase their capital ratios and fast – given the increasing "moral suasion" of regulators and the penalising valuations applied to equity research analysts to most "NPL heavy" banks. In fact, another opportunity was related to the inability of most banks of doing well their credit workout activities internally and to the following need for them to outsource or seek alliances with independent, specialised and excellent third-party players.

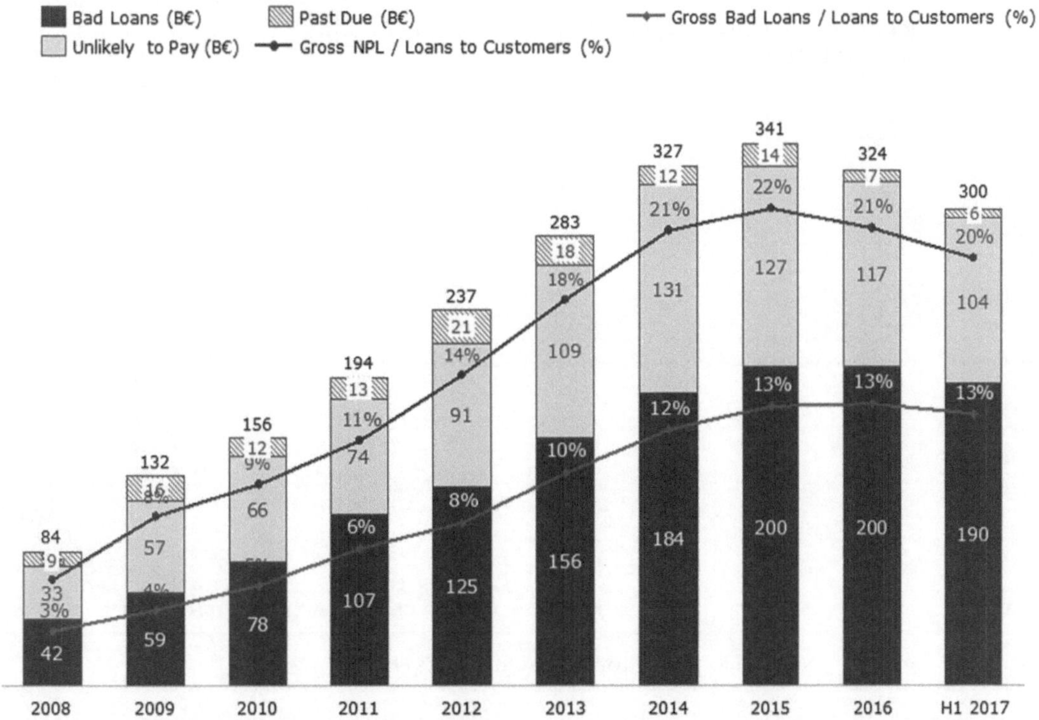

Figure 6.1 Italian gross bad loans and non-performing exposure trend.
Source: Bollettino Statistico di Banca d'Italia, ABI Monthly Outlook.

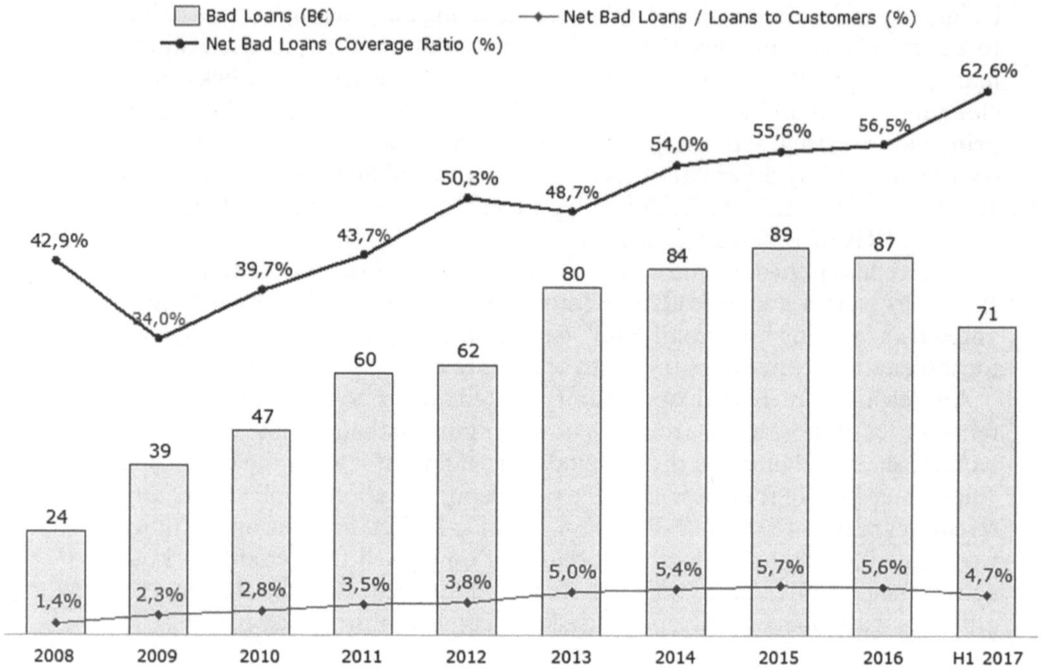

Figure 6.2 Italian net bad loans trend.
Source: ABI Monthly Outlook.

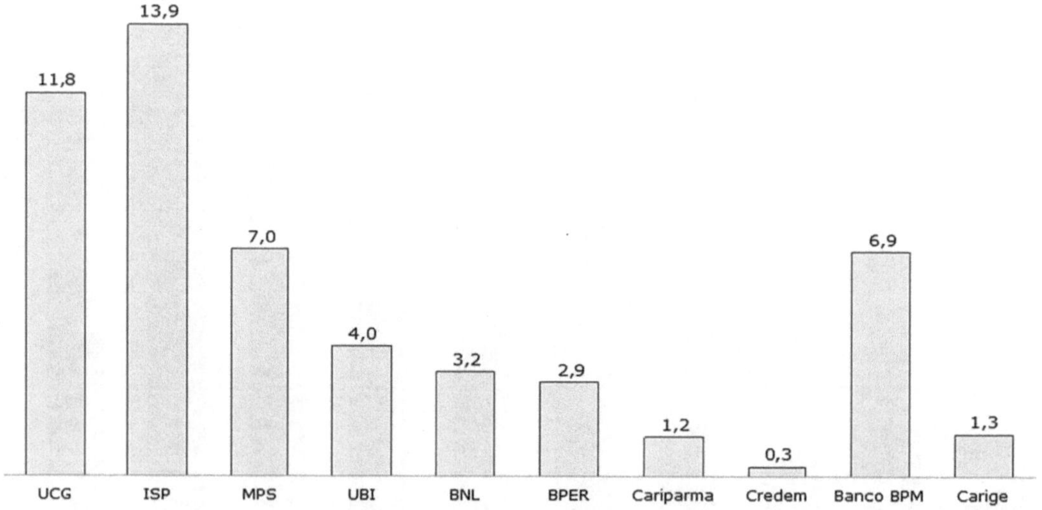

Figure 6.3 Net bad loans for top 10 Italian banks (Bn).

6.2 The search for "alpha"

The underlying hypothesis was pretty simple and agreed by most bankers and practitioners.

Banks were simply not the best holder of their NPL assets and of their related recovery activities as well. For regulatory and market reasons for the NPL assets, and for cultural ones mainly for their recovery activities.

Credit workout (the process of collecting loans and recovering as much value as possible from NPL) had been considered a "murky business" for years, in Italy and across continental Europe, as it was largely characterised by opacity, limited liquidity and trades that were done "amongst friends and family" and usually not at market value – hence sometimes perceived as a good place to cut corners and get rich fast, buying on the side a collateralised yacht for a song, or favouring the acquisition of a real estate trophy asset by some partners attending a judiciary public auction that was not particularly competitive, to say the least.

Credit workout had also become the "refugium peccatorum" at banks under stress, often hosting the redundancies coming from the other businesses of the bank – a nice way to avoid the expensive lay off procedures required by the law and to incentivise these people to look for something else in life.

It was not just a matter of culture (with good bankers keen to dedicate themselves to "good banking" only) and of approach (with most of the managers of the bank' credit workout being lawyers, hence keen to go judiciary on most dossier, notwithstanding the long delays in the Italian judiciary system and the likely negative impact on the NPV coming from most of the dossier being denounced, to then increase their never ending burden of work and hence perceived power inside the bank).

In fact, it was also a matter of "skin in the game." People working in the credit workout were performing better if they were thinking and acting with a private equity mindset – i.e. driven by the "carried interested" they could get from maximising the IRR generated by their collection activities on the managed portfolio, no matter what the effort put into it.

That "private equity mindset" was something that the bank could not assure, given its bureaucratic-styled, wait-and-see–driven career management favoured approach and the constraints on the (very limited) maximum contribution of the success-driven, cash-based bonus component paid as part of their employees' total compensation.

For a bank, it was also a matter of avoiding potential "conflict of interests" (e.g. the non-performing counterpart to a loan could be a very wealthy entrepreneur: how could the bank denounce the corporate client if it valued so much the owner as a "VIP" private client?) and of limiting further "moral hazard" (if the bank agreed on an extrajudiciary settlement, waiving part of the loan, the client could be incentivised to try it again in the future and spread words that the bank was unable to "play balls").

Not to mention the new frontiers of the excellence in credit workout, driven by big data management and applied analytics (including the use of machine learning and artificial intelligence techniques) and by the "active management" of the underlying collateral (mostly real estate, but also equipment, shipping, aviation etc.) requiring talented experts from these fields that were hard for a bank to attract – almost an oxymoron, given what banks (and bankers) were expecting from each other.

In a nutshell, not only the Italian credit workout market was ripe for disruption, but it also looked like new professional expertise (of people coming from investment banking, asset management, real estate, data science… and with an "Anglo-Saxon" mentality) could have brought a refreshing view and new energies in a service that had become quite critical, because of the oversized NPL problem that was now affecting the chances of recovery of the banking system and of the Italian economy.

Credit workout, Andrea was thinking, was at the end of the day just a very specialised sub-sector of the "alternative asset management" industry, where a lot of "alpha" (defined as superior recoveries that could be obtained from collection, uncorrelated with the overall market performance and sustainable through time) could be created, given the right strategy, culture, approach, tool kit and team of "eager practitioners," acting honestly and professionally and mainly driven by the maximisation of the NPV coming from NPL – hitting directly their bottom line as if they were "private equity" people investing their own "sweat" instead of equity.

Everything was about the search of the "holy grail" of alpha, as in many other sectors of the financial services industry. The opportunity here was just that there were still too few good people chasing the opportunity and too many bad assets to be served.

It could just be an easy win – you just had to play it smart if, as a notorious Italian add of the times was reciting, you liked to win it easy ("Ti piace viñcere facile").

6.3 A call from the "eternal city"

The call from the Capital of the Republic of Italy (and "eternal city" of the Catholic Church) had come unexpected, as his turnaround and transformation plan of CCM was starting to pay off.

As Andrea was summoned at UOB, at the time still headquartered in Via Condotti, for an interview with the long-timer Chairman Ottaviano Ottaviani, he thought of the colourful and languid description of the city played by his omonymous, the main character of "Il Piacere" – *The Pleasure* – by Gabriele D'Annunzio.

He o was also reminiscent of the easy, enjoyable life famously captured by the legendary movie director Federico Fellini ("La dolce vita" – sweet and easy life); and the one still sweet and easy but also penetrated by decadence, corruption and fatalism famously narrated 40 years later by the Oscar-winning filmmaker Paolo Sorrentino in "La Grande Bellezza – the big beauty" – filmed just at the pick of the economic crisis in Italy.

All that sounded to him fascinating and worrying at the same time, as he was finally pondering on whether to take on the offer and leave the small but entrepreneurial CCM to become the CEO of one of the largest and most well-known banks in Italy (once famous and very well respected for being "the bank of the Italian Treasury") and now fully owned by the mighty German WFS group – one of the largest bank in Europe and globally, with its notorious Cartesian approach to planning and control.

It was kind of funny, he was discussing a few months later with one of his long-timer trusted advisors, at Cova, a coffee shop in Milan and on an early Saturday morning, that he had now to manage the NPL business of UOB as one of his most pressing needs – and this time on the other side of the table!

And this just after he had left the asset management and financial reinsurance businesses at some of the most profitable companies in the world... to become a full-fledged retail and commercial banker, focusing on the management of the good bank as opposed to the wind down of the bad one.

What was the "alpha" to be searched for then, now that he "owned" the NPL book, one of the largest in Italy as UOB had been also heavily impacted by the financial crisis but – differently from other players – had decided so far to sell less than the regulators and the equity analysts had expected?

What was the "beta" of the NPL legacy portfolio then, had UOB been able to perform like the market?

What would have been the best recovery strategy that would have targeted and optimised such performances? With which governance and organisational approach? And senior management team?

More importantly, had the bank – his bank – a chance to do it all alone, or the only way forward was to consider an accelerated sell-off of the NPL portfolio, or its massive outsourcing, or a light alliance with third-party partners, or a mix of the above? Or should he consider now the development of a JV with a financial investor willing to create a competitive "alpha" credit collection platform out of the carve-out of the existing captive capabilities of the bank?

As Andrea was used to repeat to his team, a bad loan is born out of a bad decision in underwriting.

Similarly, a bad NPL strategy could have likely been taken on the basis of a bad re-underwriting of the troubled portfolio under management. Put it in another way, UOB had now to define its best strategy starting from the review and update of the business plan of its legacy NPL portfolio (the "re-underwriting" analysis leading to its revaluation on a fair value basis) and take it from there.

The introduction of the new IFRS 9 principle (suggesting a valuation of the NBV of the NPL on the basis of the expected discounted recovery value and not of the incurred losses), due to take place in January 2018, was perfectly timed, as the bank was expected to review the value of its portfolio on that basis anyway, and the new accounting principle would have allowed for a set of "first-time adoption" rules that could have eased its execution and following application at group level (see Figure 6.4 and Table 6.1).

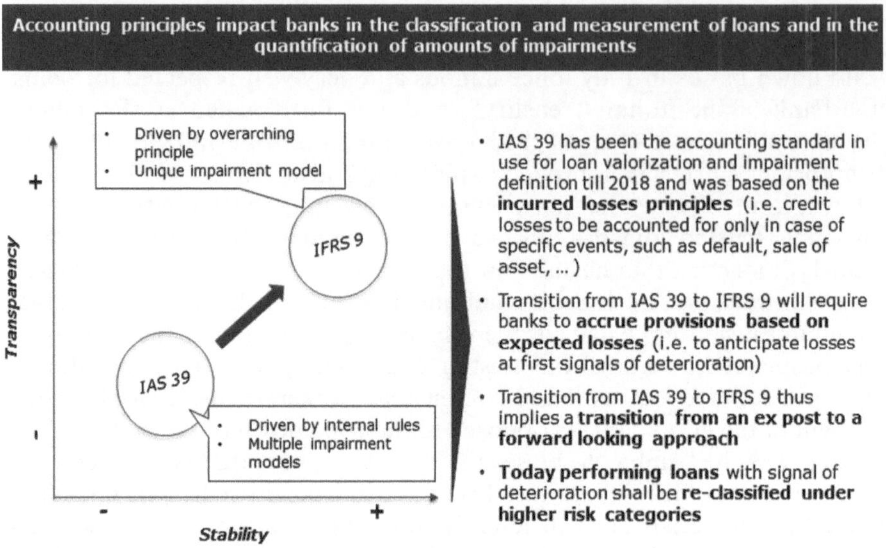

Figure 6.4 Transition principles from IAS39 to IFRS9.
Source: IFRS 9 for banks, KPMG, September 2019.

Table 6.1 IFRS9 impacts and FTA

Classification	*Impairment*
Three new classes of NPL: (i) hold to collect, (ii) hold to collect and sale and (iii) trading The need to properly **classify the non-performing exposures based on selected workout strategy** will require **banks** to **review** and strategically refine their **business model** associated with non-performing loans' management • "portfolio to hold" → strengthen the internal credit monitoring functions in terms of expertise as well as of renovated tools of credit risk measurement (e.g. KPI, index, advanced CRM solutions) • "portfolio to sell" → implement specialised units in charge of the structuring and execution of loans' sale transactions (e.g. data preparation and remediation, securitisation).	• **New impairment criteria**, based on the "expected loss" and "forward-looking" approach, will result in the **shift of certain portions of current portfolio towards more higher risk categories** (e.g. from performing to UTP/bad loan) • **Higher impairment** (both through an analytical and statistical provisioning) will result **through a "forward-looking" approach,** which will **anticipate losses** to be incurred over the loans' lifetime • Need to foresee the lifetime losses will require banks to **implement proactive actions to preliminarily assess borrowers' likelihood to pay their debts** to be associated with the reduction of the loans default rate from performing to UTP and bad loans

Source: IFRS 9 for banks, KPMG, September 2019.

As the case with other significant accounting rules transitions, the transition from IAS 39 to IFRS 9 allows banks to indicate a "first-time adoption" impact (i.e. negative, in this instance) on their books.

6.3 Taking stock

A number of moving parts were already at work at UOB anyway as – following an early internal review of the audit function of the group, a number of recommendations had already been formulated, to pursue the strengthening of its credit department and credit workout function specifically. That was hardly rocket science for any Italian bank – it all just made a lot of sense.

A new organisation, leading to the creation of "Crediti Speciali" (Special Credits), had been released and filled with new hires from the market to bring new perspectives and fresh energies to the effort.

Following this, Felix Krull, a long timer at WFS, with strong acumen on numbers and a well-rounded professional past in lending, risk management and credit workout, had been appointed as head of Special Credits. Felix had also been, prior to join WFS a dedicated, investment professional in the credit workout space, with extensive experience across Europe. He had then been hired by WFS to run its German credit workout unit, before being asked, just few months ago, to do the same for UOB, a much smaller bank than the German parent company, but with a much larger NPL portfolio.

Felix, supported by an international, specialised, trusted advisor, was then asked to undertake the gigantic effort to revaluate the NPL legacy portfolio, "taking stock" of what was in there, in accordance with international best practices and with the new IFRS 9 principle coming into place.

An NPL portfolio of well over Euro 15 billion of gross book value, encompassing more than 150,000 dossiers, across all kind of segments and collaterals was the object of the effort. The business plan had then to take into consideration not just the expected cash flow coming from the UOB recovery activities and related costs but also the discount rate (the IAS – International Accounting Standard – rate, a 3%–4% circa) that would have produced a proxy of NPV as "fair value" to be accounted for as NBV.

The effort would have lasted more than six months, with a bottom-up review of more than 15,000 loans evaluations and over 20,000 updated appraisals on the real estate collaterals spread across the country, representing more than 70% of the overall gross book value and most of the expected recovery value, as typical in the Italian banking system.

The revaluation would have followed a rigorous "statistical approach" to define the best sampling approach and to target a level of confidence of 95% and a related standard deviation of 2%. Also, a specific effort would have been considered to ensure the standardised, homogeneous and "best practice" application of the real estate valuation methodologies to be used, to address the many vagaries observed in the market and across multiple professional appraisal companies.

To that end, a notorious Italian University was also to be engaged to work with the international advisor as part of the half-year effort, to design the methodology, proof testing it and challenging on an ad hoc basis the bottom-up revaluation for the largest dossiers, including also land, equipment and else.

Finally, the idea pursued by Felix was also to make the overall effort as dynamic and easy to update as possible, with the build-up of a digital database linking the key information with the source files and with external market parameters, so as to also allow stress testing simulation analysis and a faster and simpler re-run of the valuation in the future.

It had been a very hot summer that year, as "la dolce vita" of a bygone era had been taken over by a frenzy more typical of Milan or London – as the bank was also moving its headquarters at the same time, from the glamorous Via Condotti to the less mundane, but more efficient new building at Roma Centrale, just a stone-throw away from the "fast trains" leading to Milan in little more than three hours.

That was also a sign of the time changing fast and of the impossibility to revert to an old era and to past behaviours, as nothing (not even a "Great Beauty") was granted anymore, in banking as in life.

6.4 Bid low, don't ask

After a shorter than usual holiday break, Andrea Sperelli, the CEO of UOB, was now discussing with Felix Krull the results of the business plan of the legacy NPL portfolio, completed of a "beta" scenario (or "baseline") that was basically depicting the trajectory in recovery values, assuming all major but "standard" constraints at UOB were released, to allow it to perform like the market.

Standard constraints included the required hiring of new people and with different skill sets (as for most of Italian banks, UOB credit workout had not been sized to deal with such extraordinary "peaks" in the NPL stock), the development in technology – systems, software, databases and applied analytics – and a few others: nothing obvious and to be taken for granted, but also far from being impossible to overcome if well addressed.

More interesting was instead the "alpha" scenario (or "upside") that had been developed also including the extra value that could have been attainable in the recoveries of the NPL portfolio, should the bank be able to develop some distinctive capabilities in credit workout such as, an applied analytics advanced approach to data mining, a greater focus on extrajudicial and commercial activities, and a proactive approach to the management of the real estate collaterals as, for UOB and similarly to any other Italian bank, most of the value attainable was coming from properties – highly fragmented, often characterised by low liquidity and located in marginal areas, hence difficult to treat.

These "beta" and "alpha" were then constituting the pillars of the "fair value" and optimal valuation of the NPL portfolio of UOB, assuming a consistent strategy and set of investments were put quickly in place and executed in a timely manner and "close to flawless" way.

Still, banks' NPL "fair values" were far from the respective market values, as a number of recent sale transactions had shown to be the case in Italy and elsewhere in continental Europe (see Figure 6.5).

That was not a "cooking the books" issue (or at least, not only), as few perfectly rational reasons were able to explain most of the differences.

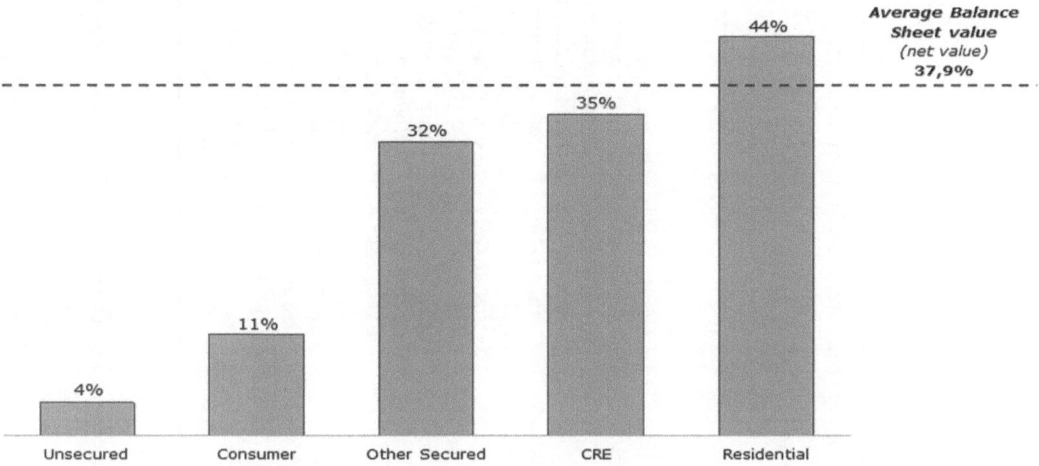

Figure 6.5 Weighted average price of transacted portfolios in 2017 (%).
Source: Banca Ifis Market Watch NPL, September 2017.

First, banks were accounting recoveries gross of their management costs, as they would have been accounting for such expenses (e.g. the lawyers' fees) as incurred. Second, banks were discounting cash flows at an average IAS rate of 3%–4%, versus the target IRR of professional investors ranging at 15%–20%. Third, data quality and analytics were key in the valuation and typically third-party investors would have discounted the less than optimal data set offered by banks in the sale virtual data room (VDR).

Finally, as the value of the portfolio was driven by the beta and alpha capabilities at work in serving this, a further discount was given by investors on portfolios managed by banks' captive workout units, or by other independent – but still less than well-performing – platforms, particularly for the secured part of NPL (a number of good unsecured, independent credit workout platform was present in Italy in 2017, but not as many – if not at all – on the beleaguered real estate secured side).

Ceding an NPL portfolio via a true sale on such a basis would have then resulted in a major loss of accounting and economic value, as other banks, like Jean Paul Mustier's Unicredit, had actually done, when forced, to perform radical clean-ups of their balance sheet and unclog some of their fairly constrained funding capacity.

Usually, they had also achieved at the same time a better appreciation in the stock market, higher credit ratings and the implicit regulators' approval – as new rules (dubbed Basel 4) and suggested principles (the ECB proposal on the NPL write-off maximum timeline) were now all converging to make the incentive for top bankers to think of a quick sale of their troubled assets even bigger (see Table 6.2 and Figure 6.6).

Table 6.2 Basle IV versus Basle III and impacts on RWA

Context and objectives	• Completion/integration of Basel III reform with significant increase in capital requirement and implementation of stricter rules • Provision of additional guidance on calculations models for RWAs and willingness to toughen approach to stress testing					
Key measures	*Revision of internal models and standardisation of RWAs calculations*					
	Credit risk	*Securitisation*	*CVA*[1]	*Ops. risk*	*Leverage*	*Output floor*
	• Increase in risk sensitivity by basing risk weights on risk drivers • Reduction of national discretions • Maintenance of simplicity of application and avoidance of reliance on internal modelling	• Reduction of complexity • Reduction of mechanistic reliance on external ratings • Introduction of minimum risk weight for securitisation (15%) and re-securitisation (100%)	• Limitation on use of internal models • Allowance of firms with up to € 100 billion in non-centrally cleared derivative to calculate the CVA charge as a simple scalar of the counterparty credit risk	• Removal of existing approaches and requirement of a single, risk-sensitive standardised approach calculated using a combination of the bank's income and its historical losses	• Introduction of a higher leverage ratio for Global Systematically Important Banks (G-SIBs), with the increase equal to 50% of the risk-adjusted capital ratio	• Introduction of capital floors to reduce model risk, increase comparability of RWA, and limit its scope of action • Revision of capital floors based on the results of the new approaches to valuation

[1]Credit Valuation Adjustments.

Source: Basel IV: The Next Generation of RWA, PwC May 15, 2018.
Basel IV completes Basel III framework and focuses on the revision of bank internal models to enhance and uniform RWAs calculation methodologies.

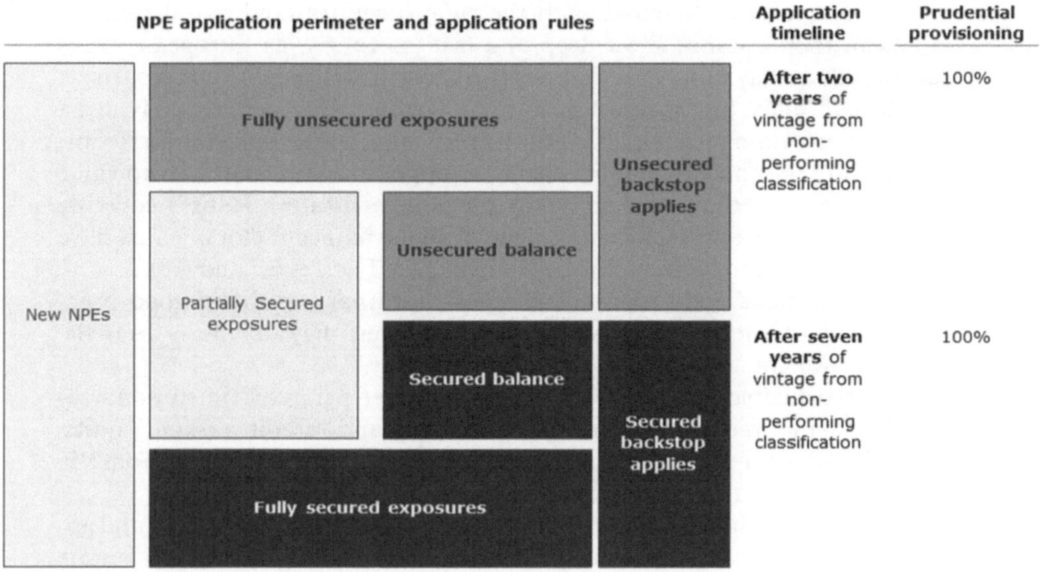

Figure 6.6 Prudential backstop for NPEs: new prudential provisioning rules.
Source: Addendum to the ECB guidance to banks on non-performing loans: prudential provisioning backstop for non-performing exposures, ECB, October 2017.

Should UOB have then considered a quick sale of its legacy portfolio as well? Starting from its newly released IFRS 9 revaluation, but also knowing how a market price was inevitably going to destroy shareholders' value – but potentially with a positive know-on effect on the stock price?

Or, should the bank just stand still and hold on the assets, working everything internally to maturity, to secure at least the "beta" and maybe aiming even higher at the "alpha"?

Was then the "hold and build" the best strategy for UOB? Or the suboptimal one, and under which market scenario? And what about the "exit and partner" strategy, to exit the NPL stock and JV the recovery capabilities at the same time? Confirming what Andrea had thought about who was the best holder of this business, when acting on the other side of the table, as principle investor and asset manager?

An overarching strategy was due, with clear interlinkages between the portfolio and the platform destinies, against a market and regulatory scenario that kept changing and sometimes in unpredictable ways, given the often-conflicting perspectives of policymakers at European and Italian level.

6.5 Not built in a day

Rome was certainly not built in a day, nor was the ECB – even more so with specific regard to all its regulatory effort to reign-in the several market dislocations matured after the global financial crisis.

Most of this re-regulation wave had actually been targeted on NPL, to make sure to provide banks with the right incentive (and moral suasion) to clean their balance sheet deep and fast (so to say, as European banks appeared already quite late vis-à-vis their North American counterparts).

More recently, and specifically in early March 2017, the ECB had issued a number of guiding principles on the overall management of troubled loans, addressing the "how to manage them" as opposed to just the "how to value them" (i.e. the "Guidance to banks on non-performing loans") covering most exogenous and endogenous critical performance factors, which have to be assessed and addressed by each bank (see Figures 6.7 and 6.8).

They all made good sense, nothing extraordinary or that a good practitioner would not have known in advance – but they obviously bear the different weight attributed to the "regulators say."

These principles were now presenting another perfectly timed opportunity to further reorganise the "Special Credit" and "credit workout" units, Felix Krull was now discussing in a late night internal meeting, far from Via Condotti and near the "speedy trains" station.

"What about the new organisational set-up? The data management and applied analytics scientist and the team for the active management of real estate collaterals we need to get?" – was asking Felix to his team. "And what about the new processes and workflows, to stir more extrajudicial activities and allow the closing of judicial ones in a much shorter time frame?" It was the right opportunity to think all of this through and over again and to position their functions to become, if not best practice, at least market competitive.

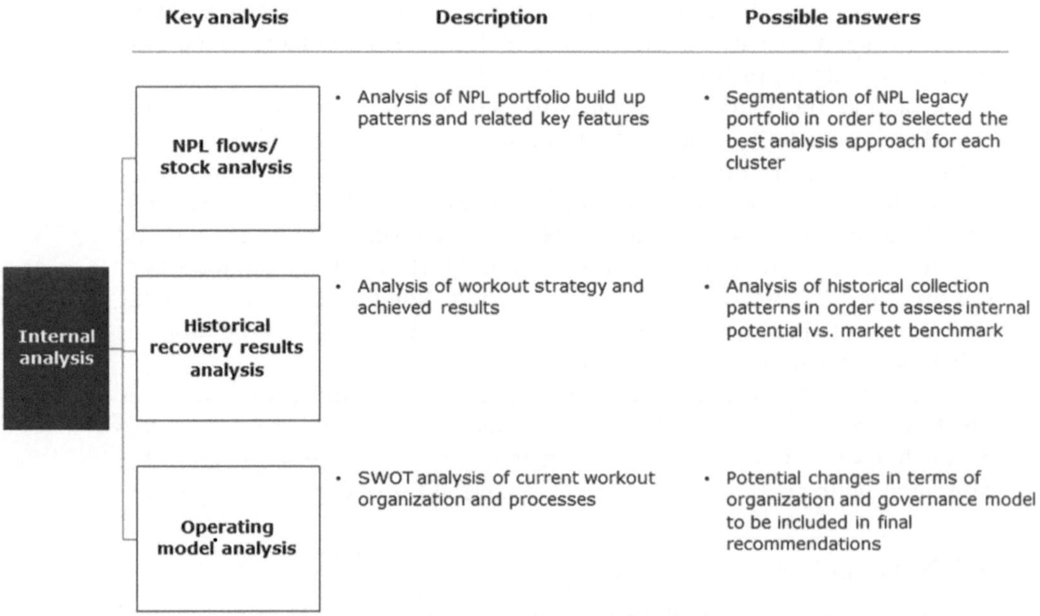

Figure 6.7 ECB principles on credit workout: endogenous factors assessment.
Source: Guidance to banks on non-performing loans, ECB, March 2017.

	Key analysis	Description	Possible answers
External analysis	**Macro-economic trends analysis**	• Potential evolution impacts of key industries – such as Real Estate – to be included in NPLs assessment	• Proprietary sensitivity model calculating bottom up impacts on collection based on RE market evolution
	Market analysis	• Potential market evolution assessment based on external expert opinions (e.g. rating agencies)	• Top down assessment of impact on portfolio value based on expected market evolution
	Special servicing analysis	• Analysis of the status/ maturity of the special servicing market and evaluation of potential partnerships	• Potential agreements with special servicers
	Legal framework evolution analysis	• Analysis of the impacts of judicial systems evolution in terms of courts timeline and legal costs	• Proprietary sensitivity model calculating bottom up impacts on changing legal frameworks
	NPL demand growth analysis	• Analysis of investors appetite for NPLs portfolio sales to define potential market price	• Market appetite assessed in case of potential sale of selected portfolio segment
	Fiscal impact analysis	• Analysis of potential fiscal impacts for selected NPL strategies	• Evaluation of fiscal impacts (if any) related to potential management strategies

Figure 6.8 ECB principles on credit workout: exogenous factors assessment.
Source: Guidance to banks on non-performing loans, ECB, March 2017.

At the end of the day, extraordinary powers were required to overcome extraordinary challenging periods, and this was certainly one – may be "the one" in his professional lifetime in this business.

Based on the NPL portfolio overall business plan, the organisation, processes and capabilities of the UOB credit workout were now to be reviewed, to make its overall strategy, development plan and organisational behaviour consistent with its set recovery targets. Setting up tight deadlines and planning detailed new hiring and development of IT and data management system, e.g.

Crafting, in short, an industrial plan for the credit workout, internal platform that would have robustly sustained the "baseline" and "upside" valuation scenarios, leveraging the ("regulators say") recommendations of the ECB and on the basis of the other overarching decision of not to sell the legacy portfolio, that Andrea Sperelli, the CEO, had just publicly announced a few weeks earlier.

Wasn't that a luxury that UOB could well afford, avoiding the gyrations of the stock market (being fully owned by WFS and part of a very large and well-capitalised European group with above average asset quality)?

Wasn't that the perfect opportunity to realise and prove the thesis that the "alpha" was attainable, even in that specific sub-segment of the alternative asset management industry called "credit workout" by professionals (and defined as "murky business" by others)? And, even more, wasn't that the perfect opportunity to show that there was still life in banking, after all, and some light at the end of the tunnel, as “fair values” (accounted for by the new IFRS 9 principles) were actually turning into real cash flows and economic values, year after year, as the workout mission progressed?

6.6 Barbarians at the gate

The Italian banking system could have been well described as an Empire under siege, Andrea Sperelli was discussing, tipping his croissant into his “cappuccino” at another early Saturday morning breakfast at Cova in Milan. A crippled empire maybe, but still worth a lot.

“There is plenty of ‘barbarians’ looking to buy anything worth that the Country has left,” he said, “starting from NPL and real estate assets, for a few cents on the Euro.”

“Banks have been cornered and have been buying time, sometimes putting everything under the proverbial Turkish carpet and kicking the next, big UTP (Unlikely To Pay) can down the road” – was arguing one of his long-time trusted advisors.

> The only way out is neither to buy other time, making up excuses, nor to sell at market prices, as the IRR sought by these private equities will be enough to kill the value of the bank – throwing the baby away along with the dirty water.

“The solution is the alpha” was replying Andrea.

> If we can create and control that, we are out of the woods, or at least we can see where the path of the next growth cycle is leading to, so to speak. But how can I create alpha? Inside my bank? With the people and IT systems I have got, including the impossibility to pay them on success, as this business would suggest and warrant?

Christmas holidays were approaching and again promising a very short break in the mountains, often interrupted by conference calls and email marked “important/ urgent.”

The “strategic plan” for the credit workout had been delivered and well received and shared with the ECB as well, as it was addressing its key principles and recommendations and setting forward a plan that was really aiming to change things in Rome, anticipating the Barbarians and actually beating them at their own game. Playing beta and alpha and another few tricks of the job.

Still, a number of worries persisted in the mind of the CEO and of his team with regard to the execution risk and the transformational challenge required to perform.

Assuming the right decision on the NPL portfolio was set in stone (“let’s keep it, we can afford the luxury and avoid destroying economic value”), was it better then to go it alone, developing all required capabilities internally, to track the market beta and gain alpha as well?

Or, was it an unsurmountable challenge for UOB? And for any bank in the world?

A long history of outsourcing contracts (something UOB was already doing, albeit on a marginal basis) had recently been overcome by one made of JV, were banks across Europe, and most recently in Italy, had carved out their credit workout unit into an SPV, to be sold (as a majority stake) to a financial or industrial counterpart, or a mix of the two, with a local presence in the market served by UOB, or else. Multiple taxonomies were in fact available for consideration.

A private equity company investing just on operating companies (e.g. a là Advent International, that had bought JFKL in Germany and Ultimo in Poland) would have had an interest in the target company to make it more efficient and effective, developing its extra-captive business and spurring its EBITDA – to finally exit from the investment at a high multiple of the money invested.

On a different note, a private equity also interested in the acquisition of NPL portfolios (like Apollo that had bought Altamira in Spain) could have instead sought the full control of the platform, not only to get a window on the market and access to valuable information on recovery curves but also to use the "captured" platform to serve its own investments and not really caring about the "extra captive."

An industrial counterpart present in the country of interest (not owned by a private equity fund) would also have considered differently the deal, typically targeting the "carved-out" entity as an opportunity to get the final and ultimate outsourcing of the parent bank, not really caring much about what the platform was really about and what its development plans were. Then, it would have been likely focused just on the opportunity to make easy cost synergies against its cost structure, basically sharing the same IT platform and some other economies of scale and laying off people.

Finally, an industrial counterpart, not owned by a private equity, or owned by one interested only in the equity investment side, could have instead considered the carved-out entity of the bank to develop a new platform "in loco," following an internationalisation strategy, e.g., or an extension of its offerings across multiple lending lines and typologies of collateral, with limited social impacts at the bank level and less conflict of interest vis-à-vis its other platforms competing in the same market (none, in this case) or with its principal investing activities (none, as it would otherwise prioritise its care and energy in serving its own NPL portfolios so as to maximise their recovery values, and offering a far worst service to the banking partner and to the open, extra-captive market).

With the Christmas holidays quickly approaching, and Andrea Sperelli still mulling over the multiple options available for its bank, a cold call came from a German man, Gustav Ashenbach, Chairman of Recovery

Express – Delivered (RED), a well-reputed and even better-connected entrepreneur and business person based in Frankfurt, with the request of a meeting to discuss a potential alliance on credit workout in Italy.

6.7 Sister company

Whether the option of a partnership with an industrial counterpart, not present in Italy, was now being considered as the "best option" or the "least worst option" was not yet fully clear in Andrea's mind.

Certainly, the opportunity was worth the trying and the timing of Gustav's call had been ideal. Also, thinking of it, a few factors were suggesting that this was more than about good timing.

In fact, RED, a leading independent credit servicer mainly based in Germany and almost exclusively focused on the recovery activities for unsecured portfolios, owned by Venice Capital Partners, a mid-cap private equity also based in Frankfurt, was something different than an "average" industrial counterpart.

RED was in fact to UOB more than a simple "industrial partner not present in Italy" as it had become, just a few years earlier, the industrial partner of choice for unsecured credit servicing for WFS in Germany, after the JV with the recovery unit of the German banking group, that was now owned by RED for a 75.5% (with WFS owning the remaining minority stake) and with a large outsourcing contract.

It had certainly worked in favour of Gustav his good reputation as a serial entrepreneur and his top relationships matured in Frankfurt's financial inner circles. But it was also helping the fact that the JV was deemed a success, with good performances recorded in the first NPL portfolios managed by the RED JV, under the helm of Ashenbach and of its progressively expanding management team.

RED could have a kind of qualify as "sister company" to WFS in Germany, so Andrea was thinking.

Why not then consider doing the same thing in Italy, were the NPL market was large and profitable for industrialised independent servicers? There could have been value in the recovery skills RED could have brought to the table, leveraging its expertise in unsecured NPL recovery management.

And there could have been value in the minority share UOB would have retained, similarly to WFS, if RED had then been able to grow the extra-captive business, addressing other potential clients not only in banking but also in the telecom and multi-utility space – where RED had experienced and was already active in Germany, including with international subsidiaries of large Italian companies.

Also, from a cultural point of view, RED was ringing two interesting bells.

On one side, it was an entrepreneurial venture, with a private equity minded mentality (and actually owned by a private equity), hence offering the opportunity to clear the workout unit of its "banking" imprinting – subject as it was to the many regulatory and compliance-related constraints – not to mention its conflict of interest vis-à-vis the ongoing commercial activities of the "good bank."

On the other side, it was, however, close to the culture of the parent company, as it was owned and run by German people and with lots of experience in dealing with and managing the heavily syndication-based internal approach to decision-making of the WFS group in Berlin.

Gustav Ashenbach was also a naturally likeable person and with a gift in building relationships quickly, and "smart" in understanding how winds were changing around him and with the sensitivity to adapt to different contexts and cultures – something valuable to consider when doing business in Rome – a fascinating but tricky city and in need of some change.

Following a first meeting in Milan, and a few phone calls exchanged during the Christmas break, the bank and RED had finally formally agreed on a Memo of Understanding to run a joint feasibility study to consider the potential alliance opportunity, mandating an independent international advisor to run the study, highlighting options and recommending the best way forward – if any, assuming that an economic convenience was to be found from the business plan of the potential JV.

The study would have covered all the strategic, financial and operational key issues, including the target end state governance and organisation of the JV, the reference perimeter of the portfolio to be worked out (the NPL legacy stock portfolio or parts of it, the new NPL flows that the bank would have originated in the future etc.) and the reference organisational perimeter to be involved in the alliance from UOB's side (including people, contracts, IT systems, processes and procedures).

It would also have covered the pricing structure regulating the servicing, setting a clear incentive scheme for the workout to perform well, getting well paid on the basis of success fees, and differently set on the "baseline" and "upside" recovery scenarios. And it would have defined in detail the required investments that the partner should have considered to develop the platform capabilities and an high-level SLA governing the quality and quantity of services that the NewCo (the JV company, incorporated into a special purpose new legal entity vehicle) should have offered through time to UOB and vice versa (the bank could have offered to the NewCo certain general and administrative services to ensure its short-term successful start-up).

Finally, the feasibility study would have defined high-level projections on the market share and related revenues that the JV could have attained in the open market, leading to an overall EBITDA and profitability trajectory for the five years business plan that would have been used by the counterparts to determine their respective firm's values and negotiate the price of the transaction on day one.

From this standpoint, a few methodological questions would have been addressed by the counterparts to determine the most appropriate valuation approach to price the JV and hence the NewCo. Should have they followed a "pure" DCF approach? Or another one driven primarily by the NPL volumes contributed as servicing to the platform? Or some kind of "goodwill" driven by UOB's portfolio and franchise that could have shorten a lot the Italian time-to-entry strategy for RED?

Of course, different answers would have been considered as "best" by the buy and sell side. For example, assuming a DCF approach on the agreed business plan, would the seller and the buyer have considered all of the different revenue streams (i.e. the fixed fees on the UOB contract, the success fees on the "baseline" and "upside," the revenues coming from the extra captive) on the same basis?

What discount rate then would the bank and the servicer have been using? The IAS one (at 3%–4%), or the average cost of capital of the WFS group (at 10%–12%), or the one used by PE companies on similar transactions (15%–20%)? Or different ones for different revenues streams?

Also, were the two business plans for the bank and the servicer similar, or did they need to consider extra components, such as the VAT cost that UOB would have been forced to pay in the future on top of the commissions contributed to the JV, or the investments on the credit workout that it could have avoided in case of large outsourcing of the NPL management to the JV?

How would, as a result of all this, the emerging price structure have compared with recent, similar transactions observed in Italy (see Figure 6.9). And, given the likely high bid – ask difference on the transaction price, how much would have these weighted in the decision of UOB, given the size of the "alpha" to be attained?

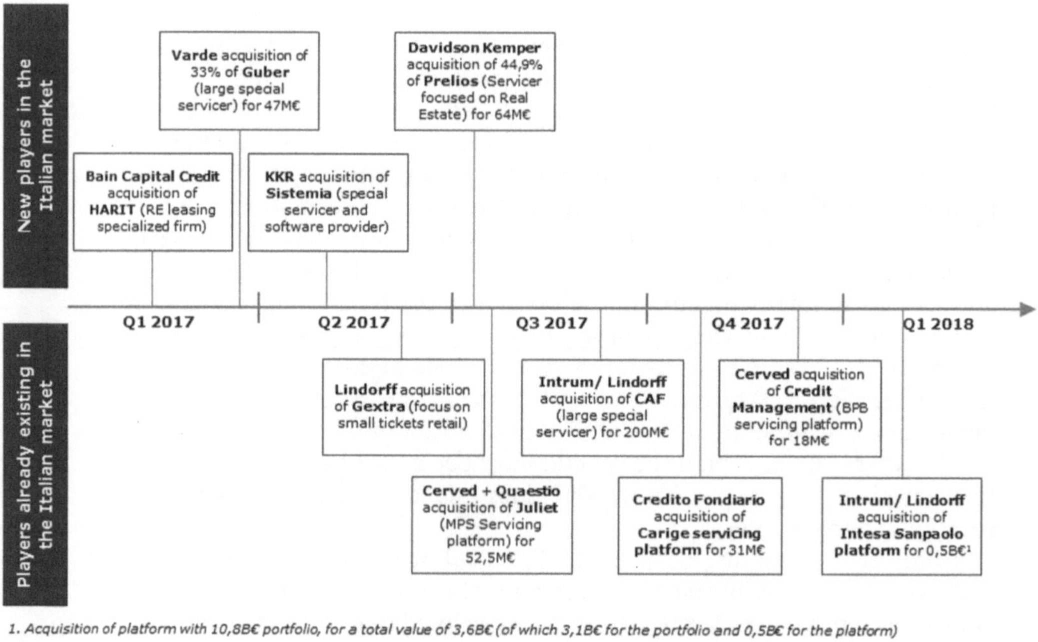

Figure 6.9 Recent transactions in the Italian servicing sector.
Source: Banca Ifis Market Watch NPL, January 2018; Intrum press release, 18/04/2018.

And how much would the price have weighted on the decision of RED that was also considering other, smaller and "bolt on" M&A investments in this space in Italy, as a way to ramp up quickly all the capabilities needed to deliver on the NPL "alpha" (and therefore get paid further commissions)?

Would an Italian servicer been able to pay more for the same transaction, and was this a really important and favourable outcome for UOB, or to be considered at the light of other components?

6.8 Vexata quaestio

A new Easter holiday was fast approaching, with the soft and warm sun of a sprawling spring bathing the eternal city with its unmatchable history and artistic beauties.

It was just marking a couple of years since Andrea Sperelli had started to consider alternative options to solve the "vexata quaestio" posed by the UOB legacy NPL portfolio – i.e. how to maximise the economic value, considering the accounting and regulatory implications in between?

Actually, in addressing this challenging question, a new one had come up, almost uncrackable as the first. If the solution to the first question was indeed the creation of "alpha", what would have then been the best way to maximise it? What was the best path forward to get to that "holy grail"?

In other words, should he now consider and take up the proposal he had just received from Gustav Ashenbach and RED, drawn on the basis of the jointly developed feasibility study, but also considering potentially different scenarios, defined in terms of a "weak" JV (with RED buying a local unsecured/small ticket credit workout platform it was already negotiating and then outsourcing on this just a small portfolio from UOB); a "semi-weak" JV (with RED extending the outsourcing from OUB to all kind of small and mid-ticket, including the secured ones, with some more contribution of people, IT and activities from UOB); a "semi-strong" JV (with RED doing all this and also progressively extending its advisory to part of the mid-large ticket portfolio, as it would have progressively developed the real estate capabilities required to do just that). Or, finally, of a "strong" JV (with RED buying into the almost full carve-out of the workout unit of UOB and serving all of its NPL legacy portfolio and the new flows – across all sizes, counterparts and collaterals).

Or, would the bank be better off just keeping everything internally, doing by itself the investments that were anyway required to be done anew – implying money, time and execution risk, as UOB had no presence in Italy and almost no experience in real estate management, if not a mere ambition?

Or, should he now open up the competitive process and consider the bid of other potential parties? An Italian servicer, e.g., could have likely been offering more, on the transaction value – but without offering the upside of the extra-captive revenues and with some conflict of interest to address?

Or a private equity specialised in NPL principal investments could have maybe offered an interesting "packaged" solution, were the buyer could have bought the servicer at a premium, if bundled with a "true sale" of large NPL portfolio from UOB (as a direct sale or via a securitisation)?

Should he go now the "MPS way" or the "Unicredit one" (likely followed by IntesaSanPaolo that, according to press report, was mulling over a similar transaction with the Nordic player Lindorff-Intrum)?

Or just build an inside out "new credit carve-out," at the UOB premises, overcoming the technical and professional challenges and, most importantly, the multiple constraints coming from a culture that was a mix of the former "bank of the Italian treasury" and based in the eternal "urbe" of Roma, and of the Kantian logical reasoning of WFS, the "uber alles" in banking by definition?

What would have been the impacts on its P&L statement on the first and coming years? And what on its regulatory capital ratio? And what on the overall ROE of the bank?

And what about the spillover effects on the way the bank, the good bank, was going to do lending in the future, learning from its past mistakes and developing new underwriting approaches that required "big data," applied analytics and "intelligence" on counterparts, collaterals and troubled situations' optimal management? Was this going to be better with everything out or in or with a mix?

Was it really possible for him? Andrea was now pondering, looking out from his office located at the top floor of the new headquarters of the bank in Rome, to just forget – by packaging some kind of solution – about the "bad bank" and focus only on the "good bank" – the main reason he had considered when, in answering another "vexata quaestio," a few years earlier, he had finally accepted to leave his job at the entrepreneurial CCM, to join ranks at the structured and hyper-regulated UOB, to become a fully-fledged retail and commercial banker and CEO?

Was it possible, in other words – Andrea was asking now to himself – to separate good and bad banks, and the good bank' and bad bank' CEO jobs and roles? Or, where they the two faces of the proverbial Ianus, the unsurmountable trade-off that he, as any other bank CEO, needed to manage anyway?

As he was now looking far afield, gazing in turn at the "speedy train," new and also hyper-technological Central Station on one side, and at the "Cupolone," the Church of San Pietro, home of the Catholic Church and beautifully realised by Michelangelo on the other, Andrea was now considering if there were no such things as "good banks" and "bad banks," but just good bankers and bad bankers at their helm, with the right ones ultimately able to take few critical decisions, in the right way, at the right time, with the right team of internal colleagues and external partners.

Reference

Bank of Italy, 2017, Rapporto sulla stabilità finanziaria, Novembre 2017.

7 Real estate

Market analysis, international evidence and strategic planning

Alessia Bezzecchi

7.1 Real estate market analysis

The real estate market is divided into sub-segments that differ in terms of use, physical characteristics that imply heterogeneous functioning, business models, key performance indicators (KPIs), and as a result interest for various stakeholders. In order to have an overall understanding of the main characteristics of the real estate space market, it is useful to single out, on a preliminary basis, the economic and financial fundamentals of the different segments associated with property usage types.

The main KPIs to understand the dynamics of the real estate market are elements like:

- Selling price
- Rent (the ratio of the rent to the price is the capitalisation rate, similar to the current yield on a bond)
- Average sales time: number of periods (months/annuity fractions)
- Number of transactions
- Discount: differential between asking price and actual price

As shown in Figure 7.1, observing such KPIs, it is possible to understand the phase of the real estate market:

- The market is in a downturn (recession) if the number of transactions is decreasing, average sales times are larger than usual and the average price discount/rent is rising;
- The market is rising (expansion) if the number of transactions is increasing, average selling times are lower than usual and the average price discount/rent is decreasing.

The selling price and the rent (economic value indicators) usually lag other indicators.

The various KPIs have different uses in different segments of the market, e.g. unit prices are the core indicator of the residential sector, whilst rents are the reference indicator for offices.

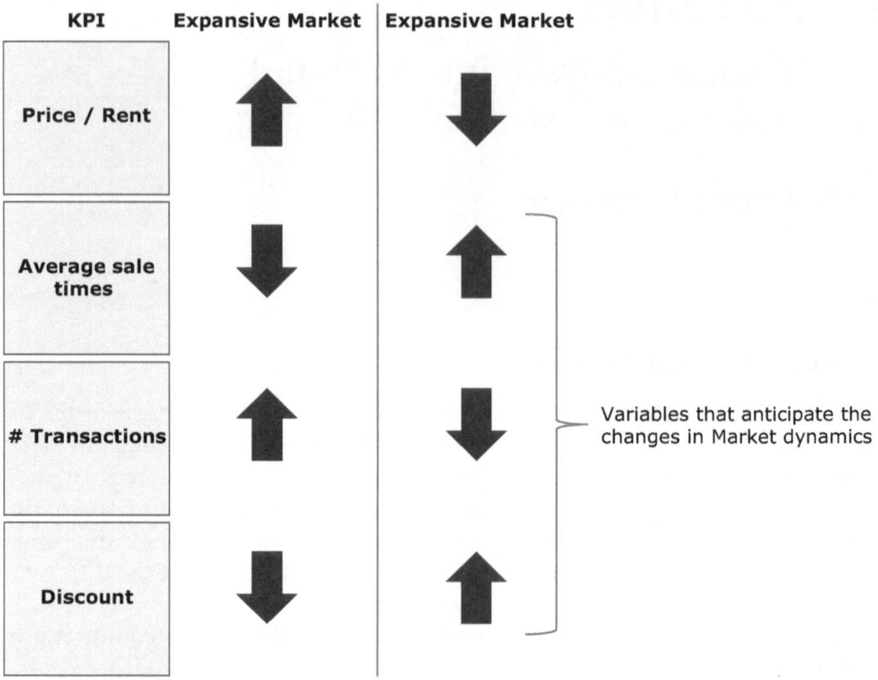

Figure 7.1 Real estate market variables.

Table 7.1 highlights the main characteristics of the various segments of the real estate market from the point of view of various elements such as use, physical characteristics, economic characteristics, KPIs and stakeholders:

- *Use*, i.e. the purpose for which the asset is intended: consumption, productive/instrumental use, direct/ indirect investment;
- *Physical characteristics* describing the structure of real estate units that can be differentiated into:
  - "All-round" property, referring to the whole building from the top floor to the covered surface,
  - Real estate portion (e.g. an apartment),
  - Real estate complex: consisting of different units belonging to a complex with a specific destination (e.g. hospital complex, shopping centre).
- *Economic characteristics* describing the economic purpose of the property in terms of the economic benefits generation process:
  - Personal use: direct use by the landlord;
  - Instrumental: in the hypothesis of a core business building use (e.g. bank agency, mass market retailers);
  - Lease: the asset is intended for income use and therefore as a fee generator (e.g. offices leased to third parties.

Table 7.1 Real estate sectors characteristics

Sector	*Use*	*Physical constitution*	*Economic characteristics*	*KPI*	*Stakeholders*
Residential	Consumption good	Real estate portion/ whole building	Personal use	Selling price	Families, retail market
Offices	Productive good	Real estate portion	Instrumental good (e.g. branch)	Selling price	Companies/banks
	Investment	Whole building	Rent to another subject	Rent/capitalisation rate	Real estate funds, property companies, insurance companies
Retail	Productive good	Real estate portion (e.g. small retail businesses)	Instrumental good (e.g. MMR)	Rent	Companies
	Investment	Real estate complex (e.g. shopping centre)	Rent to another subject (e.g. mall)	Rent to another subject (e.g. mall)	Real estate funds, property companies, insurance companies
Industrial/Logistic	Productive good	Whole building	Instrumental good	Selling price	Companies
	Investment	Whole building	Rent to another subject (residual especially for logistics)	Rent/capitalisation rate	Investors
Special properties (e.g. hotels, multiplex, healthcare residence)	Productive good/ investment	Whole building/real estate complex	Instrumental good (e.g. hotel)	Representational lease	Hotel chain, management multiplex company etc.
			Rent to another subject (e.g. hotel, multiplex)		Real estate funds, property companies

- *KPI*: main reference indicators used for the real estate–specific segment in order to clarify or identify the asset value;
- *Stakeholders*: main subjects who are going to use the building or will invest in the building. For example, companies or banks can use buildings for their standard operations, but the same buildings can be used by real estate funds and property companies as an investment object.

The real estate market can be segmented also from the point of view of the risk profile of the asset classes, which can be defined in terms of the following indicators:

- Level of substitutability of the property;
- Number of potential users;
- Life cycle of the asset.

The first two elements are useful to identify an expected average return positively correlated to the risk component. In particular:

1 The degree of substitutability of the property is the capacity of the asset to be converted into another destination. A high level of substitutability (e.g. the attitude of a building in the residential sector to be converted into an office use) is associated with a low level of risk; a low level of substitutability (e.g. a healthcare residence has a high degree of uncertainty and high conversion costs) implies a high risk;
2 The number of potential users of the asset in the current state. Properties with a high number of interested subjects have low risk, whilst real estate assets with a low level of potential users present a high level of risk.

As shown in Figure 7.2, analysing the real estate assets on the basis of the first two indicators (the degree of substitutability and the number of potential users) is useful to classify properties according to their use, i.e. a special use (e.g. low substitutability, low number of potential users implying larger risk), and a residential use (high substitutability, large number of potential buyers/users and therefore less risk). The other asset classes are positioned at intermediate levels.

Investments in real estate assets are characterised by different "investment styles":

- Core: investment in properties in excellent condition or new construction. Core investments are able to generate an income with a high level of solvency. Leases are long-term and the asset is purchased with a low use of debt capital (low level of leverage). These elements lead to defining the risk profile of core investments as low/medium.

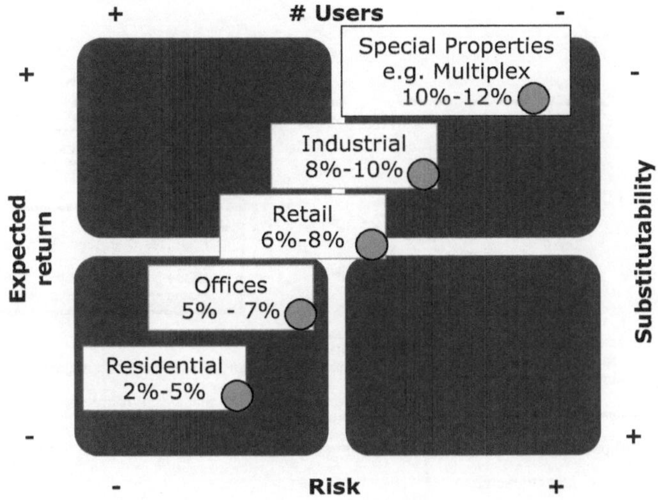

Figure 7.2 Real estate correlation of risk/return by intended use.

- Core plus: it differs from the core, especially because of the physical properties of the asset, i.e. good conditions but requiring "soft" maintenance. The leases are characterised by medium-term maturities, whilst the level of financial leverage is moderate. The risk underlying the core plus investment is medium/high.
- Value added: properties in this category require substantial extraordinary maintenance and include lease contracts that are due to expire or need to be renegotiated. The management activity of this type of assets requires more skills. The level of leverage is generally moderate, whilst the risk profile is high.
- Opportunistic: it is a type of investment that presents the highest level of management complexity, focused on the development of areas or the redevelopment of existing assets. The level of risk is considerable, and leverage is greater than the other investment profiles.

Figures 7.3 and 7.4 show the correlation between risk and return and the type of investment activity that is carried out in the asset, respectively.

7.1.2 Real estate prices: international evidence

Real property (land or built space) prices are determined by the interaction of decisions made by agents acting in the space market and in the asset market. The space market, also known as rental market, is the market for the

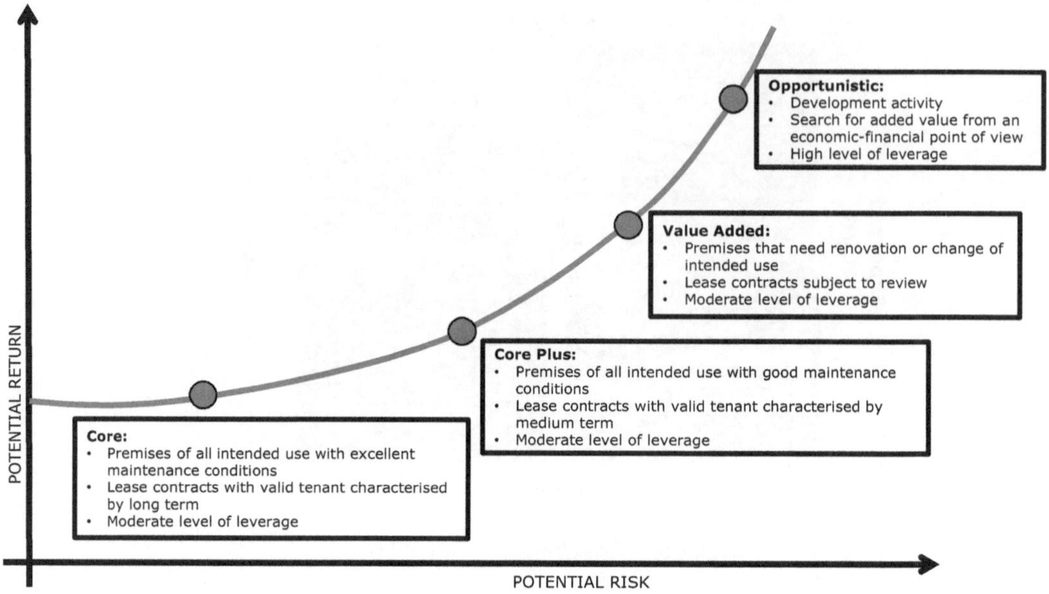

Figure 7.3 Correlation between risk and return in the real estate sector.

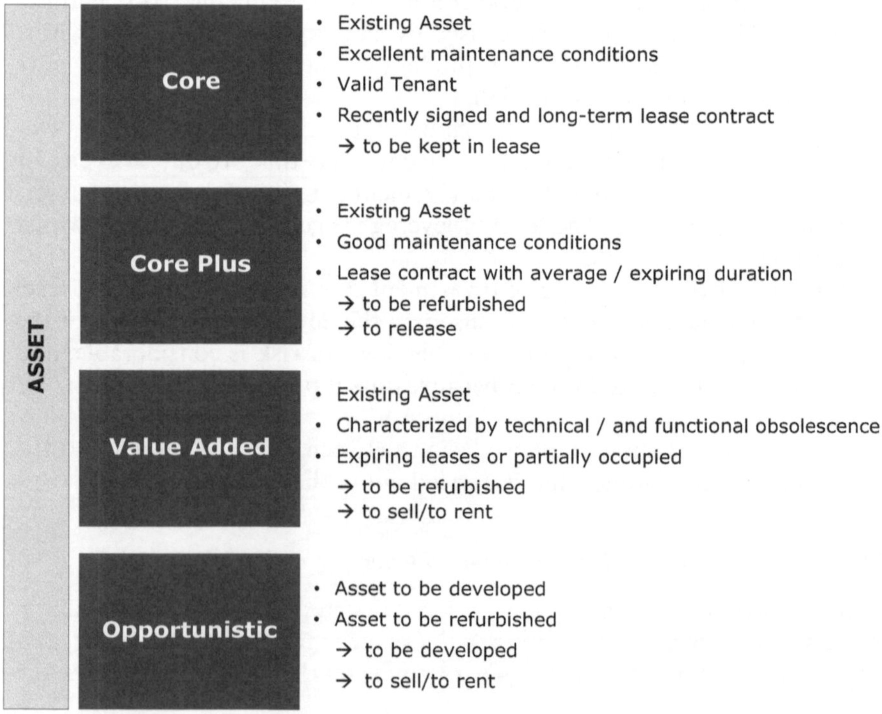

Figure 7.4 Opportunity to invest in the asset life cycle: conceptual exemplification.

usage of property. The real estate asset market is the market for ownership of real estate assets that provide claims to future cash flows.

The past couple of decades have been remarkable for global real estate prices. As shown in Figure 7.5, residential prices have shown a pattern that had never been observed in modern times.

From their peak in the first quarter of 2008, prices have declined until mid-2012 and then started a recovery with a new peak in the third quarter of 2017. A ten-year period with real estate prices that have been flat in nominal terms is highly unusual in a long-run basis. There is no shortage of explanations for this evolution, amongst which the unstable geopolitical context, the global financial crisis of 2008–2009 and the peripheral crises of 2011–2012.

Figure 7.6 presents a focus on the US real estate market in the period 2000–2018, showing a similar trend than the global market but in the context of higher volatility and a much larger overall price appreciation. If the index is set to 1 at the beginning of 2000, it reaches a maximum of 2.06 in April 2006 and then falls to a minimum of 1.36 in March 2012 to then increase to 2.13 at the end of October 2018, an incredible average annual increase of 4% regardless of the most severe economic crisis of modern times.

Figure 7.7 reports the evolution of commercial real estate prices in 1998–2018 in the USA, showing that commercial real estate prices have a pattern similar to residential prices up to the 2008 crisis. Over the same period, both residential and commercial real estate prices approximately double. Commercial prices lose more than residential prices in the aftermath of 2008 (−40% vs. −30%), but towards the end of the sample they are way above (+30%) the 2007 maximum.

The most recent period 2011–2017 has been a good one for most real estate markets around the world. Figure 7.8 reports the average percentage annual

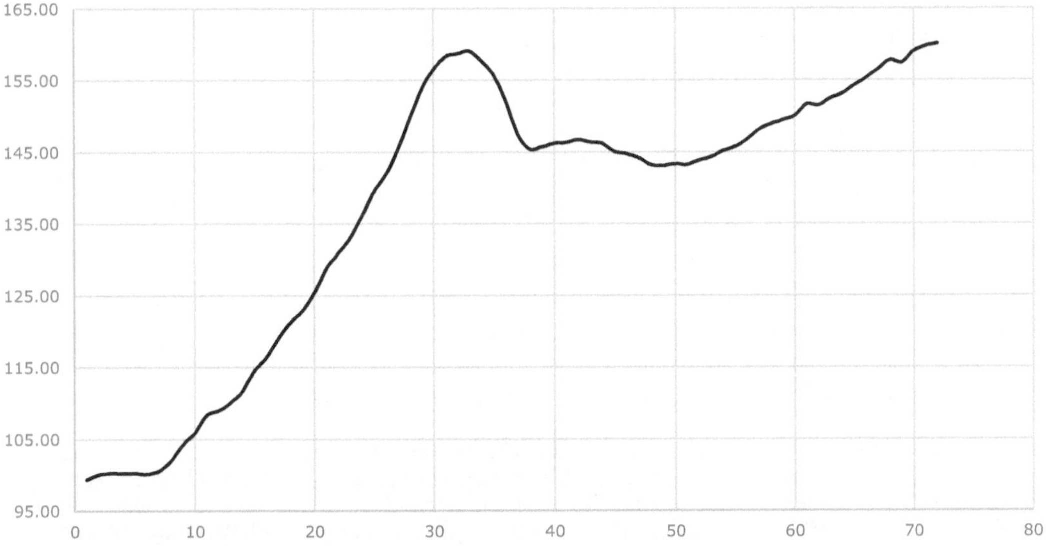

Figure 7.5 Global prices. Quarterly data, 2000–2017.
Source: IMF.

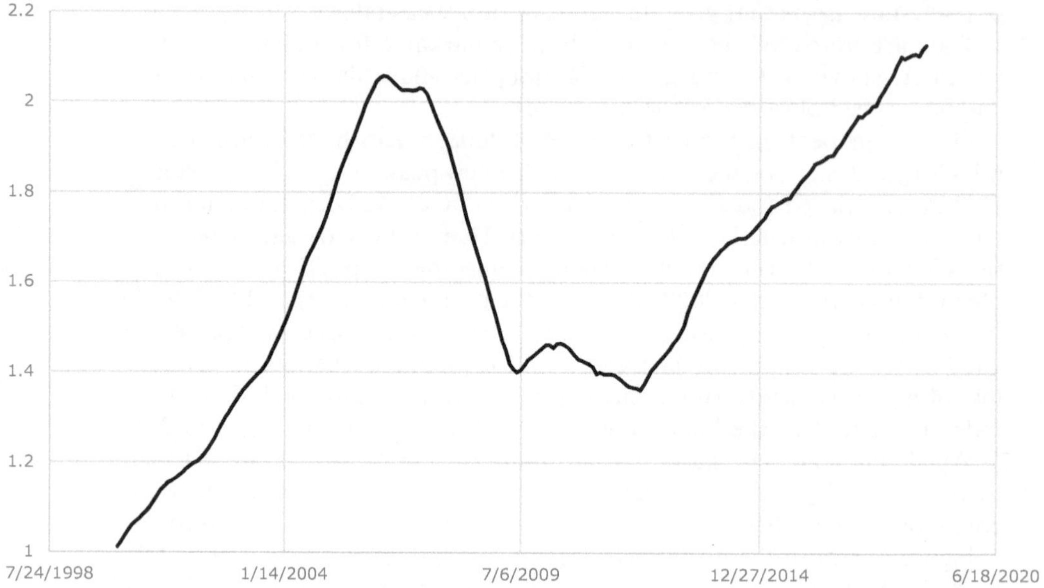

Figure 7.6 US housing prices.
Source: S&P/case Shiller price index.

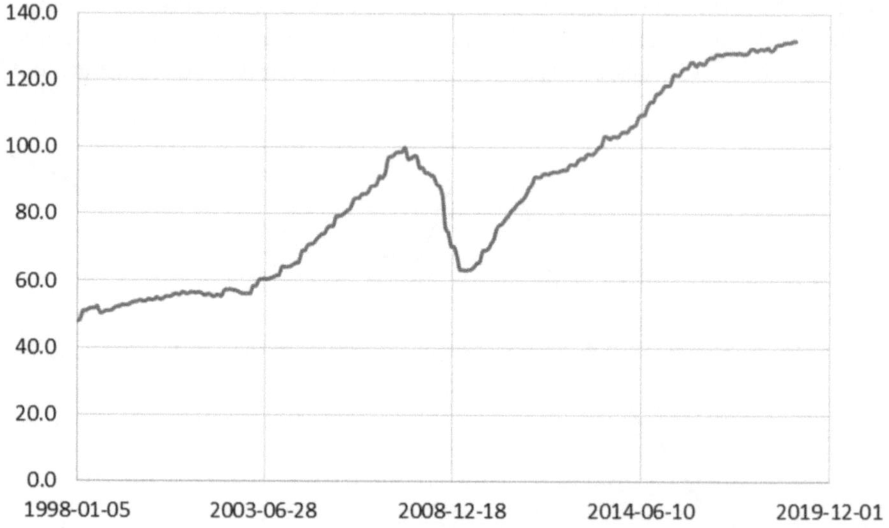

Figure 7.7 US commercial real estate prices. All property Constant Proportion Portfolio Insurance (CPPI) weights: retail (20%), office (17.5%), apartment (15%), healthcare (15%), industrial (10%), lodging (7.5%), net lease (5%), self-storage (5%), manufactured home park (2.5%) and student housing (2.5%).
Source: Green State Advisors.

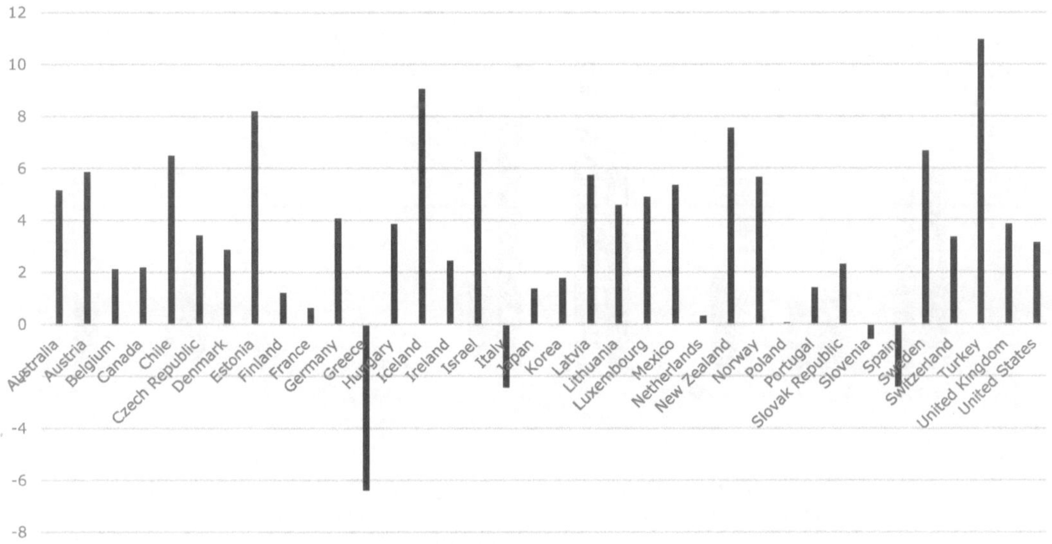

Figure 7.8 International residential prices.
Source: Residential property prices indicators, OECD.

change in the price of the total stock of newly built and existing residential dwellings. Remarkably, only in three countries (Greece, Italy and Spain), prices have declined in nominal terms, and such countries have been subject to deep economic and financial crises associated with the crisis in the local sovereign debt.

Incidentally, all three countries are characterised by a deep interrelation between the real estate market and the banking system. Interestingly, in other two peripheral countries, Ireland and Portugal, prices have managed to increase even in the presence of long and deep economic recessions.

Figure 7.9 reports the percentage change of quarterly commercial property prices (in local currency) over various sub-periods. The blue bar indicates the percentage change over country-specific sub-periods. The orange bar indicates the percentage change over the period 2007–2018.

It is remarkable that commercial prices in the recent decade have grown in most countries, regardless of being measured from a starting point representing the pre-crisis peak prices.

This evidence shows that investors have learnt that real estate prices can suffer from periods of prolonged volatility, similarly to what happens to other asset classes such as stocks and bonds. The negative news that real estate prices may fall heavily during crisis is offset by the good news that recovery may be rather quick. Investors have maintained their interest in real estate as an asset class in the context of global diversified portfolios and have looked at the different segments such as logistics, healthcare, social and student housing. These investments represent non-traditional asset classes.

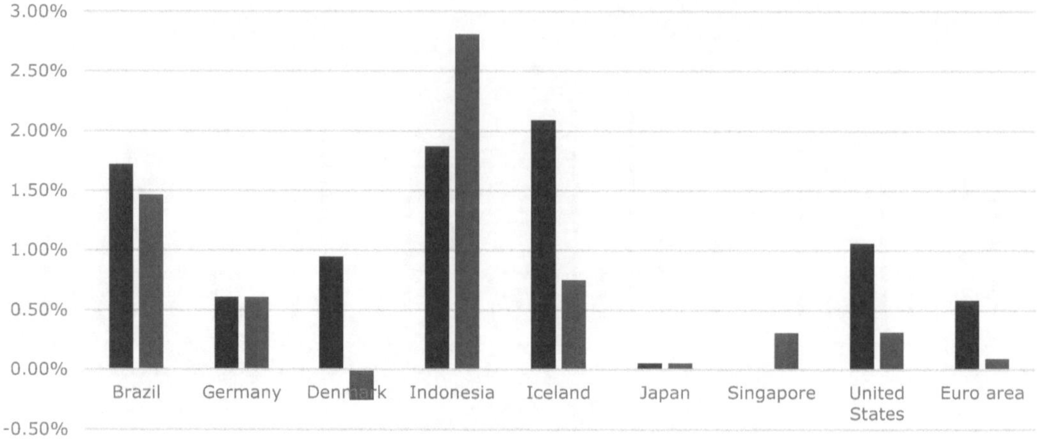

Figure 7.9 International commercial property prices: Brazil (March 2000 to December 2017), Germany (March 2008 to December 2017), Denmark (March 1992 to June 2018), Indonesia (March 2002 to March 2017), Iceland (March 1995 to June 2018), Japan (June 2008 to June 2018), Singapore (March 1998 to September 2018), the USA (December 1945 to September 2018) and Euro area (March 2000 to June 2018).

Source: Commercial property prices, bank for International Settlements.

7.2 Strategic planning in real estate

From a different perspective looking at the relevant areas, one can say that the analysis of an asset (or an asset portfolio) must include:

- Strategy, organisation and business model: this analysis aims at understanding the competitive sector, the business model and the development plans;
- Finance: financial analysis aims at assessing the relationship between debt and value, analysing valuation techniques to express judgments about economic-financial convenience and providing valuation methodologies for the listing of assets;
- Macroeconomic environment: this analysis tries to forecast and monitor macro- and microeconomic variables that have a substantial impact on company and investment development plans.

Appraisal is also related to the stakeholder interested in the valuation and to the actions taken by such stakeholder. As shown in Figure 7.10, strategic planning is the last step in the overall process that starts from valuation and ends with management. The distinctive feature of a good manager is the ability to grasp the essence of each individual area by understanding its peculiarities and interrelations.

Figure 7.10 The process of analysis, strategic planning and management of real estate.

7.3 Risk management and real estate

Figure 7.11 outlines some points of attention with respect to activities and investment in risk management carried out by real estate operators.

The main advantages of active risk management are as follows:

- Transparency: greater transparency in decision-making and knowledge of the real risk drivers underlying investment dynamics;
- Safety: less uncertainty for foreign and domestic institutional investors and for banks financing the funds. Consequently, facilitated access to equity and debt;
- Proactive management: proactive management of the risks, both recurring and "tail risk," also in terms of their coverage/insurance;
- Long-term vision: multi-year development path.

The main risks faced by players operating in the real estate market are as follows:

- Operational risks: risks in procedures/processes and internal organisational structures as well as compliance risks;
- Economic and financial risks: risks on the investments made by the individual funds and risks of the entire portfolio, also with respect to the financial structure adopted by this fund;

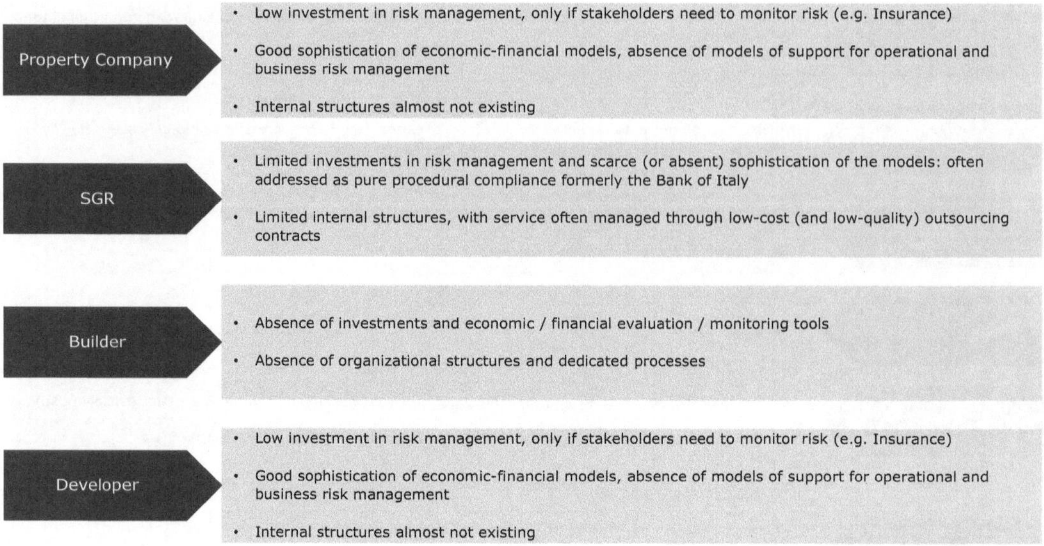

Figure 7.11 Activities and investments in risk management carried out by real estate operators.

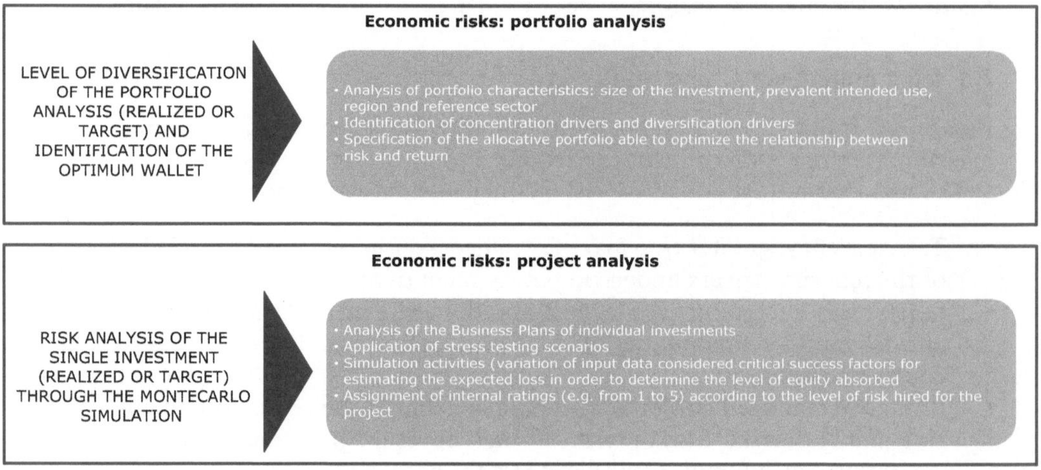

Figure 7.12 Economic risks and portfolio analysis.

For the purposes of this discussion, attention is drawn to the analysis of economic risk, i.e. the analysis of risks directly linked to the fundamental value of the real estate asset (e.g. urban risk, construction site risk, risk of non-compliance with the tenant; Figure 7.12).

The risk management system should, therefore, evaluate and identify solutions to hedge the main sources of risks generated by the individual investments, or by the investment portfolio (i.e. insurance contracts on specific operational risks).

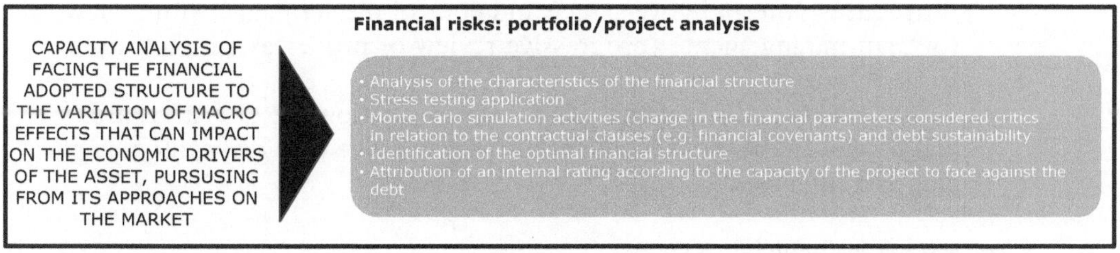

Figure 7.13 Financial risks and portfolio analysis

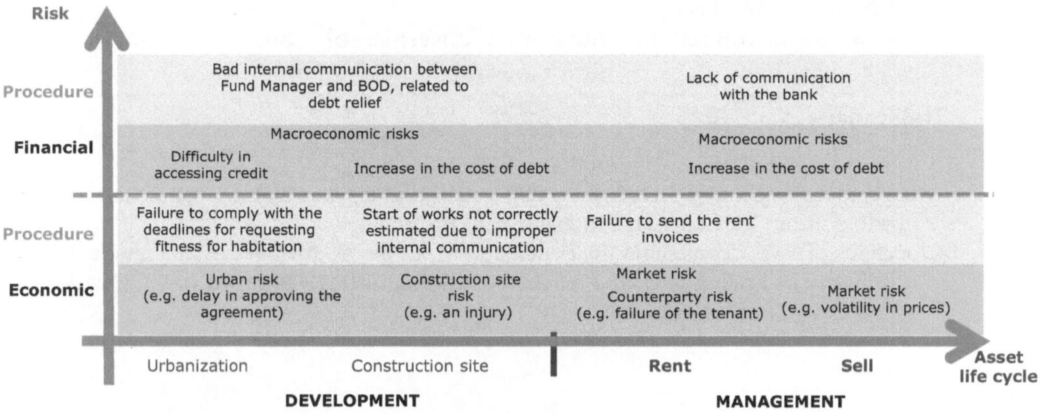

Figure 7.14 Risk management in the asset life cycle.

The analysis of financial risk includes the analysis of risks related to macroeconomic variables and, in particular, those that are more relevant for the adopted financing structure (e.g. interest rate risk, exchange rate risk, debt renegotiation; Figure 7.13).

The risk management system activates ad hoc hedging instruments for such cases, like insurance contracts on interest rate and exchange rate derivative risks, and renegotiation clauses at the time of debt assumption.

Risk management, in order to be "active," must be offered at each stage of the asset's life cycle (from the urbanisation to the sale phase), since each of these is subject to economic, financial and procedural risks (Figure 7.14).

Proactive risk management consists of a systematic monitoring activity of both operating and financial factors. Briefly,

For operational risks:

- Top-down identification of the main factors that generate costs related to operational risk and reworking, with a focus on the most recurring ones, generating costs that are not justified by any output produced;

- Identification of solutions of an organisational nature (interventions on procedures, internal governance and control mechanisms) with a view to "lean management" (progressive review of processes with a "front-to-back" view);
- Cross section statistical analysis for the evaluation of key critical areas and for the analysis of specific insurance coverage with respect to recurring and tail costs.

For economic-financial risks:

- Drafting and analysing the business plans of individual investments;
- Sensitivity analysis;
- Portfolio analysis;
- Evaluation and recommendation of coverage solutions.

References

Borghi, A., 2009, Finanza Immobiliare, EGEA.

Brueggeman, W.B., and J.D. Fisher, 2016, *Real estate finance and investments*, fifteenth edition, McGraw-Hill International Edition.

Ciocchetta, F., W. Cornacchia, R. Felici, and M. Loberto, 2016, Assessing financial stability risks arising from the real estate market in Italy, Banca d'Italia, Quaderni di Economia e Finanza No. 323.

8 Real estate appraisal

Fundamentals, appraisal process and valuation

Alessia Bezzecchi

8.1 Valuation fundamental and appraisal process

In very general terms, the *valuation process* can be defined as the methodology-based process that ends up with the determination of the value that can be assigned to a real estate asset. The process involves some objective and some subjective phases. In a preliminary phase, the evaluator must identify the valuation object, scope and time. In the operational phase, the evaluator collects and analyses all the relevant information sources, makes a decision about the methodology and carries out the valuation process. In the final phase, the evaluator verifies the results and writes up a formal report.

The fundamentals of the valuation process can be described as follows[1]:

1. The valuation object (what): in order to identify the property rights, one needs to study the property from the physical (e.g. square meters, maintenance quality, location...), legal (e.g. existence of a mortgage) and economic (e.g. vacant possession or occupied property and characteristics of the associated contracts) points of view.
2. The goal of valuation (why): specification of the purpose of the appraisal.
3. Which value (category): it is particularly important to be clear about the category, because "value" can refer to (a) the market value, i.e. the transaction price that the two parties may agree on under "normal" conditions; (b) the liquidation value, i.e. the transaction price that the two parties may agree on under a stress scenario, e.g. in the case of a fire sale, accounting for net debt; (c) the book value as reported in the balance sheet; (d) the replacement value associated with the construction cost of the same asset; (e) insurance value included in an insurance policy; (f) the collateral value, i.e. the price that might be taken as collateral in a financing operation; and (g) the high and best use, i.e. the price that may be paid by the buyer who is in the best position to extract value from that asset.
4. What moment should apply to valuation (when): specification of the effective date of value estimation.
5. Which approach should be used (how): the sales comparison approach, the income approach and the cost approach.

The "market value" is the most likely price that a real estate asset should bring in a competitive and open market under the following conditions:

1 The buyer and the seller are rational agents
2 No information asymmetries
3 Equal contractual power amongst the two parties
4 Reasonable time is allowed for exposure in the open market
5 The value is in monetary terms
6 Not affected by special financial conditions (e.g. financing, sales concession)

8.2 Real estate appraisal

Depending on the valuation manuals or financial analysis that are taken into account, different methodologies can be listed, which often, although based on the same principles and similar methods of application, differ in name.

For this reason, it is proposed a conceptual outline, which combines the methodologies discussed in this chapter with the basic principles on which they are based and the purpose of application of them: it is also necessary to underline that the financial method lends itself both to evaluating real estate assets and to expressing judgments of convenience in evaluating investments, whilst the other methodologies are used only for the first purpose (Table 8.1).

8.3 Market approach

a Definition

The market or comparable approach provides a value estimation of a real estate asset based on prices traded for physical "quantities" of comparable real estate assets ("comparable").

In a sense, the appraiser's estimate of value will help the lender determine whether the price being offered by the borrower-applicant is an "outlier," or a price that is significantly different from what would be paid by most buyers in the market for similar properties.

Table 8.1 Evaluation of real estate approaches

Fundamental	*Approach*	*Aim*
Results	Financial	Asset valuation Analysis of convenience
	Value	Asset valuation
Comparable	Market	Asset valuation
Patrimonial	Income	Asset valuation

The purpose of this method is to determine unit values (e.g. the value per square meter of GLA – gross leasable area) based on the real prices of quantities of comparable goods and to identify the relationship that binds the market value with the physical, economic and legal characteristics of the property. The determined values are multiplied by the physical "quantity" of the real estate object being valued in order to estimate the required value.

b Principles and considerations

The market approach should be applied under two main hypotheses:

- The values recorded refer to the property taken into consideration, or the transactions recorded refer to substantially similar comparable assets ("replacement principle").
- The equivalence between the market and the trading conditions that the unit price expresses ("equilibrium principle between supply and demand").

If these assumptions are valid, the market approach provides a more "neutral" measure than that determined using the methods based on cash flows (DCF) since it is based on market expectations, with regard to both the economic and financial characteristics. However, the values taken from the market rarely refer to comparable goods in the sense that:

- the characteristics used as a comparable often do not imply the selection of a homogeneous sample;
- the considered surveys frequently refer to a time horizon that is spaced over time with respect to the evaluation date;
- the analysed sample often considers a small number of surveys;
- the "quantity" used as a detection parameter is not homogeneous with reasonable certainty within the analysed samples (e.g. different definition methods of the commercial square meter).

For these reasons, the market approach is only apparently overcoming the problem of subjectivity as the selection of the sample of comparable real estate necessarily implies subjective judgments.

In this way, a tautological evaluation process is defined: the essence of the methodology in detecting the value of the asset from the market through the comparison of "replaceable" assets (objective parameter) is applied in the assignment of the choice determination to the evaluating subject.

First of all, the comparability criteria and, secondly, of the subsequent verification of the consistency of the goods comparable to the parameters outlined (subjective parameter).

The evaluation could then confirm a value more secured to subjective expectations than to market parameters.

The heterogeneous reference can be solved by setting up an evaluation process based on objective elements, not only based on comparable but also on the difference between the selected assets. The evaluation process should be formalised, motivating and making explicit the choice in terms, by way of example but not exhaustively, of:

- detection times of the selected values on which they are referred
- sample size, in terms of the number of transactions detected or indication of sources (public sources or data providers)
- reference areas.

The evaluation process can be supported by comparable tables where each criterion (comparability or differentiation) will be associated with an ad hoc judgment for comparable in qualitative terms:

- Absolutes: valuation referred to the individual asset independently of the other goods included in the sample (e.g. shoddy/sufficient/good maintenance status).
- Relatives: referenced valuation as a comparison of the asset with the other assets included in the sample (e.g. best/worst finishes).

c Formula

According to the market or comparable approach, the value of a property is equal to the product between the amount of the unit price and the appropriate quantity related to it:

$$V = P \times Q$$

where V is property value, P is unitary price, and Q is quantity.

d Use

The market or comparable approach can be divided into two application criteria according to the type of the chosen parameter and it is able to define a different relationship between quantity and value:

- Market criterion: uses "physical" quantities as a multiplicative factor. Depending on the "quantity" used, it is possible to further distinguish:
  - market principle using measures that provide value indications
  - market principle using measures that provide orders of magnitude
- Transaction multiples: it takes into account economic quantities as a multiplicative factor.

The market approach is widely used in the valuation practice mainly to determine the value of residential properties, or for asset classes in which the price is related to specific elements that, within the business model that characterises the sector, seem assume particular importance as a value index. These indicators are empirical and appreciated for certain areas in relation to specific value drivers.

The rationale of the market approach is functional to the fact that the "guides" identified as a multiplicative factor represent, in the sector considered, the actual conditions at the generation of value basis.

The transaction multiples identify the existing relationships between the value of the property and significant economic quantities. For example, revenues, net income and average gross operating profit (AGOP). These multipliers, taken from the principle of corporate finance to determine the economic capital of companies, and better defined "financial multiples," are not applied in the real estate sector due to the lack of available data but, above all, due to the lack of a correlation between economic activities sizes and the value of fully comparable assets (Table 8.2).

e Process to implement the market approach

The use of the market approach is divided into the following activities:

- Definition of comparability/differentiation criteria
- Value information collection and extraction of the sample of comparable assets
- Sample cleaning and determination of the value range
- Application of the criterion and corrections to the individual good

I Definition of comparability/differentiation criteria

The comparable elements must allow the elements of similarity/diversity to emerge. They can be divided into three different categories as follows:

- Physical characteristics of the asset (e.g. location, intended use, state of conservation, finishes, facilities, panoramic views)
- Legal characteristics (e.g. presence of third-party rights, present and future planning regulations)
- Economic-financial characteristics (e.g. rental status, macroeconomic context, operating costs, maintenance costs)

The characteristics variety could be classified to define a property in its entirety, but they are not equally significant for all buildings, but could be relevant depending on the analysed cluster and depending on the peculiarity of the asset (e.g. the physical characteristic of the "view" can be considered for the residential sector and at the same time has no relevance for the industrial sector). In the evaluation process, priority should be given to the characteristics that most identify the property

Table 8.2 Market approach: examples of multiple market principles

Criteria	*Price × Physical quantity*	*Asset class*
Market	(*measure that provides a value indicator*)	
	Price per square meter	Residential
	Price per hector	Field
	Price per parking space	Parking
Market	(*measure that provides an indication of order of magnitude*)	
	Price per hole	Golf course
	Price per theatre	Multiplex
	Price per seat	Theatre, restaurant, cinema
	Price per room	Hotel, motel, nursing home
Multiples	Revenue multiple	Hotel, multiplex, restaurant, nursing home, motel
	Gross operating margin revenue	
	Net income multiple	

subject to valuation in terms of values. It is good to highlight the comparable approach used, motivating the necessarily functional choice to the specific characteristics of the asset, first of all the intended use, location and maintenance status.

II Value information collection and extraction of the sample of comparable assets

The market approach assumes that prices are determined as the elaboration of a sufficiently large historical series of transactions involving identical assets. As highlighted above, the fungibility and the comparability of the asset is identified with reference to the main characteristics of the asset that contribute to determining its attractiveness. In order to collect the value information, there are basically two ways to list:

- Extraction of value data using databases of professional data providers.
- Appreciation of transactions of comparable assets favouring some selective criteria of comparability according to the asset peculiarity (e.g. location and maintenance status for the residential, quality standards and services offered for the hotels).

III Application of the criterion and corrections to the individual good

Once the values of the transactions obtained from the databases of the available data providers have been found, on the basis of the "comparability grid," it is, therefore, necessary to remove some observations/findings that are distinguishable to the object of assessment despite referring to assets that meet the criteria of comparability. For example, a new residential complex belonging to a redevelopment project could lead to the exclusion of data provider values that return functional ranges to property transactions that, for the same location, use and maintenance status, may not be comparable. The sample cleaning process could also lead to the exclusion of transaction values whose amount was determined by strategic choices or by choice relating to other business areas (e.g. purchase price of a strategic logistics area for the industrial core business: it is likely that the strategic purpose may imply a premium price at the strictly market value).

To clarify the reasons behind the cleanliness of the sample, or the elimination of certain observations, it is advisable to make explicit the considerations made.

Once the reference value range has been determined, to apply profitably the market criterion, it is necessary to do the following:

- Identification of the measure: as previously highlighted, each different type of real estate has its own unit of measurement. Moreover, it is important to verify the "quantity" even in the cases in which the measure is defined at theoretical level (e.g. commercial area), but not necessarily homogeneous at the level of computation (e.g. weighting coefficients of the accessory surfaces for the determination of the commercial area are different).

- Implementation of adjustment process: derived from the need to have homogeneous and significant information for the assessment. The adjustment process can be:
- Qualitative: application of corrective measures at the judgment of the evaluator;
- Percentage: application of corrective percentages based on deviations in terms of the characteristics determined by the comparability criterion (e.g. maintenance, presence of green areas);
- For merit points: application of value adjustments according to deviations in terms of ad hoc "scores" for characteristics determined by the comparability criterion.

The adjustment process is characterised in all its forms by a high subjectivity, as the quantification of the differentials of value/percentage/merit points are not based on universal standards and/or shared by the practice but on the sensitivity of the evaluator. The percentage methodologies and for merit points are very useful if you need to simultaneously assess a real estate portfolio characterised by similar real estate units, so as to be consistent in the application of the criterion (e.g. in the assessment of a residential building, allocation of 20 basis points decreased in the absence of the lift).

The market or comparable approach is appreciable for the ability to synthesise and for the assumptions of objectivity derived from extracting directly from the "market" values referring to comparable and recently traded real estate assets. The considerations made highlight how, moreover, this methodology is difficult to apply: for the limited number of transactions, the difficulty of extracting samples of comparable goods, and the lack of transparency on the amounts actually traded. For these reasons, it is advisable to clarify the assumptions and motivations of certain evaluation choices in all phases that constitute the evaluation process: from the definition of the comparability criteria to the choice of the unit of measurement, and from the extraction of values from the market to the adjustments to the adjustment process.

8.4 Cost approach

a Definition

The cost approach involves estimating the cost to reproduce the structure (less depreciation) and then adding the value of the land (site) to it in arriving at a value. The rationale for this approach is that no knowledgeable buyer would pay more for a property than the cost at which it can be reproduced.

This methodology is based on the detection of three components:

- Value of the land on which the improvement is located
- Cost of reproducing the improvement

- Adjustment factors which take into account any depreciation due to physical deterioration, functional obsolescence (e.g. excessive amounts of hallway space) and external obsolescence (e.g. changing land uses in a neighbourhood that cause a structure to become obsolete before the actual building wears out)

b Principles and points of attention

The cost approach is based on two assumptions:

- First, no rational subject is willing to pay a price higher than the purchase price of an area in the same location and the subsequent costs of realising an asset that has comparable characteristics of use (substitution principle).
- Second, the value of the asset derives from the most probable use of the good that is physically feasible, legally permitted and that offers the highest rate of return (principle of high and best use).

The cost approach is a valuation method that is difficult to determine the fair value of an asset for the following problems:

- The sum of construction costs may differ substantially from market value,
- There is no correlation between realisation cost and market value,
- The depreciation factor for functional and external obsolescence, in addition to being difficult to evaluate, in most cases involves a depreciation of the building equal to or greater than the cost of realisation: the asset is no longer suitable to carry out the use to which is intended (e.g. building without elevator, building with obsolete heating system) or, at worst, is no longer "attractive" for the market (e.g. hotel with almost no employment rate).

c Formula, areas of use and employment criteria

The cost methodology can be effectively used in order to determine the value of the area through its natural corollary: the extraction criterion. The objective of this method is to determine the value per square meter of the surface not built, but with intended use already defined and approved.

The main assumptions to be taken into consideration are as follows:

- The area should have definitive license and approved development plan.
- Any existing buildings on the area cannot be recovered and that they must be demolished: if a recovery of the buildings is assumed, the extraction method can be used to estimate the value of the properties themselves in the current state.
- That the current intended use is maintained and that a change of intended use is not foreseen.

This method makes it possible to obtain a fair value for the area, starting from the unit market value of the finished product and subsequently separating from it all the unit cost items that comprise it.

The assumption of this methodology is based on the idea that no rational operator is willing to pay a price to acquire an area to be transformed

Table 8.3 Cost approach: extraction criteria

+	Value of the product
+	Profit of the entrepreneur
+	Construction costs
+	General management costs
+	Project and construction supervision costs
+	Demolishing costs
+	Infrastructure costs
+	Contribution on the cost of construction
+	Infrastructure costs
+	Reclamation costs
=	VALUE OF THE AREA

that is higher than the sum of the revenues that can be obtained from the sale of the asset net of all the costs necessary to produce it.

More specifically, the cost items and the calculation methodology that allow to determine the value of an area using the extraction method are presented in Table 8.3.

Once the determination of the reference unit of measurement is reached, probably identifiable with the value per square meter of an area (potential object of real estate development), the appraiser has to multiply this by the square meters of the area (expression of the building capacity of the area itself) in order to obtain the value of the real estate under analysis.

8.5 Income approach

a Definition

The income approach establishes the market value of property by determining how much an investor is willing to pay for the income stream that a property produces. Using this method, the appraiser attempts to establish the relationship between a property's sale price and the monthly income stream it would produce if rented.

It is based on the underlying hypothesis that a rational buyer is not willing to pay a price higher than the current value of the economic benefits that the real estate will be able to produce during its useful life.

b Principles

The income approach is also based on the following two principles:

- Replacement principle": the recorded values as referable to the property in question refer to perfectly comparable assets.
- Principle of equilibrium between supply and demand": the values are determined in hypothesis of the equality of market conditions and negotiation.

Being the same as the comparative approach, reference is made to the relevant paragraph.

c Algorithm and points of attention

The property value is given by the ratio of the rent and the capitalisation rate:

$$W_0 = \frac{C_l}{r}$$

where W_0 is the property value, C_l is the rent, and r is the "Cap rate."

In the case of a leased asset with a new contract at a market rent, at standard conditions, to a lessee level suitable for the asset, the value of the property found by the previous formula expresses the most probable price that a rational subject is willing to pay for the property being assessed.

The "Cap rate" can be determined either on a comparative basis or on an economic basis. In terms of mere economic theory, this rate is determined by the composition of two distinct factors: (1) the pre-tax return on risk-free investments (government bonds), symbolised *Rf*; (2) the risk premium (the value of which can be determined in a subjective manner, by comparison or using statistical models). This second factor is, in turn, subdivided into two distinct components:

- The risk premium deriving from the comparison between the real estate sector and the other sectors, *Pi*.
- The risk premium for the specific property, additional risk premium (ARP).

The formula that determines the discount rate is therefore as follows:

$$r = Rf + Pi + \text{ARP}$$

The corrective factor ARP derives from the application of the parameters that distinguishes the specific asset taken into consideration: location, type, size, rental status and fungibility.

For properties with suitable characteristics for an optimal and lasting positioning on the market, this factor is close to zero, whilst the maximum values distinguish buildings with high levels of risk.

For properties that present different risk conditions with respect to market conditions (e.g. lessor with a low level of solvency), increasing correction coefficients (ARP) of the capitalisation rate of income must be adopted in order to adapt it to the real characteristics of the asset and therefore to appropriately decrease the overall value of it. In the case of different income conditions (e.g. higher market rent than the contractual one), the present value of the greater/lower retractable rent must be determined, with respect to the market rent, depending on the lease in place up to the income of the building at market conditions.

In the case of different risk conditions, the capitalisation rate determined on a comparative basis must be adjusted directly proportional to the increase in risk and the Cap rate determined on an economic basis will have to change the ARP factor, increasing it or depreciating it on the basis of the greater/lesser risk determined by the different conditions from those of the market.

In practice, the income approach is used by the formula of "limited rent" where the value of the asset is given by the capitalisation of the "rent" (rent) at a given rate "Cap rate" (yield) related to the risk/return profile of the numerator. This method has strong limits if the contractual rent differs substantially from the market rent and, at the same time, the duration is long term; at the same Cap rate, the application of the limited annuity determines significantly different values of the property depending on the rent used (potential rent – market rent vs. passing rent – contract fee).

8.6 Economic and financial approach

a Definition

The financial valuation method assumes that the value of a real estate asset is given by the ability to generate expected future economic benefits in terms of cash flows related to a specific time horizon functional to the characteristics of the asset being valued.

b Principles and points of attention

The financial method, similar to the income approach, is based on the:

- hypothesis that a rational buyer is not willing to pay a price higher than the current value of the economic benefits (declined in cash flows) that the real estate will be able to produce during its useful life;
- "substitution principle";
- "balance principle" between supply and demand.

c Algorithm, areas of use and criteria

The value of the property is given by the sum of the active and passive cash flows generated over time, discounted at an appropriate rate (discount rate):

$$W = \sum_{t=1}^{T} \frac{F_t}{(1+k)^t}$$

where W is the value of the asset, F_t is the cash flow for period t, t is the time period, T is the relevant time horizon, and k is the discount rate.

The financial approach is used to both determine the value of existing real estate assets and express opinions of the economic-financial advantage of an investment.

8.7 Valuation case study: Augustus Luxury Resort

Ms. Orchidea Vinadio and Mr. Oliver Dawson mandated to prepare a Valuation of the Augustus Luxury Resort, and a business plan post-debt service and income taxes based on the valuation's cash flows to an International Real Estate Company called Taebes Corp.

8.7.1 Location and asset description

Augustus Luxury Resort is located on the island of Wingapo, located on Greece's west coast. The island is a well-established tourist destination, internationally known for its white sand beaches, natural landscapes, rich cultural, gastronomic, historical and architectural heritage as well as its jet set nightlife. The city in which the Resort is located is well serviced by an international airport and seaport, which are located at 10 and 12 km, respectively, from the Resort. The location, therefore, benefits from good accessibility and retains a high degree of privacy. The Resort was first opened in 1993 and has constantly benefited regular refurbishment and structural changes, which have contributed to its positioning as the best resort in its market of relevance.

Augustus Luxury Resort is located in a sparsely populated area mostly covered by agricultural lands and is surrounded by a mix of low-rise residential units. The Resort occupies a rectangular site characterised by lush vegetation, covering an area of approximately 50 hectares. The site occupies a prominent position with frontage on the Mediterranean Sea.

The terrain, mostly flat, spreads from the resort to the seaside. Within its perimeters, the Resort offers 16 prime freehold properties and a range of sport and recreational facilities, amongst others are 10 pools, a spa, a basketball court, a paddle tennis court, 12 tennis courts, 3 football fields, a volleyball court and a karting track. It offers eight different accommodation facilities ranging between 4 and 5 stars. The rooms inventory comprises of 296 rooms, 375 bungalows, 20 suites and 11 villas (comprising of 32 accommodations), for a total rooms stock of 723 accommodations.

The sub-tropical climate allows an eight-month opening seasonality, attracting an internationally diversified clientele base, mainly referring to discerning wealthy families. Demand mix is well diversified and made up by 54% leisure and 46% conference, allowing mitigation during low-seasonality periods.

Augustus Resort offers sport courses through academies such as football, tennis, bike, boxing, cricket and basketball amongst others, often associated to major teams and sportspeople.

The Resort's restaurants and bars are signed by Michelin star and celebrity chefs, allowing an increased popularity for non-resident guests.

The Hotel's shops offer Greek and international designer labels as well as displaying items of local production.

8.7.2 Rooms

With regard to the rooms stock, the hotel management has been carried out a strategy aiming at improving the average level of the accommodations, refurbishing the oldest rooms and merging the smallest rooms to create larger lodgings.

The mix of accommodation at Augustus Resort is truly unique in that it provides numerous types of accommodations appealing to affluent families travelling with children, as well as couples, representing a differentiator for the Resort (Table 8.4).

8.7.3 Capital expenditure

In recent years, the Resort has undergone constant and significant capital expenditures confirming the management commitment to maintain its high-quality standards. Major works through the period of relevance were allocated to the refurbishment of the room stock, the common areas, the spa, the IT, the back of the house areas, the air-conditioning systems, the development of the arena, the pools, the go-kart, the sport facilities, the offices and the staff houses.

In the period 2012 and 2017, Capex costs amounted to approximately € 70 million, corresponding to € 96,000 on a per room basis, which is substantially in line for hotels of similar positioning.

According to the information received by the Augustus Resort Management, the total investment planned from 2018 to 2020 is mainly represented by the room inventory refurbishment, upgrades of the go-kart, tennis and pool areas, public areas configuration, meeting rooms and laundry.

The total capital expenditure deduction assumed by Taebes Corp. for the valuation is of approximately € 16 million (or € 14.2 in today's value), including an estimated contingency fee of € 615,000 or 4.0% of the total Capex.

Table 8.4 Augustus Luxury Resort: mix accommodation

#	*Name*	*Number of rooms*	*Size (square meter)*	*Category*
1	Petra	133	32	4-star
2	Clessydra (rooms/bungalows)	31	37	4-star
3	Altera (bungalows)	94	38	4-star
4	Tinya	102	39	5-star
5	Moliere (rooms/bungalows)	45	55	5-star
6	Waterfront Suites	12	73	5-star
7	Laos	218	41	5-star
8	Menos (bungalows + villas)	88	67	5-star
	Total	723	44	

8.7.4 Operating structure

Taebes Corp. has assumed a purchaser would appoint a competent hotel management company on prevailing market terms (Table 8.5).

8.7.5 Resort performance over years

Ms. Orchidea Vinadio and Mr. Oliver Dawson provide to the valuators of Taebes Corp. the key historic trading results (Table 8.6).

Table 8.5 Augustus Luxury Resort: terms

	Terms
Management fee Base fee	2.0% of total sales
Management fee Incentive fee	5.0% of AGOP (gross operating profit minus base fee)
FF&E Reserve	3.0% of total sales

Table 8.6 Augustus Luxury Resort: performance over years

All Values In (EUR)	**2013**	**2014**	**2015**	**2016**	**2017**	**2018 a/f thru August**
Period Ending	December 31	December 31	December 31	December 31	December 31	December 31
Days Open in Period	244	245	230	227	230	230
Available Hotel Rooms	750	750	740	728	712	723
Available Room Nights	151,872	166,110	153,640	165,256	163,760	176,155
Occupied Room Nights	68,929	69,614	79,730	84,643	90,029	103,177
Occupancy	45.4%	41.9%	51.9%	51.2%	55.0%	58.6%
Average Daily Rate	575.77	554.34	534.63	567.00	572.78	544.16
RevPAR	261.32	232.32	277.44	290.42	314.89	318.72
OPERATING REVENUE	**Amount**	**Amount**	**Amount**	**Amount**	**Amount**	**Amount**
Rooms Revenue	39,687,000	38,590,000	42,626,000	47,993,000	51,567,000	56,145,000
Food & Beverage Revenue	12,899,000	13,455,000	17,382,000	17,231,000	17,946,000	23,451,000
Other Operated Departments Revenue	11,205,000	9,776,000	9,656,000	9,439,000	10,461,000	10,681,000
Total Operating Revenue	63,791,000	61,821,000	69,664,000	74,663,000	79,974,000	90,277,000
DEPARTMENTAL EXPENSES						
Rooms Expenses	6,132,000	6,041,000	6,847,000	7,395,000	7,706,000	9,184,000
Food & Beverage Expenses	9,845,000	9,682,000	11,657,000	12,428,000	13,928,000	16,741,000
Other Operated Departments Expenses	9,584,000	8,272,000	8,073,000	8,098,000	8,422,000	8,465,000
Total Departmental Expenses	25,561,000	23,995,000	26,577,000	27,921,000	30,056,000	34,390,000
Total Departmental Income	38,230,000	37,826,000	43,087,000	46,742,000	49,918,000	55,887,000
UNDISTRIBUTED EXPENSES						
Administrative & General	4,963,000	4,743,000	4,850,000	5,127,000	5,298,000	5,597,000
Sales & Marketing	2,706,000	2,784,000	2,854,000	2,973,000	2,966,000	2,976,000
Property Operations and Maintenance (POM)	3,939,000	3,846,000	4,628,000	4,512,000	4,572,000	5,028,000
Utilities	1,903,000	1,889,000	1,786,000	1,563,000	1,894,000	1,976,000
Total Undistributed Expenses	13,511,000	13,262,000	14,118,000	14,175,000	14,730,000	15,577,000
Gross Operating Profit	24,719,000	24,564,000	28,969,000	32,567,000	35,188,000	40,310,000
Management Fee	0	1,068,000	1,465,000	1,760,000	2,179,000	2,718,000
Base Mgmt. Fee	0	1,068,000	1,465,000	1,760,000	2,179,000	2,718,000
Income Before Non-Operating Income & Expenses	24,719,000	23,496,000	27,504,000	30,807,000	33,009,000	37,592,000
NON-OPERATING INCOME & EXPENSES						
Property Taxes	1,098,000	1,361,000	1,361,000	1,417,000	1,717,000	1,625,000
Insurance	0	0	0	222,550	463,936	463,936
ASD Sponsorship	0	439,000	367,000	370,000	524,000	525,000
Arena	0	0	0	490,000	328,000	-104,000
Total Non-Operating Income & Expenses[2]	1,098,000	1,800,000	1,728,000	2,499,550	3,032,936	2,509,936
EBITDA[3]	23,621,000	21,696,000	25,776,000	28,307,450	29,976,064	35,082,064
Replacement Reserves (FF&E)	2,551,640	1,854,630	2,089,920	2,239,890	2,399,220	2,682,360
Management School	202,000	167,000	120,000	103,000	244,000	39,000
EBITDA Less Replacement Reserve[4]	21,271,360	20,008,370	23,806,080	26,170,560	27,820,844	32,438,704

- The Resort recorded an average opening period of 230 days over the past years, which is higher than the average opening period of its competitive market (approximately 220 days).
- Since 2014, the overall trading performance has recorded an annual growth in revenue per available room (RevPAR) averaging 5.4%, mainly driven by an increase in occupancy of 5.5% in the same period, with average room rates remaining stable (−0.1%), resulting in a forecasted average daily rate (ADR) of € 544 in 2018.
- Food & beverage revenue ratio at 26% of total sales is roughly aligned to the market benchmark (25.6%). The subject costs result to be 71.4% of total revenue, as opposed to 73.6% of the benchmark. This higher departmental profit is mostly due to the significant economies of scale the Resort can achieve.
- Minor Operating Department mainly including spa, transfers, laundry, revenues from the boutique, kids club, language courses and beach revenue is expected to equal to 11.8% of total sales in 2018 that is significantly higher than benchmark average (7% of total sales), reflecting the unique and wider range of sports and leisure facilities available at the Augustus Resort. The profitability of these facilities is, however, lower than benchmark evidence.
- A&G costs are forecast at € 5.6 million in 2018 corresponding to c.€≈7,700 per available room (PAR), lower when compared to comparable resorts. This lower level can be attributed to the relevant economies of scales associated to the large size of the Resort, when compared to the benchmarked properties.
- Overall, the Hotel has improved its performance, growing adjusted Earnings Before Interests Taxes Depreciations and Amortization (EBITDA) from € 27.8 million in 2017 (or 34.8% of total sales) to € 32.4 million expected in 2018 (36% profit margin).

8.7.6 Profit and loss projection

Taebes Corp. basic assumptions behind the projections on which they have based the valuation represent the valuators opinion of the likely projections that would be adopted by a potential purchaser and do not necessarily match those that might be forecast by Ms. Orchidea Vinadio and Mr. Oliver Dawson.

Valuators have, where relevant, benchmarked the operating performance of the Augustus Luxury Resort against similar hotels in order to analyse revenues and costs on a per occupied room (POR) and PAR basis.

The forecasted operating performance made by Taebes Valuators is summarised in Table 8.7.

8.7.7 Asset valuation

Taebes valuators have applied an exit capitalisation rate to the projected 11th years' net operating profit of 5.50% and a discount rate to this amount

Table 8.7 Augustus Luxury Resort: forecasted operating performance

Summary (EUR)	2019	2020	2021	2022	2023
Days Open in Period	240	240	240	240	240
Available Hotel Rooms	723	723	723	723	723
Occupancy	60.0%	60.0%	60.0%	60.0%	60.0%
Average Daily Rate	570.00	581.40	593.03	604.89	616.99
% Change	*4.7%*	*2.0%*	*2.0%*	*2.0%*	*2.0%*
RevPAR	342.00	348.84	355.82	362.93	370.19
% Change	*7.3%*	*2.0%*	*2.0%*	*2.0%*	*2.0%*
Rooms Revenue	59,343,840	60,530,717	61,741,331	62,976,158	64,235,681
Rooms Expenses	9,161,856	9,328,223	9,495,190	9,671,124	9,851,211
Rooms Profit	50,181,984	51,202,494	52,246,141	53,305,033	54,384,470
Food & Beverage Revenue	23,945,760	24,380,582	24,816,974	25,276,802	25,747,482
Food & Beverage Expenses	16,657,920	16,960,405	17,263,982	17,583,862	17,911,292
Food & Beverage Profit	7,287,840	7,420,177	7,552,992	7,692,940	7,836,190
Other Operated Departments Revenue	11,972,880	12,190,291	12,408,487	12,638,401	12,873,741
Other Operated Departments Expenses	8,328,960	8,480,202	8,631,991	8,791,931	8,955,646
Other Operated Departments Profit	3,643,920	3,710,089	3,776,496	3,846,470	3,918,095
Total Operating Revenue	95,262,480	97,101,590	98,966,792	100,891,361	102,856,904
Net Operating Revenue	95,262,480	97,101,590	98,966,792	100,891,361	102,856,904
Total Departmental Expenses	34,148,736	34,768,830	35,391,163	36,046,918	36,718,149
Total Departmental Income	61,113,744	62,332,760	63,575,629	64,844,443	66,138,756
Total Undistributed Expenses	16,163,391	16,467,295	16,774,148	17,093,596	17,420,161
Management Fee	4,057,505	4,138,203	4,220,443	4,304,478	4,390,211
Gross Operating Profit	44,950,353	45,865,465	46,801,482	47,750,847	48,718,595
Total Non-Operating Income & Expenses	2,515,510	2,561,188	2,607,031	2,655,336	2,704,781
EBITDA	38,377,338	39,166,073	39,974,008	40,791,033	41,623,603
Replacement Reserves (FF&E)	2,857,874	2,913,048	2,969,004	3,026,741	3,085,707
Other Income	39,624	40,344	41,066	41,827	42,605
EBITDA Less Replacement Reserve	35,559,088	36,293,369	37,046,069	37,806,118	38,580,501
Adj. EBITDA/Room	49,183	50,198	51,239	52,291	53,362
Adj. EBITDA Margin	37.3%	37.4%	37.4%	37.5%	37.5%

and to first ten years of projections of 7.50%. This produces a gross investment valuation of € 650,000,000 (€ 900,000/room) and the following running yield profile (Table 8.8).

Valuators then made a deduction for capital expenditure, which in discounted value is roundly € 14,200,000.

The market value of the freehold interest in Augustus Luxury Resort, together with all fixtures, fittings, furniture and equipment, as a fully equipped

Table 8.8 Augustus Luxury Resort: Cap rate

Exit capitalisation rate	5.50%
Discount rate	7.5%
Year	Running yield (%)
Year 1	5.6
Year 2	5.7
Year 3	5.8

operational entity, having regard to trading potential, assuming that the property is offered with the benefit of vacant possession as on August 31, 2018, on the bases and assumptions set out above, is:

€ 640,000,000
(Six Hundred Forty Million Euro)

This equates to a price per room of € 890,000.

The valuation made by Taebes Corp. is net of purchaser's costs and therefore represents the contract sum that would be negotiated between a purchaser and a vendor. However, it makes no allowance for expenses of sale, which may be considerable, or liability to taxation (including VAT), which might arise on a disposal. No allowance is made for transfer costs in disposing of the property (whether payable by the vendor or purchaser) as these often depend on the way the sale is conducted, nor for any interest, which might accrue prior to a disposal.

Note

1 For a description of the appraisal process, see also Brueggeman and Fisher (2016).

References

Brueggeman, W. B., and J. D. Fisher, 2016, *Real estate finance and investments*, fifteenth edition, McGraw-Hill International Edition.

Ciocchetta, F., W. Cornacchia, R. Felici, and M. Loberto, 2016, Assessing financial stability risks arising from the real estate market in Italy, Banca d'Italia, Quaderni di Economia e Finanza No. 323.

9 Stress testing a real estate portfolio through value at risk

Andrea Beltratti and Alessia Bezzecchi

9.1 Introduction

Real estate assets are traditionally the collateral to most loans issued by banks worldwide. Paradoxically, they have become even more important in the past decades due to the increasing relevance of intangible assets in firms' business models. In some sectors, the key asset is human capital and its ability to deploy technology. It is, however, hard to use human capital as collateral, and this has reinforced the role of real estate assets in lending relationships. The paradox is that in an economy heavily relying on technology and human capital, real estate has become even more central to obtain external financing.

The centrality of real estate as collateral is particularly important in countries whose financial system relies on financial intermediaries more than on markets in order channel to companies. Continental European countries like Italy, Germany and France are examples of large economies that have relied on banks to channel funding to the corporations. It is estimated that in continental Europe, 80% of corporate financing come from banks and only 20% from markets. The opposite is true in countries like the USA and the UK, where corporations mainly rely on markets.

It is no wonder that the combination of bank financing and the increasing relevance of real estate as collateral has increased the link between the banking and the corporate sectors in several countries, especially after the 2008 credit crisis and the 2011 peripheral European countries. In the past decade, banks have gained increasing exposure to real estate assets due to repossessions of collateral posted by firms that were unable to repay bank debt according to the original schedule set in the loan contract. The Bank of Italy (2017) clarifies that at the end of the first half of 2017, the ratio of net non-performing loans and total loans for the Italian banking system was equal to 8.4% (16.4% if gross non-performing loans are considered). Most non-performing loans have a real estate collateral. As a consequence, the sensitivity of the Italian banking system to real estate dynamics was at the highest level since the 1990s.

During an economic expansion, banks only repossess collateral assets belonging to firms that for specific and idiosyncratic reasons are unable to honour their debt. However, an economic recession may create a "perfect storm" from the point of view of creditors. Not only a recession increases the probability that each company may be unable to repay its debt and therefore that the bank gets the collateral assets. Even worse, an economic recession may decrease the value of real estate assets, particularly when a declining level of economic activity is associated with increasing interest rate: this has indeed been the case for peripheral European countries like Italy and Spain where the 2011–2012 recession has been associated with a booming spread on sovereign bonds that has been transmitted to companies through the banking systems. The Bank of Italy (2017) notices that in 2017, real estate prices in real terms were 30% lower than prices in 2007.

The resulting covariance between the economy and the real estate market is the worst enemy for the banking system: banks repossess real estate assets at a time of falling real estate values and declining liquidity. This prevents banks from following the standard management policy based on quick turnaround of the repossessed assets, which need to be kept in the banks' balance sheet in order to prevent further capital losses that would materialise of the assets were sold. At the aggregate level, this is bad for banks that involuntary need to increase their real estate exposure at a time when they would like to cut their sensitivity to the real estate market. It is quite likely, even though no formal econometric evidence had been produced to our knowledge, that this is regarded by stock market investors as an extra source of systematic risk that needs to be priced in stock prices. In turn, pricing real estate–related systematic risk increases the risk premium required to hold bank stocks ultimately the cost of capital for banks.

This situation has several crucial implications for banks. Scardovi (2017) notices that banks should change their organisation in order to account for their large exposure to real estate assets after/during an economic crisis. This re-organisation may require the appointment of a chief real estate officer that may look at all real estate assets of a bank in a systematic and comprehensive way, even though there are other possible organisational choices that are described in Chapter 5. There are serious implications also from the point of view of valuation. The experts that have to deal with real estate assets in banks' balance sheets and/or in borrowers balance sheet may suffer from behavioural biases and rely too much on historical valuations and too little on the current market prices. Such conservativeness bias may prevent prompt recognition of the true value of the real estate exposure and decrease the trust of investors on the banks' balance sheets. On the contrary, expert may become victim to the "law of small numbers" and may overextend their forecast of a weak real estate market, with an excessive mark down of asset values.

Last but not least, and central for this chapter, there is an issue of efficient valuation of the overall risk associated with the real estate exposure. The use of models that are unable to deal with risk at the real estate portfolio level may imply an overestimation of risk, e.g. because portfolio diversification benefits are totally ignored. This may be bad for investors, who do not get a true picture of the banks situation, and may be even worse for clients. Under these conditions, bank managers may decide to cut the exposure to real estate assets by giving up on new loans to companies working in the real estate sector. The resulting credit crunch towards companies belonging to the real estate sector may exacerbate corporate problems and negatively affect economic activity and market prices, in a vicious circle connecting the banking system and the corporate sector.

Increasing exposure to real estate assets in turn has alerted banks to the need to use better models for managing risk at the portfolio level. This chapter discusses the application of the value at risk (VaR) methodology to the real estate sector. This is crucial to quantify the diversification benefits at the bank portfolio level. We comment on the estimation of both market risk and the urbanisation risk typical of real estate development projects. The VaR due to market risk is estimated through an application of the standard methodology that has been developed in the banking and asset management sector. The VaR due to urbanisation risk is derived from an application of Monte Carlo simulation, due to lack of data. We also discuss an application of the overall framework to risk measurement to a portfolio of real assets acquired by a large Italian bank in the context of a restructuring operation.

The VaR methodology may be used not only to compute on a purely data-driven, statistical basis, the maximum loss associated with market and urbanisation risks but also to compute the probabilities associated with well-specified intervals (these may be defined as "resistance intervals" because they are associated with lower bounds that represent the price of real estate assets under liquidation scenarios) that are derived from independent experts' opinions about the fair value of a real estate asset and portfolio. It is interesting to supplement experts' valuations with a purely statistical analysis because experts are unlikely to be able to quantify probabilities that the value lies in a given interval, and it is important for a bank to quantify the probability that the worst-case scenario for an asset will be worse than the liquidation value derived from an expert. This is totally consistent with the stress test methodology carried out by banks and asset management companies to deal with worst-case scenarios for their portfolios of assets.

This is not the first application of VaR to the real estate market, an early example being represented by Gordon and Tse (2003) measuring leverage risk for a portfolio of real estate assets. Jin and Ziobrowski (2011) show that in high volatility regimes, the maximum loss estimate obtained from the VaR methodology is more conservative than the estimate obtained from other estimators and may also be used for portfolio optimisation. Amédée-Manesme et al. (2015) apply VaR to the residential sector with a correction to deal with non-normality of prices, whilst Amédée-Manesme and Barthelemy (2018) apply stress test analysis using a simulation model that may yield an estimate of future volatility in the real estate market under study.

Some researchers compute the VaR of listed real estate vehicles (REITs) (for an application to risk measurement in high volatility regimes, see e.g. Zhou and Anderson, 2012).

9.2 Valuation process in restructuring

In order to restructure the various strategic areas, there is a need to separately identify the operational results of the corporate (in the specific case construction activities of the OpCo Operating Company) and the results due to ancillary activities (in the specific case activities associated with the development and management of real estate assets on the part of PropCo Property Company). This may be done through a spin-off of the real estate assets in a specific vehicle, with the purpose of managing and increasing the value of the portfolio. An independent expert provides an external valuation of the restructuring plan for both the OpCo (restructuring plan of the corporate) and the PropCo (real estate restructuring plan).

The main focus of this chapter is the PropCo real estate restructuring plan, which in complex cases involves assets divided into two clusters: (a) real estate properties and (b) real estate development projects. Usually, the OpCo business plan has a time horizon that is consistent with the business plan of the corporate and the real estate restructuring plan involves the sale of the assets starting from the ones that are regarded as more liquid, under the hypothesis of a "normal" sale process (different from a liquidation procedure).

The expert in charge with the valuation of the overall plan needs to have comfort opinions about the current valuation of the assets on the part of advisors, consistent with the business plan and the associated risk analysis. A possible methodology involves the following two activities to be carried out on a representative sample of assets:

1 Sensitivity analysis aimed at determining the "resistance interval" characterised by an upper value and a lower value that should contain the values of the various assets given their business and risk profile.
2 An estimate of the maximum potential loss taking into accounts two elements: (a) the operational risks of the assets (urbanisation risk, building risk and market risk)[1] and (b) the estimation of the portfolio diversification effect (associated with characteristics such as geography, use, life-cycle stage).

In order to carry out its evaluation task, the advisor starts from all available data, analyses the specific market in the relevant area and finally uses valuation methodologies accounting for the characteristics of each asset, thus establishing the "resistance interval" and the maximum and minimum vales that define it. The lower bound represents a liquidation scenario under the hypothesis of a relevant cut in ordinary sale times, and the upper bound represents a standard scenario that accounts for the economic upside and the risks associated with each asset. Development areas are particularly the subject to urbanisation risk, and their outcome is a binary one (1 actual development, 0 the project is scrapped). For development areas, the advisor needs to estimate not only the value of the area in each of the two scenarios but also the probability of each scenario.

9.3 REVaR: VaR computation in real estate

Value at risk (VaR) is defined as "the maximum potential loss in the value of a portfolio with a certain probability over a given time horizon" (JP Morgan/ Reuters, 1996). There are various methodologies for VaR computation. In the simplest case, it is assumed that the return of each asset is conditionally normal and the VaR is computed multiplying the return volatility times a multiplier that is consistent with the identification of the maximum loss probability. The return volatility may be estimated on the basis of historical data, using exponentially weighted moving average techniques giving more weight to recent observations. More sophisticated models use GARCH-based econometric models in order to better describe long-run mean reversion of any volatility shock. When conditional normality does not hold, e.g. in the case of derivative contracts with non-linear pay-offs, historical or Monte Carlo simulation techniques are used. Jorion (2006) reviews the various techniques and their use on the part of financial institutions.

It may be useful to recall that there are peculiarities to the computation of indices of real estate markets. Whilst the indices are derived from experts' assessments and not from actual transaction prices, their dynamics may be characterised by excess persistency due to the tendency of valuation experts to anchor the current estimates to the previous estimates and insufficiently revised them in the light of new information. Such phenomenon, also present in other illiquid markets, is called "smoothing." Smoothing increases measurement errors and reduces the measured volatility of returns. Naïve statistical models may, therefore, incorrectly assume that the real estate market is less risky than it actually is, both from the point of view of its variance and from the point of view of its covariance with the returns of other real and financial assets. It is possible to use statistical "unsmoothing" techniques in order to measure variances and covariances that account for the true dynamics of average prices (see e.g. Getmansky et al., 2004). Here, we will not use unsmoothing techniques but will limit ourselves to the use of standard time series data on prices and returns. Appropriate use of unsmoothing techniques may result in increased of the volatility and therefore the VaR of the real estate portfolios.

The estimation of volatility from the time series of prices delivers the VaR from market risk only, for each asset and for the portfolio as a whole, defining the maximum loss on the basis of the product of volatility and a multiplier equal to 1.645, which is associated with a probability of losing more than the VaR in only 55 of the cases.[2] For example, a real estate asset whose initial value is equal to 100, localised in an area where the volatility of the percentage price change is equal to 5%, is characterised by a measure of VaR equal to $100 \times 0.05 \times 1.645 = 8.225$. The interpretation is that the value of the asset at the end of the horizon will have a value below 91.775, only 5% of the times. A different real estate asset with initial value equal to 50, localised in an area where volatility of percentage price change is equal to 3%, has a VaR equal to $50 \times 0.03 \times 1.645 = 2.467$, i.e. at the end of the horizon, the asset will have a value lower than 47.532, only 5% of the times.

The volatility of a portfolio composed of the two real estate assets will be less than the weighted average of the two volatilities if the correlation between assets is less than 1. In the previous example, if the correlation coefficient between the two assets is 5%, then the volatility of the portfolio is 3.5%, which is lower than the 4.3% weighted average of the two volatilities. It follows that the VaR, obtained from the multiplication of the overall portfolio value, is equal to 150, only 3.5% of the times. The resulting number, equal to 8.636, leaves a 5% left tail probability. Note that the portfolio VaR, 8.636, is lower than the sum of the two individual asset-specific VaR, equal to 8.225 + 2.476 = 10.702. It follows that the value of the overall portfolio will be lower than 141.364 (larger than 141.364 equal to the sum of the two individual VaRs, only 5% of the times). The difference between 141.364 and 139.307 is a way to quantify the portfolio diversification benefits.

We use a Monte Carlo simulation methodology to quantify the operational risk due to urbanisation and construction risks because of lack of data that may be of help to estimate the relevant parameters. The methodology involves the generation of random numbers from a probability distribution chosen in such a way as to generate different development scenarios. The analysis of the dispersion of portfolio values across scenarios allows for a measurement of risk. Overall, the Monte Carlo methodology involves three steps: (1) scenario generation, (2) portfolio valuation in each scenario and (3) VaR computation.

The methodology, named REVaR, is as follows. For each area that is intended to go to the development stage, we use the resistance interval estimated by the advisor (i.e. values of the assets in case of both development and no development) as well as the development probability p qualitatively estimated by the advisor. We next assume that urbanisation risk is uncorrelated amongst the assets in the portfolio. We simulate k scenarios on the basis of a binary random variable that may take on values 0 and 1. For the ith project, the value 1 is realised with probability p_i and is associated with a project value V_i equal to $P_{i,\,S}$ (the project is developed), whilst when the value is equal to 0 the project value is $P_{i,\,NS}$ (the project is not developed). Of course, the two values account for different sources of risk: $P_{i,\,S}$ includes both market risk and all risks associated with the execution of the project, amongst which risks due to the construction activity, including all the risks due to urbanisation and the need to improve the infrastructure of the area, whereas $P_{i,NS}$ only includes the risks associated with the execution of the project (market risk is irrelevant in case the area does not go through the development phase).

If the value of the *i*th project in the *k*th scenario is equal to V_i^k (where V_i^k is equal to $P_{i,S}$ with probability p_i and to $P_{i,NS}$ with probability $1-p_i$), it follows that the value of the portfolio in the *k*th scenario is equal to the sum of the values of the different projects in that scenario, i.e. $V^k = \sum_{i=1}^{I} V_i^k$. In the *k*th scenario, the overall portfolio value will be obtained from the value of projects that are developed as well as the value of projects without development.

We estimate the volatility of the portfolio value due to non-market operational risks (i.e. urbanisation risk) as the ratio of the standard deviation of V^k (across the *k* simulations) and the average value of V^k. The portfolio VaR due to urbanisation risk is, therefore, equal to the average value of V^k times the estimated volatility times the multiplier equal to 1.645. Through this methodology, we are able to transform risks associated with development of various sites into a synthetic volatility measure that may be summed up to market volatility in order to derive a comprehensive risk measurement framework.

Under the assumption of zero correlation amongst market and urbanisation risks, we can estimate the overall VaR as the product of the portfolio value times the multiplier of 1.645 times the square root of the sum of the variance of the market risk and the variance of urbanisation risk. The assumption of no correlation between the two sources of risk may not be appropriate in those cases when the slow-down in real estate prices may induce constructors to postpone the start of the new building sites. This would be described by a positive correlation between market risk and urbanisation risk that would increase the overall risk.

9.4 REVaR case study: real estate portfolio VaR

We consider the case of a company going through a restructuring process. The restructuring plan includes the conferment of all the directly or indirectly owned real estate assets into a new vehicle (PropCo) that may manage the overall portfolio. The real estate assets belong to two clusters:

a Real estate properties directly or indirectly owned by the corporate
b Real estate development projects directly owned by the corporate or under development by vehicles controlled by the corporate

The business plan, lasting for a ten-year period until the end of 2026, includes the sale of some assets and the terminal value of the other assets in order to sell them after the end of the business plan period.

We start from the resistance intervals that have been established by the independent experts on the basis of all the available documents, the assumptions about the yields generated by the assets etc. We study a specific sub-sample composed of 23 assets that is highly representative of the overall portfolio composed of about 100 assets. The independent experts have taken the following steps:

1 Market analysis with particular attention about the absorption rate in the past decade and the typical values of sale prices, rents and cap rates.
2 Risk factor analysis and valuation analysis in which:
   a Each asset is analysed in terms of its peculiarities in order to find out any difference with the valuation initially proposed by the expert
   b Each asset is analysed from the point of view of three core operational risk factors: urbanisation risk, building risk and market risk
3 Analysis of the industrial and financial assumptions:
   a Capitalisation rates for those assets that are devoted to renting, obtained from market analysis of specific areas and types of use. The rates are adjusted to account for various asset characteristics (physical, legal, urban, economic) of the real estate asset to also include an additional risk premium,
   b Discount rates for cash flows, depending on the weighted average cost of capital obtained from the cost of equity in its levered form (in turn obtained from the unlevered cost of equity, i.e. the required return as a function of the operational risk of the asset) and from the cost of debt including any advantage associated with the tax shield.
4 Estimation of the resistance interval on the basis of the sensitivity analysis of the business plan with the definition of the upper and lower bounds that have been previously described.

The resistance interval accounts for market risk in the case of area that has already been developed and require no further intervention, whereas the valuation of the areas that are meant to be developed include urbanisation risk, construction risk and market risk. The sample analysed is described in Table 9.1, with information on the cluster (income-producing properties and areas under development), different uses and resistance intervals. In the fifth column, the lower and the upper range are based on valuations that account for all sources of risk, i.e. market risk, construction risk and urbanisation risk. In the sixth column, resistance intervals are based on valuations that only account for market risk, whereas in the seventh column we report the weighted averages of the values in the previous columns.

For example, in the case of asset #10, the upper value of the range, equal to € 2,025,700, is equal to the weighted average between € 2,290,000 (the upper bound of the interval that ignores non-market risks) and € 1,409,000 (the upper bound of the interval that accounts for non-market risks) with a weight of 70% on the former value. € 2,025,700 can, therefore, be interpreted as the value that would be offered by a bidder expecting on the short run that there is a 70% probability to develop the area. Such valuations are the ones that are more likely to be close to the market price of each single asset.

As already mentioned, the weighting is based on the probability of urbanisation risk (fourth column), i.e. the probability that the area is developed. Usually, probabilities are above 70%, but there are two projects with probabilities as low as 30%. The second of these two projects is extremely relevant to the portfolio as a whole because its value is equal to € 11,100,000 when only accounting for market risk and to € 17,100,000 in the case of the possibility to develop the site. Table 9.1 clarifies what are the assets with the larger relevance for the overall portfolio value.

As we can see from the last two rows of the table, ignoring building risk and urbanisation risk (resistance interval #2) is equivalent to increasing the lower bound of the resistance interval #1 by an amount equal to € 28,855,000 (25.2% of the value incorporating such risks) and the upper bound by € 32,975,000 (24.6%).

Overall, the total portfolio value when judged on the basis of the upper bound of the resistance range accounting for all operational risks is equal to € 134,160,000. Using the same criterion, the direct ownership portfolio accounts for 37% of the overall portfolio. This sub-portfolio has been evaluated using both the sales comparison approach and the income capitalisation approach. The development areas accounts for 63% of the overall portfolio and has been evaluated using the income approach.

Our goal is to evaluate the resistance intervals estimated on the basis of valuation models using the computation of the VaR. One of the goals of this exercise is to compute the probability that the market value is above the lower range, using the hypothesis that returns are normally distributed. We do not have data on a time series of market prices for each asset in the sample, so we use 1992–2015 time series of price indices for the various Italian Provinces where the assets are located (the source is Scenari Immobiliari). We estimate the volatility of the rate of return (the percentage change in prices) for each asset. For the portfolio as a whole, we estimate the volatility on the basis of the weighted average of single asset returns using the weights described in the second column of Table 9.2. The next column in the same table describes the value of volatility of each asset and of the portfolio (these correspond to the values reported in the last two columns of Table 9.1). The volatility of the single assets is included between 5% and 10%. The average volatility of the 23 assets in the portfolio is equal to 6.92%, whilst the volatility of the portfolio is equal to 5.39% (see the last row of the table). The difference is due to the diversification benefits amongst areas located in different geographies.

Following the methodology described above, we can compute the VaR of each asset from its initial value and the estimated volatility, using the 1.645

multiplier to estimate a loss that is exceeded only 5% of the times. The sixth column of the table reports the maximum loss for each asset.

Let's consider asset #1 as an example. The first asset is evaluated at € 871,000 when accounting for market risk. There are no other risks that need to be considered as this asset involves no future development. Given an estimated volatility equal to 5.54% and the 1.645 multiplier, we get a maximum loss (relatively to € 871.000, the upper bound of the resistance interval) equal to € 79,388 (the VaR), implying a minimum value of € 791,612 in the seventh column. There is a 95% probability that the price is above € 791,612. The probability that the price is above the lower bound (€ 862,000 from the data in the table) of the resistance interval is equal to 57.40% (such probability has been computed from the statistical tables for a normal distribution with volatility equal to 5.54%). For the portfolio as a whole, the sum of the single asset VaRs is equal to 17,611,304, whilst the portfolio VaR (see the last row) is equal to € 13,385,324. The maximum loss is way below the sum of the single asset VaRs (the ratio of the two measures is equal to 75%) due to the benefits of diversification. The probability that the value of the portfolio is above the lower bound of € 130,894,200 is equal to 99.34%.

The interpretation of this result clarifies one of the main points of our methodology. The statistical analysis that leads to the computation of the VaR includes the computation of the overall portfolio volatility. Using such volatility, it is possible to use information from the statistical tables to compute the probability that the portfolio value is above the given threshold. A particularly important threshold is the lower bound of the resistance interval computed by independent advisors. In our case, statistical analysis suggests that there is a 99.34% probability that the value of the portfolio is above the lower bound. This result is reassuring investors who may be interested to buy the portfolio only under the condition that the value of the portfolio is above the level computed by independent experts. The result is also relevant because the judgment is obtained on the basis of data of an alternative methodology that can provide comfort about the realism of the worst-case scenario described by independent experts or derived from an analysis on the part of banks that may use the information provided by non-performing loans. In our example, results show that the computation of the worst-case scenario has been very conservative.

Finally, the statistical analysis has been used to compute the estimation of the VaR associated with the urbanisation risks, excluding building risks. For each area, we have used probabilities of development described in Table 9.1. For each area, we have generated 10,000 scenarios for the realisations of a random variable that may take on value 0 or 1. For example for area #10, the random variable may take on value equal to 1 with a 70% probability. To each realisation, we have associated an estimated value for each area. Keeping with the example of area #10, it is assumed that the value of the area in case of development is equal to € 2,290,000 (see Table 9.1), whilst a random variable equal to 0, associated with the assumption of no development, takes on the value € 1,409,000.

Random variables for the various areas are drawn independently from each other, under the assumption of independence across risks. This is clearly a simplification, because areas located in the same province could be exposed to correlated urbanisation risks. The same may happen to different provinces. For example, a new national law may force different provinces to change their rules and temporarily halt projects waiting for approvals. Our hypothesis of independence is not necessarily the best, but the methodology would be simply extended to allow for other correlations.

For each area, and for the portfolio as a whole, the 10,000 simulations produce an average level and a standard deviation that may be used to estimate the volatility due to urbanisation risk. Given the volatility, the VaR can be computed for each asset and for the overall portfolio. For the portfolio, the volatility due to urbanisation risks is equal to a 9.01%, obtained from the estimate of the cross-scenario dispersion of the portfolio values using the development probabilities reported in Table 9.1. The methodology, therefore, allows to turn into a volatility estimate the urbanisation risks quantified at the area level.

Finally, assuming there is independence between market risks and urbanisation risks, we estimate overall volatility as the square root of the sum of the variances of the two sources of risk, obtaining a value equal to 10.5%.[3] Starting from a portfolio whose value is put at € 151,049,227 and using such volatility, we get a VaR equal to € 26,086,311, implying a 5% probability worst-case scenario equal to € 124,962,916 for the value of the overall portfolio. Using the minimum value estimated by independent experts for the portfolio as a whole, equal to € 130,894,200, and using the comprehensive volatility estimate equal to 10.5%, we can estimate, from statistical tables, that the value of the portfolio will be larger than the minimum value estimated by independent experts with an 89.81% probability.

9.5 Conclusion

The VaR methodology may be applied to the real estate market to compute the probability that the value of a portfolio of assets lies within a given range. In our application, we have considered the case when the range has been computed by independent experts, with an upper range that accounts for all operational risks and a lower range describing a liquidation scenario. The main goal of the exercise is to use data and models to compare experts' opinion in a risk measurement framework. We also highlight an original application of a Monte Carlo simulation methodology for estimating urbanisation risks. We do not want to present an integrated framework of risk measurement and management for the real estate sector.

When valuing real estate assets in a restructuring phase, a prudence principle requires the use of conservative values such as the ones corresponding to the lower bounds of resistance intervals determined by independent experts mainly on a qualitative basis. However, in some cases, "excess prudence" is the result of a lack of knowledge in risk quantification, or, even worse, the feeling that the decision maker finds himself in a situation of uncertainty rather than risk, where scenarios and probabilities cannot be determined. It is well known that uncertainty fosters inaction and leads to paralysis. We claim that using easily available tools, it is possible to reduce the area belonging to uncertainty in order to enlarge situations that may be characterised by risk, i.e. situations where the probabilities of various future scenarios may be determined using available data. We acknowledge that the real estate sector is less advanced than other sectors from the point of view of data availability, but we trust that applications of big data and artificial intelligence techniques will deeply improve the situation in the next future, as discussed in several chapters in this book. By getting a better measure for the risk of the overall portfolio, different parties can find out what are the true margins of disagreement regarding the transaction price. This is in line with observations made in the previous chapters of this book when observing that often the problem is not to find a theoretical value for an asset, but the buyer who is willing to extract the largest value and therefore to pay the highest price to the seller.

Using appropriate data and indicators, strongly overlapping with data and indicators that have long been used in financial institutions for risk analysis, leads all the different parties to better understand risk and to facilitate a discussion. In our example, we have three different "resistance intervals" determined by independent experts, accounting for market risk only, all operational risks (and therefore yielding the lowest of the three "resistance intervals" and coming from the weighted average using the probabilities associated with the development scenarios for each area). In practice, in such situation potential acquirers of the portfolio could look at the lowest resistance interval (€ 114–134 million), taken as the most conservative, in order to account for the existence of uncertainty rather than risk. However, our analysis, based on a data-based evaluation of market risk as well as urbanisation risk for the portfolio as a whole, including the benefits arising from diversification across geographies and across uses, finds that there is a 95% probability that the portfolio value is above € 137 million and a 99.3% probability that the portfolio value is above € 130 million.

Our methodology is based on several simplifying hypotheses, e.g. about the accuracy of the data set used for estimating asset and portfolio volatility. There are biases associated with indices of real estate values, due to factors such as a small portion of the overall stock actually being transacted each period, in particular when the index is based on the use of experts' valuation rather than market prices with the associated lags in accounting for true market information and the resulting smoothing. Our goal, however, is showing how existing data sets may be used in order to supplement valuation experts' opinions with data-based risk analyses. The underlying data may be improved by the combination of various data sources and the use of "unsmoothing" techniques that may provide a better picture of volatilities and correlations. Several papers suggest that unsmoothed data present larger volatilities (see e.g. Edelstein, 2006; Ang, 2014), suggesting that in the USA unsmoothed data have a volatility that is twice as large as the volatility of smoothed data. There are obvious implications for the computation of the VaR.

Our methodology may be of interest to several players. Banks financing real estate companies may compute VaR to determine the probability that the portfolio remains above a threshold even in negative scenarios. Real estate companies may benefit from the application of the methodology, originally proposed in finance, to better engage their creditors in an active dialogue and manage periodic stress tests on their portfolio structure. Institutional investors may use our methodology to estimate maximum loss on their financial and real assets also accounting for all sources of diversification benefits.

Table 9.1 reports the valuation of single asset and of the portfolio as a whole in different scenarios for risk factors. The first column reports the asset number. The second column describes the asset type, i.e. "real estate properties" or "real estate development areas." The third column reports the use of the assets and the fourth column the development probability. The fifth column reports the lower and upper range for values estimated accounting for all operational risks (market risk, urbanisation risk, construction risk), the sixth column reports the lower and upper range for values estimated accounting for market risk only; the values in the sixth column are identical to the values in the fifth column for "developed areas" and are larger than the corresponding values for "development areas" because they ignore urbanisation and construction risks. The seventh column reports the lower and upper range for values that are estimated accounting for market risk but accounting for non-market operational risks as the weighted average between development and non-development scenarios (with weights equal to development probabilities). The lower part of the table ("aggregate data") sums up the individual asset information. The penultimate row ("delta") reports the difference between the resistance interval in the different columns and the resistance interval accounting for all operational risks. The last row ("percentage delta") normalise the information of the previous row by dividing by the resistance interval accounting for all operational risks.

Table 9.2 reports the results for the VaR of each single asset and for the portfolio as a whole. The first column reports the asset number. The second column reports the portfolio weight due to each asset. The third column reports asset volatility. The fourth and fifth columns, respectively, present the lower and upper bound of the resistance interval accounting for market risk and for the weighted urbanisation risk where the weight is estimated through the development probability. The sixth column reports the VaR for the different assets. The seventh column reports the minimum value for

Table 9.1 Portfolio summary statistics and resistance range

# asset	Clusters	Asset class								Probability of scenario (p)	Resistance interval with operational risks (€)		Resistance interval with market risk (€)		Resistance interval with operational risks and Probability of development (€)	
(1)	(2)	(3)								(4)	(5)		(6)		(7)	
		Industrial	Warehouse	Office	Residential	Box	Parking	Retail			Min	Max	Min	Max	Min	Max
1	Properties			•	•	•	•		1	100%	862.000	871.000	862.000	871.000	862.000	871.000
2	Properties				•			•	1	100%	612.000	620.000	612.000	620.000	612.000	620.000
3	Properties				•			•	1	100%	445.000	514.000	445.000	514.000	445.000	514.000
4	Properties			•					1	100%	1.129.000	1.185.000	1.129.000	1.185.000	1.129.000	1.185.000
5	Properties		•	•					1	100%	418.000	544.000	418.000	544.000	418.000	544.000
6	Properties					•	•		1	100%	676.000	750.000	676.000	750.000	676.000	750.000
7	Properties			•					1	100%	1.967.000	2.022.000	1.967.000	2.022.000	1.967.000	2.022.000
8	Properties				•	•		•	1	100%	1.519.000	1.673.000	1.519.000	1.673.000	1.519.000	1.673.000
9	Properties				•	•			1	100%	989.000	1.222.000	989.000	1.222.000	989.000	1.222.000
10	Development projects				•				1	70%	1.154.000	1.409.000	1.976.000	2.290.000	1.729.400	2.025.700
11	Development projects	•					•		1	90%	2.028.000	2.492.000	2.100.000	2.576.000	2.092.800	2.567.600
12	Properties			•	•		•		1	100%	2.723.000	3.281.000	2.723.000	3.281.000	2.723.000	3.281.000
13	Development projects			•	•		•		1	60%	4.557.000	4.822.000	5.074.000	5.351.000	4.867.200	5.139.400
14	Development projects				•	•	•		1	70%	4.136.000	5.145.000	4.886.000	6.001.000	4.661.000	5.744.200
15	Development projects		•	•		•	•	•	1	30%	1.535.000	2.010.000	2.080.000	2.576.000	1.698.500	2.179.800
16	Development projects	•		•				•	1	80%	2.415.000	3.695.000	2.965.000	4.389.000	2.855.000	4.250.200
17	Development projects						•	•	1	70%	3.031.000	3.705.000	3.530.000	4.270.000	3.380.300	4.100.500
18	Development projects				•	•	•	•	1	70%	43.000.000	46.500.000	57.100.000	58.700.000	52.870.000	55.040.000
19	Development projects				•	•	•	•	1	80%	9.300.000	12.400.000	10.700.000	13.700.000	10.420.000	13.440.000
20	Properties	•	•				•	•	1	100%	1.300.000	1.500.000	1.300.000	1.500.000	1.300.000	1.500.000
21	Properties	•	•		•		•	•	1	100%	11.300.000	16.200.000	11.300.000	16.200.000	11.300.000	16.200.000
22	Properties			•			•	•	1	100%	18.000.000	19.800.000	18.000.000	19.800.000	18.000.000	19.800.000
23	Development projects				•	•	•	•	1	30%	1.500.000	1.800.000	11.100.000	17.100.000	4.380.000	6.390.000

Portfolio summary

	Resistance interval with operational risks (€)		Resistance interval with market risk (€)		Resistance interval with operational risks and Probability of development (€)	
	Min	Max	Min	Max	Min	Max
Totale	**114.596.000**	**134.160.000**	**143.451.000**	**167.135.000**	**130.894.200**	**151.059.400**
Properties	41.940.000	50.182.000	41.940.000	50.182.000	41.940.000	50.182.000
Development projects	72.656.000	83.978.000	101.511.000	116.953.000	88.954.200	100.877.400
Delta			28.855.000	32.975.000	16.298.200	16.899.400
Delta %			25,2%	24,6%	14,2%	14,7%

Table 9.2 VaR analysis for single assets and portfolio

# asset	% Asset value / Portfolio value (5)	Asset volatility.	Resistance interval with operational risks and Probability of development (€) Min	Max	Value at Risk (€)	Min Asset Value (€)	Probability asset value > VaR	Probability asset value > Min asset value
(1)	(2)	(3)	(4)	(5)	(6)	(7)	(8)	(9)
1	0,58%	5,54%	862.000	871.000	79.388	791.612	95,00%	57,40%
2	0,41%	6,49%	612.000	620.000	66.231	553.769	95,00%	57,88%
3	0,34%	9,44%	445.000	514.000	79.849	434.151	95,00%	92,24%
4	0,78%	5,27%	1.129.000	1.185.000	102.713	1.082.287	95,00%	81,51%
5	0,36%	7,34%	418.000	544.000	65.648	478.352	95,00%	99,92%
6	0,50%	6,91%	676.000	750.000	85.277	664.723	95,00%	92,33%
7	1,34%	5,27%	1.967.000	2.022.000	175.263	1.846.737	95,00%	69,72%
8	1,11%	7,30%	1.519.000	1.673.000	200.898	1.472.102	95,00%	89,63%
9	0,81%	7,00%	989.000	1.222.000	140.621	1.081.379	95,00%	99,68%
10	1,34%	5,97%	1.729.400	2.025.700	198.987	1.826.713	95,00%	99,28%
11	1,70%	9,36%	2.092.800	2.567.600	395.176	2.172.424	95,00%	97,59%
12	2,17%	5,18%	2.723.000	3.281.000	279.388	3.001.612	95,00%	99,95%
13	3,40%	8,56%	4.867.200	5.139.400	723.369	4.416.031	95,00%	73,20%
14	3,80%	8,13%	4.661.000	5.744.200	768.261	4.975.939	95,00%	98,98%
15	1,44%	8,21%	1.698.500	2.179.800	294.454	1.885.346	95,00%	99,64%
16	2,81%	5,21%	2.855.000	4.250.200	364.281	3.885.919	95,00%	100,00%
17	2,71%	6,61%	3.380.300	4.100.500	445.821	3.654.679	95,00%	99,61%
18	36,44%	7,30%	52.870.000	55.040.000	6.609.341	48.430.659	95,00%	70,54%
19	8,90%	7,30%	10.420.000	13.440.000	1.613.909	11.826.091	95,00%	99,90%
20	0,99%	7,39%	1.300.000	1.500.000	182.399	1.317.601	95,00%	96,44%
21	10,72%	6,32%	11.300.000	16.200.000	1.684.748	14.515.252	95,00%	100,00%
22	13,11%	6,92%	18.000.000	19.800.000	2.252.514	17.547.486	95,00%	90,57%
23	4,23%	7,64%	4.380.000	6.390.000	802.769	5.587.231	95,00%	100,00%
Total	**100,00%**		**130.894.200**	**151.059.400**	**17.611.304**	**133.448.096**		
Portfolio	**100,00%**	**5,39%**	**130.894.200**	**151.059.400**	**13.385.324**	**137.674.076**	**95%**	**99,34%**

each asset and for the portfolio as a whole obtained subtracting from the upper bound of the resistance level the estimated VaR. The eight column reports the probability that the value of each asset and of the portfolio as a whole is larger than the VaR (the probability is always equal to 95% because the VaR has been computed in order to leave 5% probability in the left tail) and the last column reports that probability that the portfolio value is above the minimum value computed in the seventh column.

Notes

1 Operational risk in real estate is defined by two main drivers: (1) specific segment to which the asset belongs to, describing the use and all the physical, economic and legal characteristics of the asset, which are the basis for determination of price and/or rent risk, and (2) product life cycle, describing the phases of the transformation of the real estate asset, including the development of the area from the point of view of infrastructure, the construction of the buildings and all issues associated with the management/sale of the asset.

2 According to the standard normal distribution, the 5th percentile, the one leaving 5% of the overall probability in the left tail, is equal to 1.645.

3 The 10.5% estimate is obtained from the square root of the sum of the variance of market risk, equal to the square of 5.39%, and the variance of urbanization risk, equal to the square of 9.01%.

References

Amédée-Manesme, C., F. Barthelemy, and D.C. Keenan, 2015, Cornish-Fisher expansion for commercial real estate value at risk, *Journal of Real Estate Finance and Economics*, 50, 439–464.

Amédée-Manesme, C., and F. Barthelemy, 2018, Ex-ante real estate value at risk calculation method, *Annals of Operations Research*, 262, 257–285.

Ang, A., 2014, *Asset Management*, Oxford University Press, Oxford.

Edelstein, R.H., 2006, How does appraisal smoothing bias real estate returns measurement? *Journal of Real Estate Finance and Economics*, 32, 41–60.

Getmansky, M., A. Lo, and I. Makarov, 2004, An econometric model of serial correlation and illiquidity in hedge fund returns, *Journal of Financial Economics*, 74, 529–609.

Gordon, J.N., and E.W.K. Tse, 2003, VaR: A tool to measure leverage risk, *Journal of Portfolio Management*, 29, 62–65.

J.P. Morgan/Reuters, 1996, Risk Metrics Technical document, New York.

Jin, C., and A.J. Ziobrowski, 2011, Using Value-at-Risk to estimate downside residential market risk, *Journal of Real Estate Research*, 33, 389–413.

Jorion, P., 2006, *Value at Risk: The new benchmark for managing financial risk*, third edition, Mc-Graw Hill.

Scardovi, C., 2017, Holistic active management of non-performing loans, Springer.

Zhou, J., and R. Anderson, 2012, Extreme risk measures for international REIT markets, *Journal of Real Estate Finance and Economics*, 45, 152–170.

Index

Note: **Bold** page numbers refer to tables; *italic* page numbers refer to figures and page numbers followed by "n" denote endnotes.